Weaving Music into Young Minds

Dedication

To all my teachers—those who taught me in childhood, teen years, and adulthood—I pass on what you have taught me. To all of you who will teach, thank you for your dedication to the children of this world.

Weaving Music into Young Minds

MARY MICHÉ

DELMAR

THOMSON LEARNING ™ Australia Canada Mexico Singapore Spain United Kingdom United States

DELMAR

THOMSON LEARNING

Weaving Music into Young Minds
Mary Miché

Business Unit Director:
Susan L. Simpfenderfer

Executive Editor:
Marlene McHugh Pratt

Acquisitions Editor:
Erin O'Connor Traylor

Developmental Editor:
Andrea Edwards

Editorial Assistant:
Alexis Ferraro

Executive Production Manager:
Wendy A. Troeger

Project Editor:
Amy E. Tucker

**Technology and
Production Assistant:**
Nina Tucciarelli

Executive Marketing Manager:
Donna J. Lewis

Channel Manager:
Nigar Hale

Cover Design:
Spear Design

Cover Images:
Courtesy of PhotoDisc

For permission to use material from this text or product, contact us by
Tel (800) 730-2214
Fax (800) 730-2215
http://www.thomsonrights.com

Library of Congress Cataloging-in-Publication Data
Miché, Mary.
　　Weaving music into young minds / Mary Miché.
　　　　p.　cm.
　　Includes bibliographical references and index.
　　ISBN 0-7668-0019-9
　　1. Music—Instruction and study—Juvenile.　2. School music—Instruction and study—Juvenile.　I. Title.
MT1 .M565 2001
372.87'044—dc21

2001047333

NOTICE TO THE READER

Publisher does not warrant or guarantee any of the products described herein or perform any independent analysis in connection with any of the product information contained herein. Publisher does not assume, and expressly disclaims, any obligation to obtain and include information other than that provided to it by the manufacturer.

The reader is expressly warned to consider and adopt all safety precautions that might be indicated by the activities herein and to avoid all potential hazards. By following the instructions contained herein, the reader willingly assumes all risks in connection with such instructions.

The Publisher makes no representation or warranties of any kind, including but not limited to, the warranties of fitness for particular purpose or merchantability, nor are any such representations implied with respect to the material set forth herein, and the publisher takes no responsibility with respect to such material. The publisher shall not be liable for any special, consequential, or exemplary damages resulting, in whole or part, from the readers' use of, or reliance upon, this material.

Contents

1075.00

CHAPTER 2

CHAPTER 3

CHAPTER 4

Music and Children with Special Needs **107**

CHAPTER 5

Integrating Science and Music **127**

CHAPTER 6
Music and Language **151**

CHAPTER 7
Music and Social Learning **169**

CHAPTER 8
Music and the Arts **191**

CHAPTER 9
Music and Movement **215**

CHAPTER 10

Music with Reading and Writing 235

Preface

This book is intended to make you aware of the impact of music on the development of young children. With this awareness, hopefully you will be motivated to learn how you can bring more music into the lives of your students. In Chapter 1, you will be introduced to the variety of ways that you can teach music to children, whether or not you have had musical training. Chapter 1 also focuses on the variety of ways to play music and the many kinds of music to play in the classroom. Chapter 2 gives an overview of musical activities and musical knowledge that nonmusically trained teachers can do with their students. Chapter 3 is an introduction to developmental milestones in music: what children can do musically at different ages. Chapter 4 discusses children with special needs. The next five chapters focus on integrating music into other subject areas. Chapter 5 covers integrating music and science. Chapter 6 discusses the interrelationship of music and language development. This chapter also gives practical ideas for teaching foreign language and English language skills through music. Chapter 7 focuses on music and social learning, giving ideas about appreciating other cultures and other historical eras through the use of music and song. Chapter 8 is about integrating music with the visual arts. Chapter 9 covers music and movement. Finally, Chapter 10 discusses how music can enhance reading and literature programs.

Each chapter includes articles about experts and artists who work with children and music. These features are called *An Expert Opinion* and *Meet the Artist.* References to awards and numbers of books or albums sold are left out because readers need to find their own favorites. Some of the artists are relatively unknown or new to the business and have not received many awards. Others have excellent recordings but never submit them for awards. Many others have long lists of awards. In short, the information about a variety of artists is provided so that you understand the great number of children's artists and the enormous variations in their focuses. Contact information for these artists is included in Appendix A. Appendix B includes the lyrics to 20 great children's songs included on the audio CD that accompanies this book.

The book includes other special features. In each chapter *A Common Question* asked by teachers is highlighted and discussed. These features are designed to assist you with the kinds of problems and questions you may face as a teacher. *Key Terms* and *Discussion Questions* at the end of each chapter help you review important information and reinforce your knowledge of the material. *Suggested Learning Activities* will help you prepare curriculum materials for teaching. Finally, *References* and *Additional Resources* help you find the sources of material suggested in the book.

Studies reportedly show that music assists children in their learning, improves their cognitive abilities, helps them read, assists their mathematics performance, encourages creativity, and aids in remembering information. Music learning has an essential role in the lives of young children. This book will not only give the reasons why music is a necessary part of a child's education, but it will also give you ideas for how to weave this music learning into the fabric of children's lives.

Acknowledgments

A book like this is the work of many people.

We will start with my mom, who sang in the car with us, and my dad, who encouraged us to take music lessons and paid for all six of us to play instruments.

My husband, Andrew, spent countless hours fixing my computer, cooking meals, washing dishes, and taking care of our son. My child, Nathan, patiently held up plants, instruments, violins, and electric pianos for many of the photos in the book.

A great thanks goes to Melody Nicholson, Meridith Roberts, Elisabeth Severson, and John Maurer, who did so much of the calling, editing, and following up on the details of this book. It would have been hard to stay sane without them.

Thank you, Helen Botnarescue, for suggesting that I write this book. You have given telephone support at critical moments over the years of its writing.

Thank you also to Jay Whitney, who was the editor at Delmar who encouraged the writing of this book and gave me confidence to continue writing.

To Sandy Westlie, one of the best preschool teachers in the world, goes a big thank you for letting me photograph students and parents at Peter Pan Preschool.

Thanks to my friends, Sarah Friga and Cindy Edwards Trueblood, who let me come to their homes and take photos of their really cute kids.

To the many teachers who have used my recordings, tried out my ideas, and sent me feedback about them, thank you for encouraging me to keep going.

Finally, thank you to Linda Jones and so many of the parents of children who have supported me over the years in my work of teaching their children to love music.

The author and Delmar wish to gratefully acknowledge the content expertise and valuable suggestions contributed by the following reviewers:

Julia Beyeler
The University of Akron-Wayne College
Orrville, Ohio

Dr. Linda Aulgur
Westminster College
Fulton, Missouri

Julie A. Bakerlis
Becker College
Leicester, Massachusetts

About the Author

Mary Miché started singing at age four when she played a ballerina record over and over and sang along with it. When she was six, she became hooked on French songs for children. That is when she learned how to make all the sounds of French, although she never spoke the language. Mary was the oldest of six children who were born within six years. Her mother encouraged the children to sing songs in the car. When Mary was ten, her parents bought a piano and waited to see who would play it. When Mary and her sister Joan started plunking out tunes, they got piano lessons. Mary took piano and violin lessons and taught herself guitar as a teenager. Then, in college, she quit playing violin and joined the university chorus.

Choral music became Mary's love. She decided to major in vocal music. Although she sang in school and church choirs from first through eighth grade, she did not begin voice lessons until age twenty.

Mary got a job teaching in an outdoor education school right after college. She loved working with the children in a nature classroom, so she got a master's degree in environmental education. That is where she discovered many great science songs.

In 1980 she started doing assembly programs in schools and taught a children's chorus at the invitation of a parent group. She needed lots of songs to teach her students, so she started collecting all kinds. After a few years, parents asked Mary to record the songs. She had so many great songs, she had to make six recordings.

During this period, Mary also began to do teacher training in music. Soon she was traveling to kindergarten conferences all over the country to share with teachers the variety of songs she had found. Mary still gives concerts and talks all over the United States.

Currently, Mary teaches what she calls *massive music,* 150 students at a time, in a school with 900 students, of whom 90 percent are bilingual. Mary really enjoys working with children, and she loves talking with teachers about music. She wants children to sing, sing, sing. If songs are really fun to sing, children will want to sing them repeatedly and get better at singing. Mary's passion is to show regular classroom teachers how easy it is to *weave music* into the fabric of a classroom curriculum.

CHAPTER

Music in the Cracks of Your Classroom

What would your life be like without music? No songs in your life when you were a young child, no rhythm, no dancing, no beating of drums, no ringing of bells. Later, no singing around campfires, no music in church, no teen romance songs, no bands, no dances. Now in your adult life, no singing in the shower, no sweet voices of nursery songs, no oldies but goodies, no music at the movies, no symphony, no rock 'n' roll on the radio, no harmony. Music is as important for the development of a whole child as it has been in the development of your own life. The importance of music begins in the early years and extends for an entire lifetime.

Why Music?

Educators encourage the use of music in the education of children for many reasons. Draper and Gayle (1987) provided a list obtained from 108 textbooks of music education published between 1887 and 1982. Music education of children is important to

1. develop self-expression and creative pleasure;
2. develop an aesthetic sense;
3. facilitate motor and rhythmic development;
4. promote cultural heritage;
5. promote vocal and language development;
6. promote cognitive development and abstract thought;
7. teach social and group skills.

As values change, the reasons for music education cited in textbooks change. For example, *cultural heritage* gained importance in American society in the '70s, while the reason *developing an aesthetic sense* appeared less frequently. There was no change in the percentage of books that listed self-expression and motor development as goals for music; 65–70 percent of all the texts over the 100-year period studied gave these reasons. The reason *promotes cognitive development and abstract thought* did increase continually and greatly over the modern period (1964–1982). This has become one of the most common reasons for teaching music. It corresponds to the current research that shows music promotes **cognitive development**, the ability of a child to think, reason, and visualize problems.

Theory of Multiple Intelligences

As the importance of music in cognitive development has become more well-known, a new model of cognitive ability in children has developed. Howard Gardner (1983) suggested that intelligence consists of more than how a student performs on tests of mathematical thinking and verbal processing. These tests do not measure talents in dance, music, visual arts, or foreign language fluency. He presented a new idea that is being considered by educators and is beginning to be applied to educational programs. His idea is called the Theory of **Multiple Intelligences**. He suggested that there are eight different kinds of intelligence.

The first two intelligences are the ones we have traditionally considered the defining characteristics of highly achieving, intellectual people.

- ♪ Logical-Mathematical intelligence
- ♪ Verbal-Linguistic intelligence

Logical-Mathematical intelligence is the ability to reason deductively, detect patterns, and think logically. This intelligence is used in scientific and mathematical applications.

Verbal-Linguistic intelligence usually relates to verbal skills. The ability to read well, understand sophisticated vocabulary, grasp the concepts presented, speak intelligently, and write well are all included here. This intelligence also includes the use of language to help remember information. It is valued in the business and academic fields.

Gardner defined intelligence as "the capacity to solve problems or to fashion products that are valued in one or more cultural setting" (Gardner & Hatch, 1989). He added six more intelligences to the traditional two. They are:

- ♪ Visual-Spatial intelligence
- ♪ Musical-Rhythmic intelligence
- ♪ Bodily-Kinesthetic intelligence
- ♪ Naturalistic intelligence, and
- ♪ Two kinds of Personal intelligence: Intrapersonal and Interpersonal.

Visual-Spatial intelligence is the ability to visualize objects or movements through space. Architects, choreographers, race car drivers, and furniture designers use this kind of intelligence. It is not limited to only visual activities. Spatial intelligence is also formed in children with blindness as they visualize rooms in a house or trips in the car.

Musical-Rhythmic intelligence is the ability to recognize and compose musical pitches, tones, and rhythms. It also includes the ability to perform music (Figure 1–1). Hearing is required to develop musical intelligence, although persons with deafness can develop rhythmic intelligence.

Bodily-Kinesthetic intelligence is the ability to use the mind to coordinate bodily movements. This intelligence includes dance and sports ability. It is difficult, but not impossible, for persons with disabilities that limit their physical movement to develop this intelligence.

Naturalistic intelligence is used when observing, understanding, and organizing patterns in the natural environment. A *naturalist* is someone who shows expertise in the recognition and classification of plants and animals. Anyone from a child watching a bird to a molecular biologist observing chemical reactions to a traditional medicine man using herbal remedies can be considered a naturalist.

Personal intelligence, sometimes also referred to as **Emotional intelligence**, includes two kinds of intelligence.

The first, *Interpersonal intelligence,* is the ability to understand communication between people: to tune in to how they feel and what they intend. The second, *Intrapersonal intelligence,* is self-knowledge: the ability to understand one's own feelings and

FIGURE 1–1 *Children's musical intelligence starts at a young age.*

motivations. Both of these intelligences are distinct; having one without the other is possible. However, people who use one of these intelligences usually also have some ability in the other.

Although each intelligence is different, Gardner suggested that the eight intelligences complement each other as individuals develop skills or solve problems. For example, a dancer has good Bodily-Kinesthetic intelligence but also uses Visual-Spatial intelligence to visualize moving through space, Musical-Rhythmic intelligence to understand the rhythm and variations of the music, and Interpersonal intelligence to understand how to emotionally connect with the audience through movement.

Gardner argued that multiple intelligences have a biological basis. Brain research shows that different kinds of learning are stored in different parts of the brain. Some kinds of activities involve knowledge stored in different locations of the brain. For example, injury to the Broca's area of the brain will result in the loss of ability to speak using proper grammar. Nevertheless, this injury will not remove the patient's understanding of correct grammar and word usage, which is stored in another part of the brain. In another example, music draws from knowledge that is located in many different places of the brain; pitch is located in one place, rhythm in another, and synthesis of the whole experience in yet another place. Because different kinds of learning are located in different areas of the brain, one can argue that intelligence is not limited to one location and that development of a variety of intelligences can lead to excellent interaction of the differently developed brain areas.

Gardner (1983) said that culture also plays a role in the development of the intelligences. Societies value different types of intelligence. Because a culture values the ability to do an activity, that culture rewards the people who can do it well. This fact provides an incentive to individuals to practice and become skilled at the activity. For example, a culture that values basketball skills and pays people well to play it will give an incentive to young persons to practice it. A culture that rewards people well for playing violins will develop violin players. Thus, though some intelligences might be highly developed in people of one culture, those same intelligences might not be as developed in another culture.

Gardner's Theory of Multiple Intelligences has several important implications for teachers. It suggests that all eight intelligences are needed for individuals to function well in society. Teachers, therefore, could think of all intelligences as equally important. This concept is in great contrast to traditional education which typically places a strong emphasis on the development and use of verbal and mathematical intelligences. Thus, the Theory of Multiple Intelligences implies that educators should recognize and teach a broad range of talents and skills.

Another implication of the theory is that teachers should present material in ways that engage most or all of the intelligences. For example, when teaching about plants, a teacher can show students detailed drawings of plants, sing songs about plants, put on a short drama about how plants grow, plant seeds and measure the growth, read books to the students about plants, go on a walk to see plants growing in their natural habitats, and make drawings and sculptures of plants. This kind of teaching not only excites students about learning, but also reinforces the same material in a variety of ways. It can also help students understand the subject material more thoroughly because it develops all of the different intelligences while helping the mind store the information in different places all over the brain.

Students come into the classroom with different sets of developed intelligences. Each child will have her own unique set of intellectual strengths and weaknesses. The set of developed intelligences influences how easy or hard it is for the student to learn information presented in class. This is commonly referred to as a *learning style*. Many learning styles can be found in each classroom. Therefore, it is impossible, as well as impractical, for a teacher to accommodate every lesson to all of the learning styles of the class. Nevertheless, a teacher can still show students how to use their more developed intelligences to assist in the understanding of a subject which normally engages their weaker intelligences (Lazear, 1992). For example, a teacher might suggest that an especially musically intelligent child learn about plants by making up a song about them.

Because the U.S. educational system stresses the importance of developing mathematical and linguistic intelligences, it often bases student success only on the measured skills in those two intelligences. Supporters of Gardner's Theory of Multiple Intelligences believe that this emphasis is unfair. For example, children whose musical intelligences are highly developed may be overlooked for gifted programs because they do not have the required math or language scores. Teachers must seek to assess their students' learning in ways that will give an accurate overview of the their strengths and weaknesses.

Since all children do not learn in the same way, they cannot be assessed in the same way. Therefore, teachers should consider creating an *intelligence profile* for each student. Knowing how each student learns will allow a teacher to properly assess a child's progress (Lazear, 1992). This individualized evaluation practice will help a teacher make more informed decisions on what to teach and how to present information.

Traditional tests such as multiple choice, short answer, and essay tests require students to show their knowledge in a predetermined manner. Supporters of Gardner's theory claim that a better approach to assessment is to allow students to explain the material in their own ways using the different intelligences. Some of the methods that can be used are student portfolios, independent projects, student journals, and assigning creative tasks. An excellent source for a more in-depth discussion on these different evaluation practices is Lazear, *Teaching for Multiple Intelligences* (1992).

Gardner's Theory of Multiple Intelligences provides a foundation for recognizing the different kinds of abilities and talents students have. This foundation will help schools develop a sense of accomplishment and self-confidence in their students (Figure 1–2).

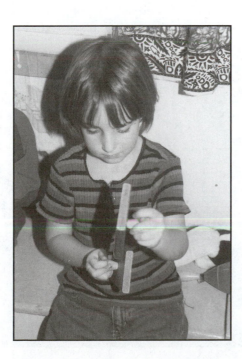

FIGURE 1–2   A child figures out how to play the sand blocks.

The theory acknowledges that all students may not be verbally or mathematically gifted, but those same children may be gifted in other areas, such as music, spatial relations, or interpersonal knowledge. Approaching and assessing learning in this manner allows a wider range of students to successfully participate in classroom learning.

How to Play Music

In light of the Theory of Multiple Intelligences, how can schools, teachers, and you provide musical experiences for young children?

First, do not panic. You can be a teacher of music no matter what your level of musical talent or skill. Talent, in particular singing ability, is helpful in teaching young children, but it is not necessary. What is necessary is interest, appreciation, and enthusiasm for music. Any music is better than no music at all. Even if the students only listen to recordings and enjoy some musical experiences, it is better than nothing. The rest of this chapter will explain how to set up a classroom environment to promote musical learning. The next chapter will explain how a teacher of any musical skill level can learn to promote musical awareness and music learning.

How can teachers create music in the classroom? Music can be sung or it can be played on a tape recorder, record player, compact disc (CD) player, computer, or instrument. There are a variety of **music delivery systems** from which to choose. Here are the pros and cons of each of these ways of using music in the classroom.

Using Records

Many teachers have used music **records** over the years (Figure 1–3). It is not unusual to meet a teacher who praises a record she has been using for 20 years. An advantage of records is the ease of finding the location of a song. The song is ready when the class is ready. While using recorded music is not a lost art among teachers, it is no longer a well-developed art.

Records are fading out of classroom use. The big disadvantage of records is that they do not hold up well over time. Sooner or later, the record gets stepped on, sat on, or

FIGURE 1–3 A varied record collection is an important teacher resource.

DENNIS AND LINDA RONBERG

Linden Tree, Music and Books for Children

Dennis Ronberg and his wife Linda started a children's music business when their children were preschoolers. Commercial music was mostly the available music for children in the '70s, with over-produced, somewhat violent, adult messages. The Ronbergs discovered a children's music artist named Raffi, and they went to teacher conferences and sold his records in the Pacific Northwest. After they moved to the San Francisco Bay Area, they opened a children's book and music store: Linden Tree. Dennis Ronberg likes getting to know children's musicians and book authors. Once a year, the store has a preschool night when teachers come to learn about new books and music. The store also sponsors concerts featuring a variety of children's musicians.

He explains that "a good children's song is a people song, folks can sing it. It's a song that doesn't require an exceptional voice to sing. It's one with wonderful harmonies and a good message that children can understand. I like a song that everyone can jump in and start singing. Music is a great way to get people together. It's also a wonderful way of calming and soothing children."

scratched. Then it can be nearly impossible to find a replacement. Because CDs are replacing records in the music market, records are becoming very expensive to make. Record players are getting older and more difficult to repair or replace. Older record players with bad needles are causing record destruction.

A teacher who does use records should keep them at home and record selections on short tapes to bring into the classroom. That way, if a child damages the tape-recorded copy, another one can be made. Older records can be kept in good condition and used much longer if they are played infrequently. Children's records are going to become more and more difficult to obtain because children's artists are now making tapes and CDs.

Using Tapes

Most teachers have switched to using a **tape recorder** or CD player. Tape recorders are inexpensive to purchase, easy to transport, and easy to store in a locked cabinet so they will be less likely to be stolen. If stolen, they are inexpensive to replace. Not all children's artists have their material available on CD, but almost all have made tapes. The great disadvantage of tapes is that it is difficult to locate the specific place on the tape for the beginning of a song. One can waste a great deal of classroom time trying to find the right place. Some teachers have corrected this problem by putting their songs onto short tapes (Figure 1–4). When they put the tape into the machine it will rewind to the right place quickly. Tapes about five minutes on each side are most effective. Most children's songs are shorter than five minutes, so one song fits on each side of the tape. Sometimes the same song can be recorded twice on one side of the tape.

Short tapes can be stored in a box with small index cards that show the song titles for easy access. It is helpful to mark codes on the outside of the short tapes and/or the index cards so that a teacher can remember which songs are a good match for different learning units. The difficulty with using short tapes is finding inexpensive ones. Do not use 30 minute tapes with 15 minutes on each side, because the rewind time is too long. See the appendix for more information about 10 minute tapes (five minutes on each side) that cost less than a dollar each.

FIGURE 1–4 Tape recorders have a special place in the preschool curriculum.

Using Compact Discs

Compact discs (**CDs**) are much more reliable and less fragile than records or tapes. An increasing number of children's recordings are becoming available on CDs, and CD players are becoming affordable for classroom use. Many teachers have CD players at home so they can make short one-song tapes to play on the tape recorder at school. Buying a CD and making copies of short selections from it for classroom use honors the rights of the music company that made the recording. It is illegal to make a copy of a whole CD or tape, especially in order to avoid paying for an original recording.

It is best to not move a CD player around too much. Players can get out of sync from too much jostling, which can cause skips in the playback. Of course, as with any other small and valuable electronic equipment, it is best to lock up a CD player so it will not be stolen. The disadvantage of CDs is that a lot of very good children's music is only available on tapes. Many new children's recording artists are not supported by a record company, so the initial investment for both tapes and CDs is too great. This problem will probably resolve itself over the next few years, as CDs become the industry standard and more affordable for artists.

A new way to create specialized CDs on the Web has been developed. A few companies will make a CD that consists only of the songs or pieces of music the customer chooses. Unfortunately, the musical selections are still limited, but this may become a viable option for classroom music in the future. Also, with a recordable CD player, teachers may be able to create customized CDs for classroom use.

Another medium for providing music in the classroom is the CD-ROM drive on a computer. Most newer computers with a CD-ROM drive can play music CDs while running other programs on the computer (unless, of course, the other programs run off CD-ROMs). With a couple of classical music CDs, one can have instant background music available in the classroom by loading a CD into the computer CD-ROM drive.

Jill Jarnow
Author, All Ears, A Parent's and Teacher's Guide to Children's Music

Jill Jarnow began listening to children's music when her son Jesse was 18 months old. Jarnow grew up listening to Pete Seeger and Tom Glazer. When Jesse was little, she played the same music for him. Through Jesse's experience, Jarnow learned that timing is everything. At first, when she tried to play Pete Seeger for him, he put his hands over his ears. She thought she was a huge failure. Six months later she tried again, and he was ready to listen to one song about trains. Six weeks later he wanted to hear the whole album. After that, he wanted to hear it all the time.

Jarnow chooses to write about kids' music because "kids are better listeners." She enjoys discovering new artists and spreading the word about them. She loves hearing from teachers and kids about the excitement they feel for something she has recommended. She loves to find music that resonates with her, even if the song is sad. Also, she gets a lot of pleasure when she finds an album that appeals to a wide age span. Albums like that are hard to find, but are worth the search.

She counsels, "Never force feed anything. It does much more harm than good. Instead, choose one song you think the child or children will like. When you play it, encourage them to sing along. Point out funny lyrics and ask them their opinions. Listen to what they say about what they like, and what they don't like." Kids are happy to talk to her about music because they know she values their opinions.

Using Instruments

Instruments are a great way to bring music into a classroom (Figure 1–5a). Teachers are encouraged to bring an instrument into a classroom even if they are not expert players. Young children are not usually very critical of a player's virtuosity. Just talking about an instrument and showing it to children broadens their experience. If you can play a few notes, that is even better. This gives the children an idea of the sound the instrument makes. Older children in school can also come to the classroom and bring an instrument. It is a very special event for first graders to have a fifth grader visit them and show off the

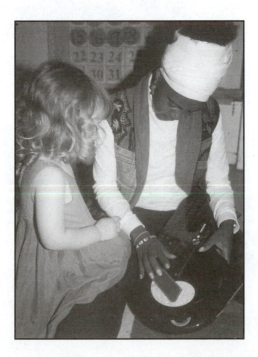

FIGURE 1–5a   A teacher and child explore the QChord. (*Photo used with permission, Suzuki Corporation*)

instrument the fifth grader is learning to play. You can even interview the older student for maximum benefit from the visit. Besides having the visitor play the instrument, ask questions and let the class ask questions to help them learn more about the instrument. After the visitor leaves, play other pieces of music with the instrument the visitor showed them. An excellent tape for featuring the sound of various instruments in short pieces of music is an album called *The Orchestra* narrated by Peter Ustinov (Ustinov, 1987).

If you do not play an instrument, consider learning one that is easy to play. Difficult instruments, like a violin, cello, or oboe, are probably not the best choices. Even a guitar is a time-consuming instrument to learn. However, many instruments are easy to play and will bring extra excitement and interest into the classroom. In the string family, an **autoharp**, on which you press a button for each chord, and a dulcimer, which has only one melody string, are excellent choices. Of the woodwinds, the recorder, kazoo, and ocarina (a small clay or gourd instrument with finger holes, played like a whistle) are all viable alternatives. Percussion instruments include the tambourine, maracas, cowbell, guiro, and drums: conga, bongo, or tom-tom. In the electronic category, a **QChord Digital Songcard Guitar** or an **electric piano** are useful in a classroom.

A great instrument to use with young children is the QChord (Figure 1–5b). This is a new instrument made for teachers. It is very easy to learn; you only have to press buttons. It has a jazzy rhythm accompaniment that can be changed to match the song. QChords are not too expensive, usually about the same cost as an inexpensive guitar. Also, preschoolers can help to play the electronic touch board at one end of the instrument, called *sonic strings or strum plate*. This is an excellent way to include children in music performance. A QChord is easier to carry and less bulky to store than a guitar. Children also really enjoy the rhythm sounds. If you already play the guitar, you can change to QChord easily because the chords have the same names.

The autoharp is another excellent selection for classroom use. It is a small wooden harp with chord bars that dampen the strings that are not part of the chord. The autoharp, like the QChord, is easy to play. It is also small and lightweight. A new autoharp

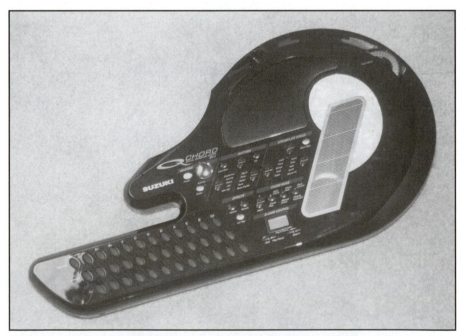

FIGURE 1–5b A QChord is inexpensive and easy to learn. *(Photo used with permission, Suzuki Corporation)*

is about the same price as a QChord. You might even find an autoharp tucked away in a school closet.

An autoharp has two disadvantages. First, it is rather difficult to tune. Second, children's fingers are small, and the strings on the autoharp are taut and can hurt their fingers when they play. For the first problem you can buy an autoharp key, bring the instrument to a music shop, and tune the autoharp by using their electronic tuner instead of tuning by ear. For the second problem, have the children use a guitar pick to strum the strings.

A third choice for a quick and easy instrument to play with students is an electric piano with pre-programmed songs and rhythms (Figure 1–6). These instruments cost a little less than a QChord or autoharp but are not as versatile unless you already play the piano. If you already play, having a keyboard instrument available will help you practice because it will encourage you to play often. An electric piano has an advantage over a real piano for classroom use: you can set it up on a small table or piano stand and play facing the children. This is a great advantage for maintaining class participation and discipline. It is also exciting for children to use the pre-programmed songs, which play with just a touch of a button. A class can make up words to go with tunes that are unfamiliar to them. The electric piano is especially useful for rhythm band time. The instrument provides background music and gives the opportunity to imitate the rhythms and guess the beat. Students can keep the beat on rhythm instruments while the electric piano plays. Best of all, an electric piano has an automatic shutoff button. With a little practice, students can learn to stop singing or playing when the piano stops playing.

Even a teacher with little musical experience can give students the experience of making music using a QChord, autoharp, or electric piano.

Additionally, a whole group of instruments has been developed for young children that are easy for them to play. These are rhythm band instruments and Orff instruments. Please see Chapter 2 to learn more about rhythm band instruments, percussion instruments, Carl Orff, and the development of Orff instruments. Chapter 7 contains a section about unique, international, and ethnic instruments.

FIGURE 1–6 An electric piano is a convenient-sized instrument for classroom use.

Using the Voice

One excellent and standard method of delivering music has not yet been discussed: singing with young children. Many adults in preschool and early elementary classrooms sing with children. However, they often sing in a voice that is comfortable for the adult, but *too low* for children's voices. This can cause serious problems for the children in developing their singing voices. Children need to be able to sing in their own **pitch range** in order to learn how to match pitch and reproduce correct pitch. If they spend most of their young lives singing with adults on low pitches, sometimes referred to as *singing in the basement,* they will learn rhythm but not pitch. By the time they are 13 years old, much of the brain flexibility will be lost, and it will be too late to easily learn how to sing on pitch.

Children's voices are about three whole steps higher in their **tessatura** (comfortable vocal range) than most adult voices. If an adult is a true soprano, her voice is in the right range for singing with children. If an adult is male, a baritone range is the best choice for singing an octave lower than the children. However, very young children have a hard time hearing and matching pitch with a voice that is an octave lower than theirs. Female altos and male high tenors sing in a range that is consistently too difficult for the children. Their tessatura is almost exactly opposite, musically speaking, of the range for children and sopranos.

If, instead of trying to sing the song at the wrong pitch level, the adult plays a recording and sings along with children, the children have a much better chance of learning to sing on pitch. This works even if an adult does not sing perfectly, especially if the recording is in the correct pitch range for children. Using a recording also provides a musical anchor for both teacher and children, so they can use their hands for motions or instruments. Also, a teacher can keep students engaged without having to worry about remembering all the words to a new song (Figure 1–7). You are encouraged to sing, sing, sing with young children, but please do it in their vocal range so they can learn and benefit from the experience.

FIGURE 1–7   *Singing a silly song encourages child participation.*

When to Play Music

In many schools, music time is considered the time to sing traditional, repetitive songs while children bang on instruments for an accompaniment. Teachers should try to broaden this idea of how to bring music into a child's life. At an unconscious level, children are continually listening to their environments. Sounds present in their environments lead to emotional and **auditory** stimulation. Even when no music is in a classroom, children still attend to the noise level, extraneous sounds, teacher's voice, and other children. If no music is being played in a classroom, an atmosphere is still set by the lack of music and the presence of noise. A teacher can begin to affect children's musical development by simply adding soothing and calming music into the classroom ambience to provide them with a feeling of safety and relaxation.

Different kinds of music are needed for different kinds of classroom activities. All children are sensitive to music, but some are more sensitive than others. Many children are distracted by jumpy, speedy, jazzy music with a strong beat. However, this kind of music is great for physical education activities and clean-up time. A teacher would not want to play rock 'n' roll music while children are trying to learn to read, but she would want to select a short piece of music with a lot of energy and not too much wildness as a clean-up song. This issue leads into the next topic: how to fit music into the classroom schedule.

Integrating Music into the Schedule

In designing music to fit a classroom activity, think about what activities the students do during their day and what music might assist in classroom management and comprehensive learning. The following section will consider the various components of the classroom schedule.

The Beginning of the Day

At the beginning of the day, children often enter the classroom either individually with their parents or as a group from the bus or play yard. In either case, children make a transition from a large motor activity to less motor activity and a quieter, calmer atmosphere. Music that will assist this transition is usually calm and quiet. With infants and very young children, a nursery atmosphere can be controlled by the kind of music played. In a preschool classroom, the beginning of the day will sometimes be as long as twenty minutes to half an hour while children arrive at school. It is helpful to provide music that sets a calm and quiet tone during this whole time. In an elementary school classroom, the transition time is much shorter. Teachers find it helpful to start music before going out to get children in the yard. If a school has a working public address system (PA system), the staff may consider playing calm music over it while children enter and settle into their classrooms. If music is already playing in the classroom, a teacher can draw children's attention to the music by commenting, "Let's listen to this beautiful music." This announcement achieves two purposes at once: getting the children to notice the music and bringing the noise in the classroom down to a manageable level. In the morning, most people, including children, like to gather their thoughts and approach their day in a relaxed way. Even if quiet and relaxing music does nothing for the students, it still helps a teacher's peace of mind.

Gathering the Group

Soon after beginning the day, it is time to turn off the quiet and relaxing music and move on to an organizing event. Teachers should ideally take charge of the tape or CD player. Otherwise, children might turn the music up and down all day. In classrooms where music is left playing, the impact of the quieting process is diminished by the background music continuing while the class proceeds. A teacher has to talk loudly over the music, and children must ignore the music in order to pay attention to the teacher.

Later in the morning, a piece of music can be used as a signal to children to begin gathering (Figure 1–8). In a child care program, a different piece of recorded music can be used to signal an announcement. In a toddler program, the organizing event of the day can be indicated by a switch to another kind of music. The same piece of music can be used each day to cue children for circle time. In preschool, music can alert children for circle time or small group time. In an elementary classroom, music can be used during attendance and lunch count. If the school staff uses a PA system for music, it is an easy transition for all the classes to hear the principal's announcement right after the music.

A simple repetitive song sung by the class rather than a recording can be used for the transition to the first group meeting of the day. In a preschool or elementary classroom, some kind of call and response song can be used. Teachers sometimes use a hello song that is very simple to greet each child, something like, "Hello, Tina, how are you? You're our friend and we like you." Other teachers use rhythmic words, without melody, in a call and response format. For example:

Teacher:	Hello there, Nathan.
Children:	Hello there, Nathan.
Teacher:	How are you today?
Children:	How are you today?
Teacher:	We're gonna have a good day.
Children:	We're gonna have a good day.

FIGURE 1–8 A group gathers around an Omnichord. *(Photo used with permission, Suzuki Corporation)*

> *Teacher:*   Hope you stay and play.
>
> *Children:*   Hope you stay and play.

It is fun for the children and good for their music learning if the teacher can incorporate music into taking attendance.

With very young children, up to age four, the consistency and safety provided by using the same piece of music every day for an entire year to signal group time is acceptable for the children. (Although teachers may need a change midway through the year.) With kindergarteners through third graders, teachers should vary the selections at least every two to three months, so children get greater exposure to a variety of music and their interest is maintained.

If flag salute is done each morning, it is an excellent time for a short interlude of patriotic music. The class could occasionally sing "The Star Spangled Banner" (Smith, 1995) or "You're a Grand Old Flag" (Cedarmont Kids, 1995). In one school, a teacher did a patriotic marching song every morning with her kindergartners. While it was wonderful that she did music so regularly, she unfortunately played the same song every day for the entire year. The record was difficult to decipher after fifteen years of everyday use. This experience would have been a great musical benefit to the children if she had made a tape of her original album so her students would not have to listen to a scratchy old record. It would have been even better if she had acquired an album of marches by John Phillip Sousa and played a different march each month.

Moving into the Day

Different kinds of music can be used for a variety of activities later in the school day. While children do a reading activity, teachers find it effective to have some very quiet classical music playing in the background. This music should be instrumental, not vocal or choral, because the words can distract children during reading time. For this kind of activity, the music must be calming. Sometimes this type of music is used as a background on spoken word recordings made for children. If the selection a teacher used when the children were entering the classroom is appropriate and nonintrusive, it can be played again.

A wonderful benefit of playing quiet instrumental music while children do activities in different centers is that a teacher can stop the class and ask students if they can hear the music. The noise level in a classroom can easily escalate, especially when children do activities they enjoy. Asking the children if they can hear the beautiful music playing in the room is a much more positive intervention than saying, "Can you please quiet down now?"

If you do not have any quiet music on hand, an excellent selection of quiet classical music has been compiled by Time-Life Music®. The set of five CDs each have ten selections of famous, relaxing classical music. You will probably recognize some of the themes as you listen. The set is called *Classics for Relaxation* (2000) and can be found at wholesale outlets for an inexpensive price. The same group also makes boxed sets of famous piano selections that work well as background music in a classroom setting.

Research suggests that mathematics learning is enhanced by listening to **classical music** (Rauscher, Shaw, & Ky, 1993). The importance of listening to **baroque music** has been promoted for many years by the people who developed SuperLearning™. Some evidence supports this concept (Rauscher, Shaw, Levine, Ky, & Wright, 1994). However, not only baroque music seems to create this effect, but possibly also music from the early classical period, such as Mozart and Schubert. The actual research showed an effect when college students listened to Mozart before taking a spatial relations mathematics test (Rauscher et al., 1993).

The Mozart Effect. The Mozart Effect is the name given to the outcome of a particular experiment done by Frances Rauscher and her colleagues at the University of California at Irvine (Rauscher et al., 1993). In their experiment they tested college students with a specific set of subtests from a standard IQ test. These are the tests that measure spatial reasoning. The students took the tests right after listening to one of three things: Mozart's Sonata for Two Pianos (catalogued as K. 488) (Haskil, 1998), a relaxation tape, or silence. A significant short-term increase in the student's ability on the spatial reasoning tests was noted for those who listened to the Mozart sonata. This was a landmark study because it showed that a particular kind of music can have a significant effect on certain intellectual skills. After they published their findings, another group, at the University of Auckland, tried to replicate their experiment but did not get the same results (Stough, Kerkin, Bates, & Mangan, 1994). Rauscher and her colleagues then did another study in 1995 with more students and three kinds of music: the same Mozart sonata, silence, and a minimalist piece by Philip Glass (1987). Again they noted the significant increase in spatial IQ score for the Mozart students that they had found in the first experiment (Rauscher, 1995).

In an interesting article by Rauscher and Shaw (1998), they discussed the various studies done by their group and others. They pointed out that other kinds of music, such as folk music, trance music, relaxation music, minimalist music, and also silence, produce no special effects. They also carefully reviewed the kinds of intelligence tests used by the various groups. The Mozart music had no effect on tests in which students had to remember numbers or on general tests of intelligence, but it did affect students' performance on tasks like recognizing visual pattern duplicates and mentally rotating objects. They came to the conclusion that the Mozart Effect is a very specific reaction of the brain that affects spatial reasoning tasks and not other kinds of intellectual tests. They did, however, leave open the possibility that other highly structured music, such as that of Bach, Schubert, or Yanni, might produce the same effect on the brain.

One caution on this research is that a number of people interpret these results as suggesting that teachers ought to play ten minutes of Mozart for their students each day. This is a misinterpretation of the experiment, and doing this probably would not be productive. The subjects were college students wearing headphones, who listened to Mozart for this one experiment. If teachers make preschoolers sit and listen to ten minutes of Mozart every day, they could be training children to hate Mozart. Most preschoolers are not ready to listen to the same music every day. Instead, teachers should put on Mozart in the background and let it set a quiet tone in the classroom.

The results of this experiment also do not mean that listening to Mozart will automatically develop spatial reasoning in young children. Research with young children points to the effectiveness of making music and not just listening to it (Gardiner, Fox, Knowles, & Jeffrey, 1996). This does not mean that listening to music is a waste of time, it only indicates how much research has not yet been done in this area. The research has not been broad enough or comprehensive enough to determine exactly the music that has an effect on mathematics and how that music should be delivered to a young child (Rauscher & Shaw, 1998). Also, it is unknown what effects different kinds of music have on different age groups. Finally, the research is unclear about whether the baroque and classical music should necessarily be played during mathematics time. It seems that an effect on mathematics learning is created by musical training, but this musical training would not necessarily be given during mathematics learning time (Gardiner et al., 1996).

Some musical composers suggested that music similar to baroque music, played at 60 beats per minute (about heart rate speed), may have the same effect. Considering that music is chosen for research because of its ability to structure the cortex of the brain, it may be the organizing effect of the music, and not the 60 beats per minute, that causes enhanced learning. Researchers theorized that the organized and structured style of baroque music (Rauscher & Shaw, 1998) affects the cortical structures of the brain, so it may not be necessary to buy specifically designed music in order to create the possible beneficial effects of listening to baroque and classical music. The people who promote specially composed music do so in an effort to promote particular products. This music may be useful in the classroom, but other classical music might have an equal benefit.

Generally, records, tapes, or CDs of baroque music are easy to find in the local library. Look for music by the most famous baroque composers: Bach, Handel, Vivaldi, Telemann, and Scarlatti. A reference librarian can be helpful in suggesting current artists who have recorded excellent performances of these works. Baroque music usually has an intricate set of notes and has a tendency to encourage toe tapping. It is a welcome change for some children from the calm music of the beginning of the day. However, a teacher must evaluate the particular class to see whether the toe tapping is helpful to the overall classroom ambience.

Transition Times

Baroque music also works well for a clean-up signal or transition time. Choose a piece of music that is fairly short, fun to listen to, and somewhat energetic, but not too wild (Figure 1–9). With this short piece, children can be energized to put away materials from the previous task and be ready for the next event. The music should be lively so that children will work on the clean-up task fairly quickly, but not so energetic that they will get out of control. The length of the piece can be used as a timing device to make classroom clean-up time short and effective. A piece about one minute in length is ideal. Also, one minute does not take undue class time. This is a piece of music that children will hear many times, so they will develop familiarity with it. For this reason, do not change the musical piece frequently. Instead, use the same short piece of music for at least a couple of months. After a few days, encourage children to hum along with the music.

Teachers who are ambitious in the musical education of children might want to change this piece of music every month. At the other extreme, the children can be exposed without harm to the same short piece of baroque music for the entire year. When selecting baroque music, choose about four short pieces for transition times and six or

FIGURE 1–9 Music aids transition times.

seven longer, quieter pieces for math time. The music will be most accessible if each piece of music is on a side of a short tape. A continuous play tape deck is useful for longer periods of listening.

Music across the Curriculum

Music can also be woven into the content areas of social studies, literature, visual arts, and language arts. Each of these subject areas is important enough to have a chapter of its own, so please see Chapters 5 through 10 for more information about how to integrate music throughout the day.

Another effective use of music is in conjunction with physical education. Particularly, if physical education has not been a favorite activity of a teacher or class, it is worth trying to combine music with physical activity. The simplest combination is the use of movement with songs the class is practicing for musical purposes. Just stand up and do large movements with the class while practicing the songs normally sung. Another possibility is to choose music that is great for dancing, and the class will be doing jazzy exercise without any complaints. Keep in mind that as a teacher, you may not have enough time to exercise as much as you should, so the opportunity to stand up and jump along with class is an extra health benefit. Chapter 9 contains more suggestions for how to incorporate movement with music, along with suggestions for particularly good songs to use for this purpose.

Having Music for Lunch

Lunchtime is another opportunity for the class to sing a short song, perhaps daily, while walking to the cafeteria. Many teachers use songs about thankfulness, such as the Girl Scout song, "For health and strength and daily bread, we give our thanks today." Be careful about using songs that have a religious reference in public schools, as some parents are upset by this. Choose the words of the song carefully to emphasize thankfulness and community. Another possibility is to do funny songs about food. Favorites for this time of day are songs such as "I am a Pizza," which is written and recorded by Peter Alsop (1983) and also recorded by Charlotte Diamond (1986). Alsop has another song called "Sandwiches" (1983). Linda Arnold has recorded one about peanut butter sandwiches (1984) and another about popcorn (1986). Lionel Bart's wonderful song "Food Glorious Food" from the musical *Oliver!* (1962) is another great one in this category.

Goodbye

Finally, at the end of the day, it is special to have a song that the students can sing together (Figure 1–10). In preschool this will probably be the same song every day for the entire year. With kindergarteners, change the song in the middle of the year so that the children will have the experience of learning two songs really well. By third grade, a change of song once every two months will provide students with the opportunity to learn five songs by the end of the year. At the end of the day, songs that are quiet, simple, repetitive, and fun to sing work well for a goodbye song. A song like "The more we get together, together, together, the more we get together, the happier we'll be" is an example of a simple song that can be sung while the children are packing up and getting ready to go home. Another favorite is "So Long, Farewell" from *The Sound of Music* (Rodgers & Hammerstein, 1965). With a song like this, you might even consider learning to say goodbye in different languages.

FIGURE 1–10 A favorite preschool farewell song.

Preschool Pointers

When it comes to preschool children, the susceptibility to music is particularly strong. It is possible to influence their emotional states simply with your choices of music.

Preschool teachers can do an experiment in their classrooms and see if the kind of music they choose sets a tone for their children. Then, they can decide what kind of tone they would like to set at the beginning of the day. It helps infants and toddlers to begin with calm and quiet, unless a different atmosphere is desired. Making the decision and purposefully planning the kind of music to play in a classroom environment is important.

The perfect time to use a regular song or short piece of music as a signal is when a group gathers in the morning. A short piece of classical music with a happy sound will help do this. The tape recorder can remain stationary if the room is small, or it can be carried around so the children can hear it, especially if the room is large or there is more than one room. This way, children can be exposed regularly to classical music without having to sit down and listen to it. Forcing young children to sit and listen to classical music can actually do damage, because then they associate the requirement to sit still with classical music. As the group gathers, a teacher can begin with an activity like tapping toes or having adults gently pat a child's back in time to the music that is playing. Do not try hand clapping at this point because the noise from the clapping will overwhelm the sound of the music. If, instead of playing music, you are singing a song, be sure to sing it in a high enough pitch so that the children can sing along. Also, choose a simple song that the children can easily imitate.

P. J. Swift
Children's Radio Programmer, Pickleberry Pie, A Public Radio Program for Children

P. J. Swift fell into children's radio in a rather unusual way. She said, "I taught next to a teacher who had a boyfriend in public radio. She told him I had quite a collection of children's music (all five records, as I recall), so he came by my classroom and asked if I would like to create a kids' program on their public station. I was so flattered I couldn't say no. I had no idea what I was getting into." That was in 1979. Since then, Swift has become one of the country's foremost experts on children's music. She is still doing radio shows and teaching.

Swift enjoys the creative aspects of producing a radio show: writing, pulling things together, and working with kids. For her, children are continually fresh and inspiring. She says, "I think if you show your enthusiasm, kids will show theirs." With Swift, kids certainly do show their enthusiasm.

Sometimes she will hear a program that she wrote several years ago, and she will chuckle. It is satisfying to do a good job. Swift also teaches radio production such as digital editing, producing, and writing, to kids and adults. She frequently serves as a mentor to other inspirational people like herself who are starting radio programs for kids.

Swift is doing an Internet project to list her program's songs on the Web. The name of her radio program is *Pickleberry Pie,* so sometimes children write and ask, "Is the pie real? Can I go there?" One fan wrote to her, "Your program is more fun than a barrel of blue grapes." Swift plays her favorite songs each week. Some are kids' songs and some are in other genres, such as world music, classical, or reggae. Swift is a sucker for songs written or sung by kids, and she also likes humorous kids' songs written by adults. To her, a great song has honesty: the freshness and resonance that comes from getting close to the truth. That is her favorite kind of song, humorous or not.

Swift feels that a happy childhood is the right of every kid. She wishes that this right were cherished and guarded by others. She would like to do her part to help the process along; she does it through her creative efforts in radio.

When asked what is important about music, Swift says, "It's like food. Everyone loves it and needs it, so it brings people together when they share it. A simple song can resonate in a person's life, and add richness, depth, and nuance. It's poetry in 3-D."

Once you begin your group, try to include at least one musical activity in group time each day. If you can, vary the musical activities from day to day. For example, on Mondays use rhythm sticks to tap out the sound of the month, day, and year. On Tuesdays, practice loud and soft (forte and piano) talking or singing. On Wednesdays, clap to the rhythm of a recorded song. On Thursdays, sing along to the song that you clapped with on Wednesday. On Fridays, bounce or dance to the rhythm of the same song. You do not have to follow a rigid plan, but remember to give children a variety of musical experiences.

Teachers also find it helpful to slip music in as a signal during the day. At the end of play time, have a clean-up song. At the beginning of snack, have a choice of one or two thank you songs. Before outside play time, have a *let's go out* song. After outside play time, have a *come on in* song. At the end of the day, have a goodbye song. You can make up your own simple songs or put new words to standard children's songs. You can sing the songs or play recordings on a boom box that can be carried around. Sneak music in whenever you can.

How do I find a recording of a song when I only know the first line?

It is more difficult than you might at first expect to find a song that fits snugly into a curriculum niche.

Many ways are available for finding songs. The first method is to remember, when you first hear a song, to ask the person who is playing it for you where they got it.

Many times, children will bring you songs. Sometimes, they have CDs or cassettes from which they learned a song. In this case, ask them to bring you the tapes or CDs so you can listen to the songs from the original recordings and perhaps even order one for your class. Please do all children's musicians a favor and do not copy songs. If a child has learned a song at camp or from a friend, you will probably have to use other methods to locate the song.

The second step is to ask children or parents if they know of any recordings of a song. Sometimes, children will have learned the same song from different sources. Also, some children are better at remembering sources from which they learned a song. Other teachers are another excellent resource at this stage. A child might even have learned a song from a previous grade level, and a former teacher might have that tape or CD.

If these attempts fail, you have a challenge on your hands. If you have an excellent children's librarian at your local library who has a good music collection, she may be able to help you to locate a song. Sometimes you can find old songs using this method. If a song was written after 1950, it is less likely to be in older song books. A folk song or historical ballad is more likely to be in a library collection. These books often have indexes of first lines of songs. Unfortunately, not many collections of more modern songs exist. One recent book that includes lyrics for children's songs is *Rise Up Singing* by Peter Blood and Annie Patterson (1988). It contains many songs from the 1960s and '70s, but hundreds more children's songs on children's artists' albums are not collected in any book. If you want a nonstandard children's song, it is like searching for a needle in a haystack.

Sometimes the organizations ASCAP and BMI, which help songwriters collect royalties for their songs, can help find the song or the author of a song. However, most children's music writers do not list their songs with either organization, since they collect royalties for songs played on radio or television. ASCAP stands for American Society of Composers, Authors and Publishers. BMI Incorporated is the full name of a nonprofit corporation created to assist musical artists.

The newest way to search for a song is on the Internet. Already, a great deal of information about children's music is available on the Web. An excellent Web site for children's music is put together by Monty Harper and called the *Children's Music Web*. Its address is http://www.childrensmusic.org. Harper and a number of other children's music specialists, including P. J. Swift, have worked for many hours to make children's music available on this site. It contains lists of children's radio stations and children's musicians, links to other Web sites, and articles about children's music. P. J. Swift is working on a comprehensive list of songs for children for this site in the future.

Another project on the Web site that may help you find a song is the Children's Music Mail List. It is an e-mail list of people who work in children's music and/or teach music to children. If you are looking for a song, someone on the e-mail list may know where to find it. If you go to the Web site and send an e-mail to Monty Harper, he can post your question on the list and someone may know the answer to your question.

If you can't find a song, the last resort is to write one yourself that fits the concepts. If you write a great song, be sure to share it with other teachers, or join the e-mail list on the Web site and share it with other children's songwriters and performers.

By the end of your search, you will probably have discovered many other songs that fit your classroom needs, so you may change your mind about what you were looking for.

Monty Harper
Webmaster, the Children's Music Web,
Internet Resources for Children's Music

Children's performer Monty Harper was excited to read about this new thing called the World Wide Web. It sounded like a great way to connect directly to his potential audience as well as with other songwriters and performers. Immediately, he saw the need for a central place to find children's music on the Web, and began a directory of other sites as part of his own Web site. He also started an e-mail discussion group for performers and educators, called the Children's Music Mail List. When children's radio producer P. J. Swift (*Pickleberry Pie*) discovered his site, she gave him a call. She was working on her own children's music site called *Pipsqueaks* and proposed that they join forces. The result was the *Children's Music Web* at http://www.childrensmusic.org.

Harper has also been a children's performer in Oklahoma since 1989. His favorite fan quote is from a kid who saw him perform at a library and wrote on a program comment slip, "Monty Harper is all that and a bag of chips!"

Harper performs his own original songs. He uses a lot of humor and never talks down to kids or shies away from interesting words or concepts. He always tries to get the audience involved with call and answer, sing-alongs, and hand motions. Many of his songs tell stories, and many promote reading and libraries, but mostly they are just fun and entertaining. His favorite audience is kindergarteners through fifth graders, but younger children and adults also enjoy his programs.

In college, Harper took some courses on writing and literature for children, thinking that he might become an author or a poet. The Beatles inspired him to combine writing and music, and he began messing around with two tape players, trying to layer different sounds. He needed something to record, so he put music to a poem he had written called "Jungle Junk." When he played the recording for some kids he knew, they went nuts over it. So, he wrote and recorded some more songs and started passing out tapes to friends and family. Pretty soon, people were asking him to perform, and it grew from there. Now performing is a full-time job!

Harper does the Web work because he enjoys getting to know fellow children's performers and recording artists. Most performers are self-employed and work from their homes, so they do not talk to colleagues on a daily basis. Harper hears from many artists who find the *Children's Music Web* site on the Internet and say, "I thought I was the only one doing children's music!" Harper says, "It's good to be able to bring people together like this."

To Harper, a great song is simple, but complex. It grabs you right away, then grows on you. It makes you laugh. It makes you cry. It makes you dance. It makes you think. It sings itself into your head when you are not looking and sticks. It is your buddy. It never gets boring. Then three years later it tells you something about itself that it never told you before.

Harper feels that children are more important than adults, and more fun. Through the *Children's Music Web,* Harper and P. J. Swift involve kids with such features as *Pipsqueaks* that include songs written by kids, as well as tips for kids about writing songs and making music. They have given children a voice through the Children's Music Web Awards, a series of awards given each year that combines both adult and kid sensibilities. Although knowledgeable children's music professionals narrow the selection of songs so that only *kid appropriate* music is considered, kids make the actual selections of the award winners.

What Music to Play

Recent research showed that it is extremely important to play music for young children and that it *does* make a difference what music is played. A small study done by a high school student illustrates this point. When the student played hard rock music to mice 10 hours a day for three weeks, their ability to run a maze they already knew decreased. A **control group**, listening to classical music, improved their maze time. Unfortunately, the experiment was cut short because the hard rock mice killed and cannibalized each other. This is a striking and powerful indication that the kind of music we feed children is vital to the development of their minds.

Teachers should have their children bring in songs they really like. This is a wonderful way to learn more about their interests. Encourage students to bring in a favorite tape or CD. *Be sure to listen to it* before you play it for the class. You might be surprised to find out what kind of music they enjoy. When one kindergartner brought in Madonna's "Like a Virgin," the teacher explained to the child that this music was inappropriate for school. If you find that your young students have a steady diet of teen pop music, you might want to gently encourage them to broaden their musical horizons.

Consider looking for music from these categories to play in your classroom. It is not necessary to cover every category, but the classical music category needs to be an essential part of every child's education. Playing music in your classroom that you enjoy listening to *yourself* is important. This will help you encourage students to open their own musical horizons (Figure 1–11).

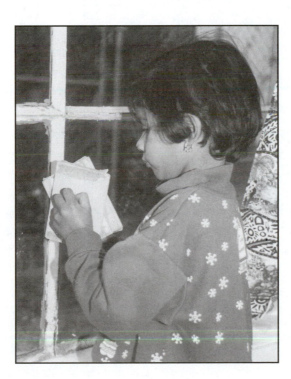

FIGURE 1–11 Take a quiet moment to enjoy listening to music.

Classical

Classical music is a top choice for children because study after study has shown that classical music, particularly baroque and early classical (e.g., Mozart and Haydn), has a significant effect on the brain (Figure 1–12). As discussed earlier, studies have clearly shown that music training and listening positively enhance learning.

Classical music can affect people's moods, memory, perceptions of spatial relationships, learning, and relaxation. Classical music that sounds happy seems to make people feel happier, especially if they listen to it for at least an hour (Lewis, Dember, Scheff, & Radenhausen, 1995). Research showed that when classical music was played in the background during study time, the ability to recall the studied material was better if the same music was played again when the person was trying to recall the information (Weinberger, 1995). A number of studies explore the relationship between music learning and spatial relationships in mathematics. They show that classical music does have a beneficial effect on the brains of young children in promoting spatial reasoning (Rauscher et al., 1994). Finally, calm classical music is one of the kinds of music that seems to promote relaxation. (Bouhuys, Bloem, & Groothuis, 1995; Stratton & Zalanowski, 1989). For all of these reasons, it is important to play classical music for young children.

FIGURE 1–12   All ages enjoy listening to classical music.

Folk Music

Folk music includes a wide variety of musical styles, but it most often consists of simple songs sung by a single voice with minimal instrumental accompaniment. One of the hallmarks of folk music is the vocal quality, usually a rather untrained, straightforward singing style. Folk music is also characterized by simple, singable melodies, often with a chorus that repeats throughout a song. The advantage of folk music for young

Peter Blood and Annie Patterson
Authors, *Rise Up Singing, Collection of Folk Song Lyrics*

Peter Blood's family had a strong interest in singing. They sang hymns regularly at the Ann Arbor Friends Quaker Meeting. They enjoyed singing campfire songs as a family. The Fireside series of songbooks were always on the piano. Blood taught himself to play guitar in ninth grade and began leading folk singing for gatherings of young Quakers.

Blood started collecting music for folk singing groups. When he was a counselor at a Quaker camp for teenagers, the campers were enthusiastic about singing folk songs as well as popular songs from groups like the Beatles. They were frustrated that the camp songbook was limited to traditional campfire songs. Blood and this group of campers developed the idea of putting together a collection of song lyrics. They never finished the project that summer, but Blood continued working on the idea.

After college, Annie Patterson moved back to her hometown area of Philadelphia and met Blood. They began working together on collections of folk songs. Patterson's degree in graphic arts and extensive knowledge of folk music were natural assets for working on a songbook. She did a weekly three-hour folk music show called *Homegrown* on the radio station WXPN. She also began to perform at many open mike coffeehouses at this time. Blood was one of Patterson's biggest fans. They have been a song leading team ever since.

Some years later Pete Seeger helped persuade a nonprofit folk music organization, Sing Out! Corporation, to publish Peter Blood's new singing-oriented collection of song lyrics and guitar chords. Seeger and his manager played a significant role in helping to acquire copyright permissions from most of the major music publishing houses in the United States. *Rise Up Singing* was born in 1988. Later, Blood and his wife, Patterson, made recordings of the songs in *Rise Up Singing*.

Blood believes a great song has a good melody and powerful lyrics. A great title even helps a song to catch on and be remembered and loved. It helps for the melody to be easy enough for people to learn and remember. Blood looks for a song that has a message that strikes a deep chord and moves humanity forward.

children is that they can usually understand the singer without the surrounding, complex instrumental music.

Young children respond well to folk songs because the melody is simple and the words are often repetitious. Many folk songs have been popular songs from a previous era that people have continued to sing. For example, one popular song from the 1960s, "Puff the Magic Dragon" (Various artists, 2000), quickly became a standard folk song. Everyone would consider it a folk song, even though it was written only thirty years ago. It became part of the folk tradition as soon as it was written, as a welcome addition to a long tradition. "Good Night Irene" (Cash, 2001) was written during the 1920s, so it has been in the folk category much longer. Sometimes songs from a previous era are adapted into folk music just because they are still popular and no longer contemporary. An example of this would be the song "I Get Around" (1964), a Beach Boys song that is really an early rock 'n' roll song. From these examples, folk music clearly has a broad definition.

Not all folk songs are good for children. An example is "Banks of the Ohio" (West & West, 2000), a lovely tune that tells the story of a man who killed his girlfriend down by the banks of the Ohio River. This is hardly a suitable song for young children, even though it has appeared more than once in folk collections for children. When looking for folk songs for young children, even the acceptable folk songs of previous eras may not be appropriate for children of this generation. For example, "The Cat Came Back" (Penner, 1992) was considered an acceptable song for second graders in the 1970s. Now, because it depicts violent acts against the cat, it would be considered inappropriate for children younger than fifth grade.

Over the years, some folk songs have been used in the classroom that, on closer examination, have questionable vocabulary or shaky moral lessons. As a teacher, you could handle this in one of two ways. If the song is really questionable, with few redeeming qualities, do not use it. However, some songs may have questionable vocabulary but provide a vehicle for discussing important issues with children. In those cases, keep the song, but make a special effort to talk with the children about the values it conveys. "The Cat Came Back" is a good example. This song is about a man who keeps trying to get rid of a cat, but no matter what, the cat always comes back. Some of the ways the man tries to get rid of the cat are violent, so the song is not recommended for preschoolers. On the other hand, fifth graders understand that hurting animals is inappropriate and harmful behavior. Besides, children often identify with an animal rather than with an adult, so this song helps them to understand that hurting animals is wrong. Children sing the song with gleeful appreciation of the cat's ability to keep coming back, and teachers have an opportunity to discuss death and nonviolence. You need to use judgment in deciding which folk songs to include in a music program and how to discuss the issues brought up by the song with children.

Two of the most famous collections of folk songs were done by Alan Lomax and Ruth Crawford Seeger. Alan Lomax published a collection of 300 folk songs in a book entitled *The Folk Songs of North America* (1960). This is one of the most extensive and well-known collections of folk songs done in the United States. Some of these folk songs are appropriate for children, but many of them are about love, jealousy, murder, death, and violence. The collection was created for adults and musicians, not necessarily for children.

Ruth Crawford Seeger did another folk song collection specifically for children in her book *American Folk Songs for Children* (1948). The collection contains some very famous songs that teachers would probably recognize. We have Ruth to thank for preserving "The Eency Weency Spider," "Froggie Went a Courtin'," "John Henry," "Hush, Little Baby," "Mary Wore Her Red Dress," "Jimmy Crack Corn," "This Old Man," and "Skip to My Lou." Her stepson, Pete Seeger, made some of those songs famous with his marvelous banjo playing and folksy voice in albums of songs for young children.

A modern folk song collection has been done by Peter Blood and Annie Patterson. *Rise Up Singing* (1988) is a collection of the words to songs with guitar chords. Many of the songs are more modern folk songs. This collection has a different flavor from Alan Lomax's and Ruth Seeger's collections, with more emphasis on songs that have values of kindness, peacefulness, and appreciation, rather than teaching history and preserving tradition.

Spirituals

Spirituals are folk songs that were originally written to convey important spiritual truths in a simple style. Spirituals were written by people from diverse backgrounds, but the tradition of preserving the singing of spirituals we owe to many African-American communities. You probably already know a number of spirituals and have probably sung some of them with young children. Such songs as "Swing Low Sweet Chariot" and "When the Saints Go Marching In" are well-known spirituals. Spirituals are both powerful and beautiful, and they are part of our heritage. Children of all ethnicities should learn a few spirituals in the course of their musical training. If you are working in an elementary school, you might consider including spirituals in a unit on the Martin Luther King Jr. holiday or Black History Month in February. However, you should include spirituals at other times so that your students understand spirituals' overall importance to music.

Ballads

A **ballad** is a song that tells a story. The ballad is one of the oldest forms of song, probably dating back earlier than the Middle Ages. Ballads preserve historical information and often convey important moral lessons to succeeding generations. A well-known example of a ballad is the song "Clementine" (Seeger, 1997). It tells the story of a gold miner's daughter. Often, ballads have dark lessons about death and danger that are not necessarily suitable for young children. Choose ballads carefully. Most ballads are too complex for preschoolers, but children in first, second, and third grades have more language ability, so the story aspect of ballads is appealing to them. An example of an appropriate ballad for young children is a song by Pete Seeger, "Abiyoyo" (1994), which tells the story of how a young boy and his father save the town from a giant.

Lullabies

Lullabies are one of the best ways to calm a group of children (Figure 1–13). Lullabies are not only for young children; the power of lullabies is effective with older children and adults. If you play a lullaby when children are entering or leaving a room, the power of the music becomes evident. An example of this occurred during a musical program for a large group of children, kindergarten through second grade, in an elementary school. As the children came into the auditorium, the teacher played her guitar quietly and started to hum a lullaby with no words. The children were unusually calm and quiet. Even the principal remarked on their attentiveness and model behavior.

The power of lullabies is the power of the human voice. The soothing quality of the voice and the simplicity of the music can focus children's attention in a way that classical instrumental music cannot. Much classical music consists of complex harmonies and a variety of instrumentation, and this appeals to adults. Young children cannot yet hear these differences, so to them, this kind of classical music may be boring. Young children are interested in the language that they are trying to learn, so the attraction to music often begins with the sound of the words, which are central to lullabies.

FIGURE 1–13 Spirituals, ballads, and lullabies help to calm children.

Country Music

Country music is similar in style to folk music, so it is often used in music programs for children. For example, country music singer John Denver composed and sang many songs for adults that are now used in children's music programs all over the country. His melodies are simple, choruses often repeat, and the themes are about home, family, and nature. This fact is not true of all country music. Some country music is not appropriate for young children, particularly the songs that focus on lost love and betrayal. These themes are not usually appealing to children because they often view the opposite sex as "yucky." Even in preschool, where opposite sex aversion has not quite set in, songs about lost love and disappointment can be confusing and upsetting. In choosing country songs, listen carefully to the lyrics before introducing the song.

Jazz and the Blues

Jazz and **the blues** are harmonically different from other Western music to which children listen. They are prevalent in our culture, so it is important for children to have exposure to them. Particularly in the elementary school years, it is important to introduce new ways of musical thinking so that children begin to try new tastes (like trying new foods). Jazz and blues music are especially good for teaching children about musical themes and musical variation. Teach them to appreciate a new sound by your own positive example. Some children have already been exposed to these musical styles, so this music may help them feel more at home in a classroom. Others will be challenged to learn how to listen and appreciate it without judging it.

Rock 'n' Roll

Rock 'n' roll is universally appealing to children. The beat captures their attention. Just try it in the classroom. Many teachers have found that the rock 'n' roll songs are great favorites. Put on a folk song version of a tune and the children say, "boring, boring." Then, the same tune in rock 'n' roll format grabs their attention (Figure 1–14). Many

FIGURE 1–14 Rock 'n' roll grabs a child's interest every time.

A Parent's Opinion

The Messages We Send Our Children
(A personal reflection printed with permission by Adam Miller)

On October 17, 1998, there was a school assembly at our elementary school for the entire student body, kindergarten through fifth grade students. The music teacher had booked an a capella rock group. I have seen them perform several times at the Harmony Sweepstakes concert. They are one of the very best adult oriented a capella vocal groups working today. The members of the band began their concert by announcing that they had never before performed during the day and never performed a children's concert. Then they launched into "Take The Money and Run," in which the lyrics state, "sit around the house, get high and watch the news / here's what happens when they decided to cut loose / take the money and run." A fine message for a nine-year-old boy, don't you think? They sang Roy Orbison's "Pretty Woman" to a blonde science teacher. (Let's teach our daughters to obsess on their appearances.) They sang "On Broadway." The only song which seemed appropriate to the children in the audience was "Wimoweh" ("The Lion Sleeps Tonight"). Throughout the concert the children were nonplused.

The program for this assembly is among my favorite examples of "music professionals" who don't get it. The issue at hand, as I see it, is just a lack of understanding on the part of parents and educators regarding the ingredients that go into healthy kids' brains, namely the messages contained in the music children are exposed to. Kids absorb and remember whatever messages they are exposed to—especially in music. How many of our kids can sing us the commercials they hear on TV? Many parents and educators lack an understanding of the messaging ingredients required for healthy children. We live in a culture where we are bombarded by the messages of advertisers and the corporate controlled media. Are these the right messages for our children? Do we want our educators reinforcing these messages? How do you effectively get folks to recognize they are teaching values through music that they, themselves, do not embrace (i.e., sexism, objectification of blonde females, discussions of cocaine among kindergarteners, etc.)? Perhaps the decision makers are unaware of what music is appropriate for children.

I am a member and participant in the Children's Music Network, an association of like-minded teachers, performers, songwriters, radio hosts, and parents who care about the quality and content of music for children. Have they ever heard of the many children's music performers who live, work, and tour? I think about how many Children's Music Network performers you can hire for the price of a commercial rock group: quite a few!

rock 'n' roll songs have good tunes, acceptable words, and tuneful singing. They also have an exciting beat and musical value. Even preschoolers love to dance to rock 'n' roll music. Dennis Westphall recorded an excellent rock 'n' roll song for kids on *Hug the Earth* (Tickle Tune Typhoon, 1985). In "Garbage Blues," a young lady describes in great detail the contents of the garbage that she sorts through in order to take out the recycling. The beat is catchy, the tune is pure rock 'n' roll, and the words are gross enough to engage any child. If teachers need an attention-grabbing device in the classroom, a rock 'n' roll song is the answer.

Educational Children's Music

Many people create songs and music just for children. Most of them have experience as educators of children: classroom teachers, preschool workers, parents, or camp counselors. They have created albums of music for children because they enjoy performing for children, discover creative new ideas that need to be expressed as songs for children, or could not find appropriate music to use in the classroom. Usually, a children's music album includes a variety of styles of music, so a teacher can find songs in different categories on one album. The purpose of most albums is to introduce children to a variety of musical styles, teach songs that appeal to children, and teach an important concept or information (Figure 1–15).

Most children's musicians work with large groups of children, either in assembly programs or concerts. Most musicians have a particular focus important to the musical and educational development of children. Some musicians who do **educational children's music** focus on music about nature, science, and the environment; others focus on music to promote self-esteem, multicultural awareness, drug and alcohol awareness, cooperation and conflict resolution, or reading readiness and language arts. Literally hundreds of musicians do this kind of work, and, unfortunately, some teachers and principals do not know about the contributions children's musicians can make to a school.

It is not unusual for famous adult performers to sing for children. Some adult performers are good with children, but many are used to working with adults and are unfamiliar with what is appropriate for children. The letter in *A Parent's Opinion* from a

FIGURE 1–15 Through the teaching of music, cooperation is learned.

parent to a school board illustrates the kind of problems a school can have when substituting adult performers for children's programs.

The letter shows the concerns many teachers and parents have about the messages we are feeding our children, both consciously and unconsciously. The parent expresses well the reason why so many people work in the field of children's music. The messages in songs make a difference to young children. Throughout this book you will read about the many musicians who are committed to offering something special for children.

Conclusion

When you are teaching children any subject, you teach at many levels at once. When you are doing a musical activity, you are teaching listening skills, vocabulary, language structure, cultural awareness, movement, morals, and values. Be aware of the morals and values you teach. Sometimes, when children do not respond to what you think you are teaching them, they are responding to some other aspect of what you are presenting. Be aware of the different levels that you are teaching so you can consciously control the curriculum at the various levels.

Become aware of the many small spaces available in your daily schedule for teaching values and thinking skills as well as facts. Consider carefully how you will fill up the musical spaces in the cracks of your own classroom and the minds of your young charges.

KEY TERMS

auditory
autoharp
ballad
baroque music
blues, the
Bodily-Kinesthetic intelligence
classical music
cognitive development
compact discs
control group
country music
educational children's music

electric piano
Emotional intelligence
folk music
instruments
jazz
Logical-Mathematical intelligence
lullabies
Multiple Intelligences
music delivery systems
Musical-Rhythmic intelligence

Naturalistic intelligence
Personal intelligence
pitch range
QChord Digital Songcard Guitar
records
rock 'n' roll
spirituals
tape recorder
tessatura
Verbal-Linguistic intelligence
Visual-Spatial intelligence

DISCUSSION QUESTIONS

1. Discuss what kind of music delivery system you plan to use and why you chose that system.

2. Give the pros and cons of using CDs and tapes in the classroom.

3. How do you plan to expose your students to instrumental music?

4. Why is it important for adults to sing with children in a higher vocal range? How can adults do this if their voices are low pitched?

5. Name five transition times when music can be incorporated into a classroom schedule.

6. Name the 10 styles of music to which children should have some exposure.

7. What is the Mozart Effect?

8. Name seven reasons why music should be included in the curriculum for the young child.

9. Name and describe the eight intelligences according to Howard Gardner's Theory of Multiple Intelligences.

10. How is spatial reasoning different from Visual-Spatial intelligence?

SUGGESTED LEARNING ACTIVITY

Choose 10 short pieces of music suitable for a variety of transition times in the educational setting in which you expect to work. List the pieces of music and discuss why you chose each one for that particular time slot. If you can, record the pieces on short tapes or order a specialized CD, so the music is ready for classroom use.

REFERENCES

Alsop, P. (1983). *Wha'd'ya wanna do?* [cassette]. Santa Cruz, CA: Flying Fish Records.

Arnold, L. (1984). *Happiness cake* [cassette]. Santa Monica, CA: A & M.

Arnold, L. (1986). *Make believe* [CD]. Santa Monica, CA: A & M.

Bart, L. (1962). *Oliver!* [CD]. Toronto, ON, Canada: Madacy.

Beach Boys, The. (1964). *All summer long* [CD]. London: EMI.

Blood, P., & Patterson, A. (1988). *Rise up singing.* Bethlehem, PA: Sing Out!

Bouhuys, A. L., Bloem, G. M., & Groothuis, T. G. G. (1995). Induction of depressed and elated mood by music influences the perception of facial emotional expressions in healthy subjects. *Journal of Affective Disorders, 33,* 215–226.

Cash, J. (2001). *Roads less traveled* [CD]. Studio City, CA: Varese.

Cedarmont Kids. (1995). *School days* [cassette]. New York: Author.

Diamond, C. (1986). *10 carrot diamond* [cassette]. Vancouver, BC, Canada: Hug Bug Records.

Draper, T. W., & Gayle, C. (1987). An analysis of historical reasons for teaching music to young children: Is it the same old song? In J. C. Perry, I. W. Perry, & T. W. Draper (Eds.), *Music and child development* (pp. 194–205). New York: Springer-Verlag.

Gardiner, M. F., Fox, A., Knowles, F., & Jeffrey, D. (1996). Learning improved by arts training. *Nature, 381,* 284.

Gardner, H. (1983). *Frames of mind.* New York: Basic Books.

Gardner, H., & Hatch, T. (1989). Multiple intelligences go to school: Educational implications of the theory of multiple intelligences. *Educational Researcher, 18*(8), 4–9.

Glass, P. (1987). *Music in twelve parts* [CD]. New York: Nonesuch.

Haskil, C. (1998). *Mozart* [CD]. New York: Uni/Philips.

Lazear, D. (1992). *Teaching for Multiple Intelligences.* Bloomington, IN: Phi Delta Kappan Educational Foundation.

Lewis, L. M., Dember, W. N., Scheff, B. K., & Radenhausen, R. A. (1995). Can experimentally induced mood affect optimism and pessimism scores? *Current Psychology: Development, Learning, Personality, Social, 14,* 29–41.

Lomax, A. (1960). *The folk songs of North America.* Garden City, NY: Doubleday.

Penner, F. (1992). *Cat came back* [cassette]. Ukiah, CA: Shoreline.

Rauscher, F. (1995). (Letters to the editor). *Neuroscience, 185,* 44–47

Rauscher, F. H., & Shaw, G. L. (1998). Key components of the Mozart Effect. *Perceptual and Motor Skills, 86,* 835–841.

Rauscher, F. H., Shaw, G . L., & Ky, K. N. (1993). Music and spatial task performance, *Nature, 365,* 611.

Rauscher, F. H., Shaw, G. L., Levine, L. J., Ky, K. N., & Wright, E. L. (1994, August). Symposium conducted at the annual meeting of the American Psychological Society. Los Angeles, CA.

Rodgers & Hammerstein. (1965). *The Sound of Music* [CD]. New York: RCA.

Seeger, P. (1994). *Stories and songs for little children* [cassette]. Lakewood, CO: High Windy Audio.

Seeger, P. (1997). *American favorite ballads* [CD]. Washington, DC: Smithsonian/Folkways.

Seeger, R. C. (1948). *American folk songs for children*. Garden City, NY: Doubleday.

Smith, K. (1995). *It's a lovely day* [CD]. New York: Sony.

Stough, C., Kerkin, B., Bates, T., & Mangan, G. (1994). Music and spatial I.Q. *Personality and Individual Differences, 17,* 695.

Stratton, V. N., & Zalanowski, A. H. (1989). The effects of music and paintings on mood. *Journal of Music Therapy, 26,* 30–41.

Tickle Tune Typhoon. (1985). *Hug the earth* [cassette]. Seattle, WA: Author.

Time-Life Music®. (2000). *Classics for relaxation* [CD]. Richmond, VA: Time-Life.

Ustinov, P. (1987). *The Orchestra* [cassette]. Toronto, ON, Canada: Mark Rubin Productions.

Various artists. (2000). *Songs for kids* [cassette]. New York: Legacy.

Weinberger, N. M. (1995). *Musica Research Newsletter.* [Retrieved from http://www.musica.uci.edu, October, 2001.]

West, J., & West, H. (2000). *Country bluegrass* [CD]. Berkeley, CA: Prestige.

ADDITIONAL RESOURCES

Blythe, T., & Gardner H. (1990). A school for all intelligences. *Educational Leadership, 47*(7), 33–37.

Chastain, G., Seibert, P. S., & Ferraro, F. R. (1995). Mood and lexical access of positive, negative, and neutral words. *Journal of General Psychology, 122,* 137–157.

Fogarty, R., & Stoehr, J. (1995). *Integrating curricula with multiple intelligences. Teams, themes, and threads. K–College.* Palatine, IL: IRI Skylight.

Gardner, H. (1991). *The unschooled mind: How children think and how schools should teach.* New York: Basic Books.

Kornhaber, M., & Gardner, H. (1993). *Varieties of excellence: Identifying and assessing children's talents. A series on authentic assessment and accountability.* New York: Columbia University, Teachers College, National Center for Restructuring Education, Schools, and Teaching.

Lazear, D. (1991). *Seven ways of teaching: The artistry of teaching with multiple intelligences.* Palatine, IL: IRI Skylight.

Martin, W. C. (1995). *Assessing multiple intelligences. Meeting of the International Conference on Educational Assessment.* Unpublished contribution. Ponce, PR.

Rauscher, F. H., Shaw, G. L., Levine, L. J., Wright, E. L., Dennis, W. R., & Newcomb, R. L. (1997). Music training causes long term enhancement of preschool children's spatial-temporal reasoning. *Neurological Research, 19,* 1.

CHAPTER **2**

Music Basics

Teachers are often surprised to find out how many ways they can teach music to young children, even if they consider themselves totally nonmusical persons. Musicians learn much about music that is just information and does not require any musical ability. Even if a teacher is well-trained musically, he might not have been exposed to the variety of ways to teach musical information simply. This chapter is a description of musical ideas that classroom teachers and preschool educators who are not musically trained can use to teach music to young children. It is also useful to musically trained teachers because it suggests new ways to teach musical information.

The Importance of Music Learning

Children begin learning about music the moment someone jiggles them up and down or they begin rocking in their cribs. According to new research, this jiggling includes experiences in the womb. By the time they are five years old, they have learned the rhythm of language—feeling the beat, keeping time to the music—and can usually distinguish between $\frac{4}{4}$ time and $\frac{3}{4}$ time, although they would not call it that. Many children at this age have learned how to sing (and pester grownups with) simple songs. As long as they are exposed to an environment with the elements of music present, almost all children will naturally have the ability to interact with that musical environment. Thus, a teacher's job is to provide a musical environment to support the natural development of a child's **musical ability** and neural growth.

In the preschool years, the musical environment is usually comprehensive enough that a child will develop a musical sense. Music is often played in classrooms. During music time, children gather to sing or move to music. Music accompanies favorite television programs. Parents often play some kind of music for their children at home or in the car. Most preschool children will glean enough music from their environments to develop some level of musical ability, even if they do not have well-organized and intentional musical experiences, such as music lessons or music specialists at their schools. All musical development is not lost if the child does not have an outstanding preschool musical experience. Many children have been known to excel at the elementary level after an unremarkable preschool musical experience.

However, a very serious concern in the preschool years is a child's physical ability to hear. Poor hearing can inhibit musical development for young children. The lack of stimulation to the brain caused by difficulty hearing can actually produce long-term hearing loss even if a child's physical ability to hear later develops to the typical level. This situation is the reason why physicians are so concerned when a young child has a series of ear infections. A child's development of hearing nerves are dependent on sound reaching them, thus ear infections in childhood can cause a lifelong hearing loss. Because teachers have experience with a wide range of children, they can often identify problems that might go unnoticed by parents. Preschool teachers should take time each year to test the hearing of the children or encourage parents to have children's hearing tested as a routine part of health screening.

Once you know the children are able to hear music, you can organize purposeful musical activities that help children progress in language, **pitch**, and **rhythm** skills. Just as children in the preschool years need gross motor opportunities to develop large muscle movement, children also need to listen to songs that have words they can hear and understand to help them develop language skills (Figure 2–1). They need music in their pitch range to help them hear tunes so they can sing along comfortably in their own **vocal range**. They need music that has a clear, unambiguous beat so they can learn to keep time to the rhythm. However, not every single song must meet all of these requirements. Children do not spend their whole time riding tricycles to develop gross motor skills; rather, they engage in a variety of physical activities. Similarly, they need a variety of musical pieces in their music program.

Experienced teachers may already have a number of favorite songs that they use with children. Inexperienced teachers can develop a set of songs for classroom use by using the

FIGURE 2–1 Purposeful musical activities start in preschool.

CD included with this textbook and by listening to a variety of recordings of children's music. Throughout this book, many children's musicians are featured. This is done for the purpose of introducing teachers to the scope of children's music currently available.

Each song in your music selection should contribute to a child's musical development in some way. Some are simple tunes, easy to learn, fun to sing, and great for pitch development. Others are jazzy dance pieces that get the kids moving in time to the beat. Still others are songs that fit seasons and help children learn about musical and social cultures.

A teacher's modeling of musical behavior through enjoyment of the songs and ease with musical activities is another important factor in a child's music education (Figure 2–2). By the teacher's participation, a preschool child learns that music is valuable. A teacher does not have to be a great singer. All that is required is enthusiasm and willingness to sing in children's vocal range.

In the elementary school years, children often have increasingly diminished exposure to music as other aspects of a curriculum, such as reading and mathematics, become more important. The period from ages five to nine is critical for musical development. The lack of music learning may eventually harm a child's reading and mathematics ability because of disuse of neural pathways in the brain. Because of a lack of stimulation to the aural nerves, the neural links that might otherwise form can be underdeveloped. As the body matures in adolescence, unused neural connections are pruned away. Because of the plastic nature of the brain during this period of child development, the window of opportunity, or developmentally appropriate time, when children are able to learn certain skills easily, is not used. This leaves the brain without the neural connections that might have been made. Such lost neural connections may not hurt performance in the elementary school years, but the advantage of musical development is likely to affect mathematical ability in the teens and early twenties.

In elementary school, it is important to have purposeful musical activities because children are ready for more sophisticated and complex music learning and the social environment does not readily provide it. The social environment of elementary school–age children provides a few commercial jingles, occasional jump rope rhymes, and incidental

Diana Zegers
Music Educator, Preschool Music Specialist, Author: Discover Music

Diana Zegers started thinking about music curriculums when her son was three years old. She searched music stores for games she could use to begin teaching him musical concepts. When she found nothing, she made her own cards and games. She then started to teach neighborhood classes once a week. Soon she was hired by a local Montessori school to teach the same lessons. After a few years, it was evident that more teachers wanted to teach the lessons she had developed. She wrote an entire curriculum for preschool music, and thus *Discover Music* was created.

Zegers shows teachers how simple it is to teach musical concepts to three- and four-year-olds. In addition to the lessons published in *Discover Music,* she has collected many other ideas that really work. Her focus has not been to teach particular songs, but to instruct teachers how to find or create their own songs to fit the units they teach.

One of Zegers's favorite ways to teach music is using *copy cat* songs. These are songs with new words to old tunes that enable a nonmusical teacher to read music. The teacher already knows the tune, so with the addition of new words, it becomes a new song. This is true for children as well. If they already know the tune, they immediately focus on the new words and concepts. Zegers has been collecting *copy cat* songs and has found them to be very popular with preschool teachers and their students.

Zegers is currently the director of two Montessori schools. However, she still enjoys training teachers in music and conducting workshops and seminars.

cartoon music. If the current trend in education continues to cut music programs from the early elementary grades, the average elementary school child is likely to get almost *no* **musical training**. Soon music education will be limited to children whose parents make the effort to take them to musical classes and events. Unlike preschoolers, elementary school–age children are usually discriminating in their musical tastes. A preschooler will learn many basic tunes indiscriminately from the variety of television programs he

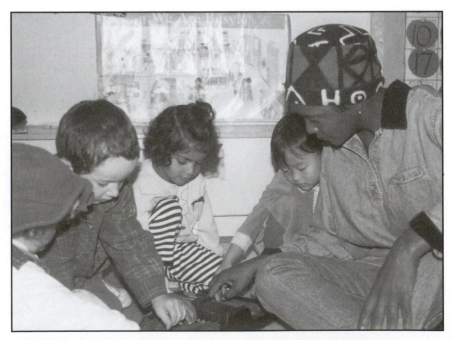

FIGURE 2–2 Model musical behavior through your own interest.

HAP PALMER'S VIEWPOINT

Hap Palmer talks about the importance of music learning:

Gardner's Theory of Multiple Intelligences suggests that music is an independent intelligence that may be helped by influences at home and school. If music is overlooked, essential learning stages may be missed in early childhood and the potential intelligence may diminish.

The concept of diminishing intelligence has been supported by the research of Edwin Gordon. He developed a test which measures the ability to retain a short melody in your mind and then compare it with a second melody. Gordon defines the ability to hear music that is not physically present as *audiation* and determines the level of musical aptitude by the ability to audiate. There are two parts to the test: tonal and rhythmic.

Gordon found the audiation of eighteen-year-olds resembled their audiation as nine-year-olds. While students may learn to perform better and develop musical coordination skills through the school years, they cannot actually enhance their basic aptitude for mentally retaining tonal or rhythmic patterns. When students between the ages of five and nine were tested, Gordon discovered that music audiation scores would *decline* if the children did not receive musical stimulation. The greatest loss occurred between the ages of five and six. Students who did not receive music stimulation between the ages of five and six and then began to receive music stimulation at age seven showed some improvement up to age nine. The audiation scores that then stabilized at age nine were slightly higher than those at age eight but noticeably lower than at age five. It appears that the longer the delay in music stimulation in the form of singing and rhythmic moving, the more the ability to audiate can be lost and the less will be regained.

Although there is currently no test to measure music aptitude in children younger than five years, there is a clear trend in Gordon's research. If children have not experienced singing and rhythmic moving by the time they reach kindergarten their music aptitudes may well have declined. If they are given a nurturing environment starting in kindergarten, their music aptitude scores can increase until age nine. For each year closer to nine, the increase is less noticeable.

In another study, a low correlation was found between the music aptitude of parents and children. It seems that the musical intelligence of children born to a family where parents provide musical experiences will be nurtured, but there is no guarantee that musical parents will pass on musical intelligence to their offspring.

As is the case with language, complete yet informal exposure is necessary for adequate musical development. According to Gordon, music achievement will depend on a number of factors. Students need a balanced diet of music experience. This includes experiences with major, minor, and other tonalities and a wide variety of rhythms. A broader range of experiences will enable children to assimilate a more complete understanding of musical organization. Formal study of meters and tonalities is not needed at this early stage. Young children should sing and move to music informally, much the way they work with language during the first five years of life. As with language, children should not be deprived of the whole musical picture because they are too young to understand it. Children learn and understand a great deal more than they can speak about during their first years, but we would never think of not speaking to infants and toddlers just because they cannot speak. The child will naturally assimilate the sophistication of the language, the grammar, and the dialect in a specific environment. When children begin to speak, they will attempt to reproduce those sounds or words that their lips and tongue can reproduce. Their comprehension of language far exceeds their ability to coordinate speech.

Music works the same way. The broader the exposure and the more sophisticated the musical vocabulary, the richer will be the child's intuitive understanding of how music is organized. Children's early attempts at singing or moving to music may show a lack of coordination, but they should not be deprived of experiences that nurture comprehension before they are able to coordinate their activities.

watches. Not as many television programs are geared to teaching music to elementary school–age children as there are musical programs for preschoolers. Finally, the lack of exposure to music leads to inexperience with music, and in the later elementary school years a child is often less willing to pursue studies in which he feels untalented. This outcome is most commonly seen in the middle school years when children begin to define their talents and areas of expertise.

In the elementary school years, the culture of children also begins to exert its influence. Each generation of children trains the next one about appropriate and acceptable behavior. Elementary school boys begin to circulate rumors among themselves that music is for girls, and girls tell the boys that they are no good at music. These factors coalesce to make music proficiency more inaccessible as children grow older.

Learning the Beat

The **beat** is the basic rhythmic pulse that steadily undergirds the music. Rhythm is the various lengths of musical sounds. Very young children, between the ages of six months and one year, begin learning to keep time to music by rocking their whole bodies. By the time they are one-year-olds, they are able to stand up and bob to the music. Two- and three-year-olds are ready to use whole body movement in a variety of ways to keep time to music. Preschoolers enjoy jumping, walking, bouncing, wiggling, dancing, and swaying to music. Some children learn to keep time to the beat as young as nine months, others do not learn this until almost five years.

With preschoolers it is important to develop keeping the beat in a variety of different ways. Children can keep the beat to a song by clapping their hands while they sing. They can keep the beat by listening to music and tapping their fingers on their knees (Figure 2–3). They can keep the beat by jumping up and down or dancing to the music. They can keep the beat to an instrument playing, particularly an instrument such as a small electric piano that has a rhythm setting. Preschoolers particularly need to learn how to stay with the beat: to bounce, jump, or clap in time. Preschoolers have a tendency, when the beat is either particularly slow or particularly fast, to lose the connection with

FIGURE 2–3
Clapping helps children learn rhythm and beats.

the beat, so begin with a moderate pace. As the beat goes faster, make sure that the children are staying with the beat and not rushing ahead or dragging behind. With preschoolers, teachers should encourage large motor movement but begin to train the finer motor movements (Figure 2–4). Encourage keeping the beat by having them just tap their hands on their knees or by simply tapping a foot or nodding their heads. This begins to develop the smaller groups of muscles as well. In summary, make sure that the activities are varied so that preschoolers are exposed to many different ways of keeping beat.

In the early elementary grades, it is helpful to learn more complicated rhythms so that children can learn to keep time with the beat and not be confused by the rhythmic patterns that overlay the beat. Many teachers have a tendency to practice rhythms that are very easy with elementary school–age children. Teachers often clap a standard *Ta titi ta ta* and have the children respond *Ta ta*. But this kind of rhythm is too easy to present any challenge to the child. It would be better to clap a different rhythm each time so that the students have to listen to what was clapped and repeat the pattern back. This would achieve the same effect of getting the children's attention while helping to develop their rhythmic abilities. Another common mistake with elementary students is spending music time playing a rhythmically straightforward folk song and clapping to the beat. This would be like singing the "Alphabet Song" (Bartels, 1980) over and over with eight-year-olds. Very few seven- to eight-year-olds have trouble keeping a straightforward, steady beat. Older children need to begin to differentiate the rhythm of the notes from the beat of the music. Unfortunately elementary school teachers have a tendency to repeat the preschool curriculum of repetitious songs and keeping the beat. Try to be aware of this fact and present elementary students with as much challenge in rhythm as possible.

One way to do this is to use a **call and response** format with clapping. A teacher claps a rhythm and the children clap the same rhythm back. Start with simple, short rhythmic patterns, then move on to longer and more complicated patterns. With numbers representing the names of the beats, say, "One, two, three and four" while clapping: one (wait), two (wait), three (wait), four (wait).

FIGURE 2–4   Keeping the beat is a preschooler's challenge.

A simple clapping pattern is long, long, short, short, long. One can also say *"ta, ta, titi, ta."* *Ta* is twice the length of *ti*. In musical terms, *ta* is a quarter note and *ti* is an eighth note. If students are Spanish-speaking, be sure to use the words *da* and *di* instead of *ta* and *ti* because of the sexual connotations of the word *titi* in Spanish. Clap this pattern:

1	2	3 +	4
/	/	/ /	/
Ta	ta	titi	ta

Do a number of different combinations of short and long patterns with the class, using both the numbers and the words. Another example is short, short, long, long, long. Say, "One *and* two, three, four." In rhythmic words that would be *"titi, ta, ta, ta."* Clap this pattern:

1 +	2	3	4
/ /	/	/	/
Titi	ta	ta	ta

When students are doing well on the four **beat patterns**, then add an additional four beats, going to an eight-beat pattern. For example, one, two, three *and* four, one *and* two, three, four is a combination of the two short patterns we have discussed, but it is harder to remember because of the length. Notice that we do not count five *and* six, seven, eight but in music we repeat one, two, three, four. This work on patterns fits right in with pattern learning for mathematics, especially in kindergarten through third grade.

A teacher can then begin to make up **rhythmic patterns** that consist of four-beat patterns that are then combined into eight-beat patterns. The strokes above the words indicate where to clap. Try to figure out how to clap the rhythmic pattern in this written example:

/	/	/ /	/
Ta	ta	titi	ta

/ /	/	/	/
Titi	ta	ta	ta

Clap this pattern and say, "One, two, three *and* four." Then clap one *and* two, three, four.

The *ta* and *titi* words are another method of counting the same rhythm. Notice that the *ta* that occurs on the first beat is capitalized. That is to help you remember which one is on the first beat. Go back now and clap the same rhythm using the *ta* and *ti* words. Here's a harder one:

/	/ /	/ /	/
Ta	titi	titi	ta

/ /	/	/ /	/
Titi	ta	titi	ta

When clapping this pattern, say "One, two *and* three *and* four." Then it changes to one *and* two, three *and* four. Practice this a few times and try out the other ones at the end of the chapter.

In the counting exercises above, the counting is four beats to a group, called a **measure**. Use the word *measure* with the students to help them understand that beats are grouped into larger units. There are normally from two to 12 beats in a measure. In most children's and folk music there are two, three, four, or six beats to a measure. The simplest music is usually four beats to a measure. The word *measure* is synonymous with the word **bar**, but children sometimes confuse this with other kinds of bars. In written music, each measure is denoted by a line, called a *bar line,* at the beginning and end of each measure.

In between each beat is the **off beat**. Most musicians say *and* when counting the off beat. Practice clapping the **on beat**, saying, "One, two, three, four" while you clap on each number. Then, practice counting, "One, two, three, four" on the beat while clapping *between* the beats, on the *off beat.* That is, say "one," then clap on the *and,* say "two," then clap on the *and,* say "three," then clap on the *and,* and say "four," then clap on the *and.* This is a somewhat difficult exercise for kindergarteners but not too hard for second graders. This exercise can also be accomplished by stamping your foot *on* the beat while clapping your hands on the *off beat.*

With second and third graders, the class can begin to move to the next level of abstraction by writing down the rhythmic patterns they are learning. Teach the pattern first, then clap it, then write it, then clap it while reading it. This is one of the basics of learning to read music. It is a skill that most nonmusical teachers can do with their classes and will find themselves getting better at it as they practice reading and writing rhythms with their classes.

The most difficult level of rhythmic practice is to take a rhythmic pattern you hear, analyze it, and then write it down so that others can read it and reproduce it. Real musicians do this when they are compose music. Short rhythmic patterns are not too difficult to remember and repeat. However, a long pattern is too hard to remember. Analyzing the beat pattern and writing it down makes it easier to remember because different areas of the brain are used to help store the information. A group of third graders with a lot of practice copying beat patterns can try figuring out a beat pattern. This activity is easier in a group. However, if a class is ready and interested in analyzing rhythmic patterns and writing them down, talk to an experienced musician or music teacher who can teach them how to do this. Teachers who wish to develop their expertise in this area can take a class in beginning musicianship at a local college.

With children of early elementary grade age, it is fun to use an electronic instrument with a strong beat and different rhythmic patterns, so the children can play *guess the beat.* Play a rhythm and have the children try to guess how many beats are in the rhythmic pattern. First have them tap to the beat while you say "one" to the strongest beat, wherever they feel the downbeat occurring. After that, count out the other beats between the downbeats. Once they have an idea of how many beats are in the rhythm, then they can begin learning how to listen for the rhythm over the beats. This listening, tapping, filling in the other beats, and figuring out the rhythm as separate from the beat are all part of learning to analyze and imitate rhythms. Children and adults can remember rhythmic patterns of about four to six beats and imitate the rhythm without doing formal analysis. However, if a student is trying to remember a long or difficult rhythmic pattern, especially one with many off beats, it is too difficult to do without analyzing the pattern and writing it down. This is why classical musicians developed the habit of writing down the music. Also, it is easy to do a rhythmic pattern that is *almost* the same as the one you heard. However, if you want the rhythmic pattern to be accurate, it needs to be written so that it can be remembered correctly.

One of the ways to help preschoolers and early elementary grade students notice the beat is by having them pop up on a particular beat. With preschoolers it is important to emphasize the downbeat, so *pop up activities* should be done to the downbeat. The greatest problem with using this technique with preschoolers is that they pop up with even the slightest encouragement and often nowhere close to the beat. The trick is to get them to sit down and listen to the music until the appropriate point comes for them to pop up. You can overcome this problem by starting with infrequent popping up on a very strong downbeat. As students get better at listening and paying attention to the appropriate time for popping up, you can add more opportunities. With elementary grade students, this activity is best done in a small group on the classroom rug, not at their desks. This activity does not work well for upper graders because of their size and the lack of classroom space, but is very popular with younger students.

Tempo

Tempo is the speed of music. This is not to be confused with the sound quality of the music. For example, music that has short, disconnected notes can be played at any speed. In classical music a variety of different words are used to describe the speed. These words are Italian. Even young children can be exposed to the words that describe tempo. Preschoolers can learn to use the words lento, moderato, and presto for slow, medium, and fast. You can practice different speeds by turning the tempo dial of an electronic instrument such as a QChord or an electronic piano. If you do not have an electronic instrument, you can use a drum to play different speeds. Children can move in time to the drum with whole body movements, and you can call out the name of the tempo while they are moving. As the children get more experienced with this activity, you can gradually speed up and slow down the music while they try to stay with the beat. You can also have them call out the tempo word that goes with the beat. This exercise is similar to the clapping and tapping activities we were doing while learning the beat. Again, with preschoolers, the great emphasis is on learning to move in time to the beat.

Elementary school–age children can learn to use a variety of different words to describe tempo. Expose them to the Italian terms used in classical music. A very slow speed can be lento, largo, or grave, with grave, pronounced *grah-vay*, being the slowest. Almost as slow is adagio, pronounced *aah-da-gee-o.* For more moderate speeds, the word moderato fits well. Andante, pronounced *on-don-tay,* is a walking speed. We gradually speed up with allegro, meaning fast, vivace, pronounced *vee-vah-chay,* meaning fast and lively, and presto, meaning super fast. Presto is generally their favorite speed. A few other terms such as leggiero, meaning lightly and airily, and allegretto, meaning playfully and fast, can be included in their musical vocabulary.

Teachers can do different kinds of activities to teach these tempo words. Use different pieces of music for each speed word. As suggested in Chapter 1, it is helpful to put the pieces of music that you want to play onto short tapes (six minutes on each side). First, have children listen to each piece of music and decide what word goes with each piece. Then do some movement activities, like dancing, tapping, moving, or marching to the music. Next, play a piece of music and have children guess the tempo word that matches the music. In order to add to the challenge, do not use the same music you used to teach the tempo words. To vary your approach, use a drum instead of recordings. You could use almost any percussion instrument for this exercise. A small electric piano or a QChord that has a tempo dial is especially enjoyable to use. Speeding up music is called *accelerando.* The word is similar to our English word *accelerate.* The word *ritardando* means to slow the music down. It is sometimes shortened to *ritard.* or *rit.* in written music. The other technical music word for slowing down music is *rallentando* or *rall.* for short.

Another method to teach tempo is to use a metronome. An old-fashioned metronome looks like a small triangle with a tail that clicks back and forth. You can move a sliding piece on the tail to make it click at different speeds. If you happen to have a metronome or find one in a closet at your school, it is an entertaining little gadget to use with your students. More likely, you will use an electric piano or QChord with a tempo setting to teach about different speeds. Metronomes and electronic instruments can keep a tempo at an exact speed. People have a tendency to either speed up or slow down the tempo, but with a machine available, students can learn to keep a steady beat. After they have practiced keeping a regular beat with a metronome or electric piano, you can turn down the sound of the beat and see if your students can keep the tempo. After a few minutes, you can turn the sound up again and see if you were able to keep the exact same tempo.

Conducting

Even very young children like to be the director of the band. Conducting is a simple affair with preschoolers. One child is the leader and waves his hands in time to the music, while other children follow and dance or move to the beat. With elementary school–age children, conducting creates new levels of understanding about rhythmic patterns (Figure 2–5). Learning the patterns that a *real* conductor uses helps children to understand the concepts of beats and measures. Teachers can begin by teaching how to conduct the downbeat. First, listen to the music and tap to the beat. Then get the feeling of where the strong downbeat is. Once students feel the downbeat, they can move their hands from the top down every time they hear it. Have students conduct just the downbeat and then count the other beats out loud until the next downbeat. Even kindergartners can learn the **conducting pattern** that real musicians use. Two-beat music is a simple down and up beat. For three beats, the hands go down, out, and then up. In conducting, the two hands mirror each other. So, for three beats, both hands do a downbeat together then point away from each other for the second beat and come up to the top for the third beat (Figure 2–6).

For four beats, we begin with a downbeat, then go in, out, up (Figure 2–7). Switch between saying the count, "One, two, three, four" and saying, "Down, in, out, up." After learning the basic conducting patterns, have the students practice conducting together as a group, first with one hand, then the other hand, then with both hands. A metronome, electronic piano, or QChord can all be used to help practice conducting. This is also a

FIGURE 2–5 Children enjoy conducting music.

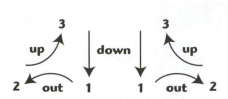

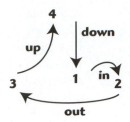

FIGURE 2–6 A conducting pattern of three beats.

FIGURE 2–7 A conducting pattern of four beats.

good time to introduce pieces of classical music for conducting. Anyone can pretend to be a famous conductor of an orchestra while conducting one of Beethoven's symphonies. You might even want to choose a piece of classical music that you already use to signal a classroom activity; refer to Chapter 1 for suggested musical selections. It is so much fun when a student comes up afterwards and says, "Haven't we heard that music before?"

After students have learned the basics of conducting, experiment with more beats and more complicated rhythms. A five-beat pattern has one extra *out* beat, making the pattern: down, in, out, out, up. However, a five-beat pattern is often conducted by alternating two beats and three beats. So, the conductor beats: down, up, down, out, up. Another very interesting pattern is one with six beats. This is usually called $\frac{6}{8}$ time and is usually divided into two groups of three beats. So, you would count one, two, three, / four, five, six, with the emphasis on numbers one and four. To conduct this pattern, only conduct two beats—down, up—but say, "One, two, three" on the first beat and, "four, five, six" on the second beat. These three numbers together form a *triplet:* three notes on one beat. A $\frac{6}{8}$ time signature can be divided into two triplets. However, $\frac{6}{8}$ time can also be divided into three groups of two beats. For this, you would count one, two, / three, four, / five, six, with the emphasis on numbers one, three, and five. To conduct this, use the pattern for three beats—down, out, up—but say, "One, two" on the first beat, "three, four" on the second beat, and "five, six" on the last beat. When these two beats occur together on one beat, they are called *duplets.*

Sometimes in $\frac{6}{8}$ time musicians switch back and forth between two beats to a bar, called conducting *in two,* and three beats to a bar, called conducting *in three.* The song "America" in *West Side Story* by Leonard Bernstein (1957) has this rhythmic pattern. Some musicians consider this fun, while others think of it as challenging. Sometimes a musical piece in $\frac{6}{8}$ will be mostly conducted *in two,* with a change to conducting *in three* for only the last few measures. This gives the music a sense of urgency at the end. This pattern of switching into three at the end is called a *hemiola* and was used fairly often in baroque music. Conducting with six beats can be done with children as young as first grade and even up to fourth or fifth grade, depending on the rhythmic experience of your children.

Children sometimes ask about the largest number of beats that can be conducted. The most this author has ever seen was 12, and that was an extremely slow 12 beats. There were so many extra ins and outs that the musicians had a hard time following the conductor. He finally gave up and conducted the piece *in four;* that is, four beats with triplets on each beat.

In addition to teaching children how to conduct, you can show them a short video of someone conducting an orchestra or chorus. Your students can also look for a program on television that features a conductor. Look in your local library for a book about conductors to show your class. Two great examples are *The Philharmonic Gets Dressed* by Karla Kuskin (1986) and Bill Martin Jr.'s *The Maestro Plays* (1994). You never know what will inspire one of your students to become the next Leonard Bernstein.

Rhythm Band

Some teachers cringe at the thought of teaching rhythm band. The usual experience of rhythm band is a terrible crashing and banging of instruments that is hard on the nerves of a teacher. This can be prevented if you lay down some basic ground rules before your students pick up the instruments. First, train them with imaginary instruments. Discuss how each child will have an instrument in front of him and how that instrument should be treated. Show children that the instruments will be picked up when the conductor's hands go up. The instruments need to be quiet until the conductor begins moving her hands. Children will play the instruments until the conductor gives a **cutoff**. Then they will put the instruments down quietly. While playing the instruments, children should follow her movements. Then practice doing a cutoff, which is done by making a large *C* in the air with the right hand. For extra emphasis, a backwards *C* is made with the left hand at the same time. The motion looks a lot like a baseball umpire's signal for *safe*. Be sure to give students some practice about how to give a cutoff. They love the power of giving a teacher a cutoff. So, talk a little, then wait for them to give you a cutoff. Of course, you should be ready to stop in mid-sentence.

The next activity is for children from four to eight. Two- and three-year-olds may not have enough impulse control for such a structured approach to rhythmic instruments. They might even injure themselves on instruments with sharp edges.

After practicing cutoffs, you are ready to get out the instruments. Have children sit on the floor in a circle, and put an instrument in front of each one. When you bring out the instruments, be very firm about the children waiting to play until everyone is ready. You may have to take an instrument away from a child who is having difficulty with impulse control. At first, remove the instrument quickly from the child who has impulsively started banging the instrument, and then return it to the child within two minutes. If random banging continues to be a problem, you may need to put the instrument *in the mush pot;* that is, take it away for a couple more minutes. Try to keep good control of the group by positively praising children who do a good job during their first experience with the instruments (Figure 2–8).

FIGURE 2–8   It takes concentration to play in a rhythm band.

As you distribute the instruments, vary the order so that children near each other do not have the same instruments. After each child has had a chance to play one instrument, the children will rotate so that each child will have opportunities to play different instruments.

Once the instruments have been placed in front of your class, have them follow you as the conductor. Practice having them pick up the instruments when you put up your arms and put the instruments back down when you put your arms down. Then you are ready to really make music. Have your students try to play the instruments in response to the gestures you make with your hands, just like real musicians. When you are finished, give a cutoff and have everyone hold the instruments up quietly, just like a real orchestra. When you put your arms down, they put their instruments on the floor or desk in front of them. After each round of play, the children can pass the instruments to the next child to the right.

Next, play a short piece of music from a recording and have the rhythm band play along. Again, have them watch the conductor for the beat and the cutoff.

When a class has some experience with the teacher as the conductor, they can learn to begin conducting themselves. Practice the conducting patterns as a group, then choose individual children to be the conductor. The children love having control, even for a short time.

More Rhythm Activities

Rhythm sticks, sometimes known as Lummie sticks, are another form of rhythm instrument. Each child has two sticks, longer and fatter than a pencil, which are used to keep time to music (Figure 2–9). With rhythm sticks, you can do a variety of stick dance patterns. The sticks can be banged together in front of the child, behind the knees, over the head, to the right, to the left, up high, down low, and in the middle. The idea is for a child to follow the pattern a teacher gives. When your students get proficient at rhythm sticks, have them do pairs patterns, with two children working together, each with a pair of rhythm sticks.

FIGURE 2–9 Chopsticks can be used in place of Lummie sticks.

The Orff Approach

Carl Orff (1895–1982) was a composer who lived in Germany. His most famous piece of music is *Carmina Burana* (Morley & Ferrante, 1999), a musical work for large chorus and orchestra with a huge percussion section. If you ever get a chance to hear it or perform it, you are in for a great musical adventure. Carl Orff wanted to create music that children can easily learn and perform. He also wanted children to be intimately involved in the process of inventing music, improvising, and participating in the experience of an ensemble (playing with a musical group). Orff felt that many adult instruments were too difficult for children to play, so he developed **Orff instruments**, percussion instruments created especially for children (Figure 2–10). Orff instruments make it easy for children to play and perform interesting music. Orff originally started with the idea of music learning in general, but much **Orff music** today focuses on rhythmic styles and rhythmic learning. Most Orff instruments are rhythm instruments, even though it was not his original intention to teach only rhythm. Nevertheless, when you listen to Carl Orff's music you can understand how his work with children is characterized by rhythmic learning.

Carl Orff began to create music for his students as part of his work with young women in a school for gymnastics and dance. He started in 1924, and by 1948 he had developed **Orff-Schulwerke**, an approach to music teaching. This work was translated into English as *Music for Children* (Orff & Keetman, 1959) in the 1950s and became popular in the United States. Because he dealt with rhythm so well, his *Orff-Schulwerke* was excellent for teaching rhythmic awareness (Bayless & Ramsey, 1991).

A number of rhythmically complicated songs are included in the *Orff-Schulwerke*. One particularly difficult clapping song consists of only claps, slaps, and finger clicks. Children are more advanced in their rhythmic abilities than in their pitch, but we normally do not give them challenging rhythmic work. This piece of music definitely challenges young children.

FIGURE 2–10   The wood block is a favorite Orff instrument.

THE ORFF APPROACH

A Short History, by Doug Goodkin

Some of the finest music written for children is in a five-volume series published in the 1950s and appropriately titled *Music for Children* (Orff & Keetman, 1959). The authors, Carl Orff and Gunild Keetman, were both composers and educators whose work with children grew to become an internationally recognized approach to music education: the *Orff-Schulwerke*. Its success can be attributed to several key factors: Carl Orff was well known as the composer of *Carmina Burana*, and his colleague, Gunild Keetman, was equally adept in the elemental style of composition, writing chamber music for recorders, percussion, and Orff instruments. Beginning with composition gave an artistic integrity to the approach. Both Orff and Keetman understood that the nature of the child is to try things out, to move, to explore, and to imagine. They built their ideas around giving structure to these natural tendencies. By beginning with the folklore of one's country—songs, rhymes, and dances—there was an assurance of quality material that has withstood the test of time.

In writing an introduction to the *Music for Children* series, Eberhard Preussner remarks, "One cannot value too highly the special fact that it is a composer who has introduced this fundamental reform in the field of music education. . . . It enables progress from the educational to the artistic to be made without a break, or rather that from the very beginning, art and education are bound together as one unity."

But what is this approach known as *Orff-Schulwerke*? We may be surprised to discover that the beginnings had nothing to do with the education of young children. The story began in Munich, Germany, in the 1920s, a time of new ideas in the arts as young Bohemian poets, writers, painters, musicians, and dancers gathered to experiment with new forms and concepts. The modern dance movement was particularly vibrant when artist Dorothy Gunther decided to open a school of gymnastics and rhythmic and expressive dance. She met Carl Orff and was impressed with his ideas that musical training should go hand in hand with the dance training. The Guntherschule opened its doors to 17 college-age women in 1924, and Orff began experimenting with his ideas. He wanted to re-imagine the ancient Greek ideal of *mousike,* the meeting point of sound, speech, and movement. The students improvised with text and vocal sounds, piano, small percussion instruments, and recorders. A few years later, inspired by African, Indonesian, and German models, specially designed Orff instruments were built: high quality xylophones, metallophones, and glockenspiels. An elemental style of improvisation and composition evolved to accompany the choreographed dances. These experiments, aided by two talented students-turned-teachers, Gunild Keetman and Maya Lex, led to the formation of a performance group in which there was no division between dancers and musicians. Dancers played and moved with percussion instruments, vocalized, and moved freely between dancing and playing the newly created Orff instruments. By the 1930s, the group had begun to tour Germany to critical acclaim. Orff began to speak with educators about applying these ideas with children, but the political climate in Germany interrupted these plans. Orff turned his attention to composing the *Carmina Burana*, which premiered in 1937. The Guntherschule was destroyed during the war in 1944. That might have been the end of the story, but in 1948, a Bavarian radio station asked Orff to compose music for a series of broadcasts designed for children. Orff called on Keetman, and the impetus for *Music for Children* was born. By 1963, their approach had attracted so much attention that an international center for the study of *Orff-Schulwerke,* the Orff Institute, was founded. It continues to be the gathering place for people all over the world carrying these ideas forward in their respective countries. In 1968, the American Orff-Schulwerke Association was founded, and AOSA now has over 5,000 members nationwide.

Following Orff's holistic vision, a typical Orff class might include playful exploration of a rhyme, a rhythmic pattern, a children's game, an object, moving freely between speech,

continued

THE ORFF APPROACH *continued*

song, body percussion, movement, folk dance, small percussion instruments, Orff instruments, recorder, and drama. The children are intimately involved in the creation of their own music, creating drones, ostinato patterns, pentatonic melodies, and often choreographing dances as well. A typical climax of a unit of study is an Orff event in which children sing, dance, and play instruments, like their predecessors in the Guntherschule, often moving freely between all three. The Orff style of children's music fits them naturally because they create much of it directly from their own experience, following the contours of their elemental sensibility. At its best, it is equally enjoyable for adults and children. One cannot detect any condescending, watered down, or cutesy childish quality. Begun with college-age dancers and filtering down many years later to elementary school children, the Orff approach is now employed with babies and toddlers, middle schoolers and high schoolers, adults and seniors. As Orff himself makes clear, "The elemental remains a foundation that is timeless."

Carl Orff's *Schulwerke* usually consists of some kind of an **ostinato**: a regular pattern that repeats and forms the basis of the musical piece. In the case of Carl Orff, the regular pattern is usually rhythmic, but an ostinato pattern could have both rhythm and melody. In actual practice, a small group of children would play the ostinato pattern, usually on wooden instruments similar to a vibraphone or gamilan (a South Pacific Islands instrument). These wooden instruments are usually hit by a mallet and generally have a choice of six to eight notes carved into the top of the instrument. The children might play only one note with a particular rhythm for the whole piece (Figure 2–11). Sometimes, the ostinato base in *Orff-Schulwerke* will consist of two notes. Other children will play a different percussive instrument with a more varied pattern while still other children will sing a tune or say a rhyme to round out the whole ensemble.

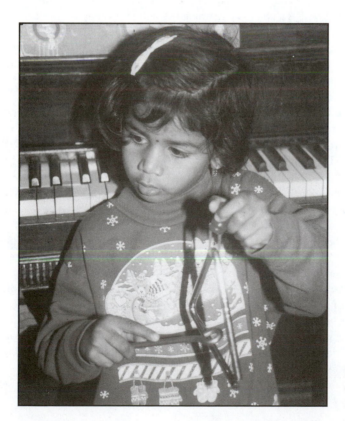

FIGURE 2–11 Playing an ostinato on the triangle, a lovely Orff accompaniment.

Doug Goodkin
*Orff Music Specialist; Director,
Mills College Orff Program, Oakland, California*

Doug Goodkin began studying the organ when he was six years old and the piano at eight years old. The lessons were the archetypal private lessons: learn to decipher those black dots on paper, curve your fingers, and every once in a while, follow those loud and soft markings. He quit his piano and organ lessons at age thirteen. Goodkin never played clapping games with the girls in the neighborhood, never danced in or out of school, never sang except in elementary school, and never had a guided lesson in improvisation. He did mess around quite a bit on the piano on his own and composed some pseudoclassic pieces. He also spent many hours with his parents' classical record collection.

Somewhere around age seventeen, Goodkin realized that:

- ♪ he did not know how to dance;
- ♪ he could not drum coherently to the beat;
- ♪ he could not sing Beatles songs in tune;
- ♪ though he could play Bach's Toccata and Fugue in D Minor on the organ, he could not decipher the simple chord chart when someone invited him to play organ on a Beach Boys song.

By the time Goodkin entered college, he began exploring musical expression on his own, drumming on bongos to the Grateful Dead, trying out a blues progression on the piano, dancing, singing, and taking music classes. He also read books like *Summerhill* (Neill, 1995) and *How Children Fail* (Holt, 1995). He became interested in the alternative education movement, and began working at various experimental schools.

In 1972, Avon Gillespie, a guest teacher, visited his class and had them singing and clapping with partners like the girls in Goodkin's neighborhood used to do. The relationship between music and the education of young children came together for him. The next year Avon Gillespie taught a full semester course in *Orff-Schulwerke* at Goodkin's college. Goodkin spent each Saturday for 10 weeks playing all the children's music games he had never played as a child and learning the natural overlap of speech, movement, games, and guided exploration on the Orff instruments.

At the time, it just seemed like great fun. He was too busy being a child immersed in the joy of the approach to think about techniques. Later, he found himself in San Francisco volunteering to teach music at a school and had to read frantically through his notes on the Orff method. In 1975, The San Francisco School had just purchased Orff instruments and needed a teacher. He was hired to teach full-time. Over twenty years later, he is still the music teacher there.

From 1983 to 1985, Goodkin took the official three-summer Orff Certification Program at the University of California at Santa Cruz. Avon Gillespie was the teacher. In 1990, Goodkin joined the Santa Cruz Orff Certification faculty and is now director of the program at Mills College. Goodkin has taught in the summer program at The Orff Institute in Salzburg, Austria, and in various courses worldwide. Teaching children at The San Francisco School is his main job, but his schedule allows him to offer teacher-training workshops on the weekends both locally and throughout the United States and Canada. In addition to the Mills course each summer, he teaches a course on jazz and *Orff-Schulwerke.* Recently, he began teaching an evening class at The San Francisco Conservatory of Music.

Goodkin has managed to find a balance between teaching children and adults. Continuing to work with children keeps the practice grounded, real, and ever evolving, while working with adults forces him to clarify and continually reflect on the ideas behind the practice. He has the satisfaction of knowing that his work will reach children beyond his own classroom, and he has the joy of watching adults rediscover a playful self that got locked away in their journey to adulthood.

continued

DOUG GOODKIN *continued*

Goodkin says:

In realizing the demands of the curriculum I've created, I must spend time with Mozart and Duke Ellington. I must keep learning new instruments to accompany songs—guitar, banjo, dulcimer—and play for folk dances—accordion, Bulgarian bagpipe. I must keep up with an expanding multicultural musical foundation, studying Balinese gamilan, Philippine kulingtang, Middle Eastern percussion, Brazilian samba, and more. I must keep playing piano and keep going to workshops and conferences. I must keep reading poetry to set for the Orff instrumentarium and myths and fairy tales to dramatize. I must keep reading books by authors as diverse and stimulating as Rudolf Steiner, Alfred North Whitehead, Joseph Chilton Pearce, Neil Postman, and Howard Gardner. I must continually search to see the genius behind each child's sparkling eyes and erratic behavior. In short, my job asks me to do everything I already love doing. Who could ask for anything more?

Goodkin has made a professionally recorded audiocassette of music the children have done each year, almost every year since 1983. The material is about one-third music from diverse cultures, one-third jazz, and one-third rhymes and poetry, all arranged for the Orff instruments and featuring children from first to the eighth grades. These tapes are quite unique, inasmuch as they represent authentic children's music: children playing at their level of understanding and hearing in an elemental style. Some pieces are entirely created by the children, and many feature some level of improvisation. These tapes are not sold commercially, but are available through The San Francisco School.

One lovely piece of music performed on the *Orff-Schulwerke* album by a group of children, probably second graders, is a poem about gemstones. Each line is said by a different child, and at the end of each line, a chime is struck. The expression in each voice is priceless. Particularly lovely is one child's line, "The ruby is a precious rose, the sapphire is a brilliant blue." At the end of the piece, all the chimes are struck randomly. A quite moving piece of music, it is well within the performance capabilities of young children.

Pitch Learning

Pitch learning is more complicated than rhythm learning and more closely related to language learning. Children must develop an ability to hear the differences between various pitches and learn to distinguish the *tonal quality* of the sound from the *pitch level* of the sound. For example, middle C can be played on a piano, a flute, or a guitar, or sung by a voice. They are all the same pitch, but they have different qualities. Most preschoolers cannot hear differences in sound qualities. They hear them as different pitches. It takes training and development for preschoolers to understand the difference between pitch and tonal quality.

Fortunately, most preschoolers have the ability to learn and hear this difference. It is very closely related to language learning. If a child is able to speak fairly well, it should not be hard for him to learn to distinguish between pitch and tonal quality. If a child has poor language ability, training his ear to hear pitch differences can help him learn language. You can train children to hear these differences by playing the same note on a variety of instruments. An electronic piano is ideal for this musical exercise. It is easy to play the same note with varying sound qualities just by changing the dials on the machine. However, if you have the instruments, it is more fun and more educational to bring in a variety of instruments and play the same pitch on each one. Be sure to include singing the same pitch.

Preschoolers usually learn to match pitch by singing along with an adult voice *in their pitch range* (Figure 2–12). Female voices seem to be the best suited for teaching pitch to young children. Children can hear them easily, and it is easy for them to imitate the adult sound. Children learn language by adults repeating words and slowing down their speech; it is also easy for children to learn pitch with a strong, clear voice that pauses to help them notice and hold a pitch. If you are an adult with reasonably good pitch, as long as you sing up in the *children's range,* they will probably progress in their **pitch matching** ability. As mentioned in Chapter 1, singing too low for children may hinder their pitch learning.

Kindergarten through second grade is the crucial period for pitch learning. An excellent preschool musical education can prepare children to do well in music, but it cannot substitute for lack of music during the early elementary years. Preschoolers are not developmentally ready to make the leap that elementary school students can make. It is as if you spent the preschool years teaching children to identify the letters and then stopped teaching them how to read when they arrived in first grade. When children fail to learn the next steps in music, they fail to progress in music. The present day failure to teach music at the elementary grade levels occurs at a critical time. This time is the window of opportunity for learning pitch and the time when the brain is developmentally ready to learn how to sing. Children are still ready and willing to sing during the early elementary years, but classroom teachers feel pressure to focus on reading and math skills. They do not know the importance of music or how to teach music. By fifth grade, some children, mostly boys, have decided that singing is not for them. By then, only children with affluent or musically attuned parents continue with a musical education. Is it surprising then, that those musically trained children go on to excel in math and sciences?

Researcher and neurobiologist Norman Weinberger stated that "the brain is specialized for the building blocks of music" (1994). In his newsletter on music research, he

FIGURE 2–12 Children sing in higher pitches than adults.

discussed the brain's perception of pitch. The brain receives information from the inner ear, which breaks down music and other complex sounds into frequency *bits*. These bits are then put together by the brain into a perception of the whole sound. In other words, the brain constructs the perception of pitch from the information it gets from the ear.

Researchers discovered this information by testing people on their perception of pitch. Here is how it works. When the note A is played on the piano, the string inside the piano vibrates at 440 hertz. But the sound of the A also produces other higher vibrations, at 880, 1320, 1760, and 2200 hertz, and up into sounds we cannot hear. The 440 hertz vibration is called the *fundamental frequency*, while the higher vibrations are called *harmonics*. When researchers play the harmonics only, without the fundamental frequency, people perceive the sound to be the same as when the fundamental frequency is presented along with the harmonics. This means that the brain is *hearing* a pitch that is not there, which shows that the brain is combining information about frequencies to construct a perception of pitch. This is also the way that birds, cats, and monkeys process pitch. Researchers found that this process in the brain occurs in the auditory cortex situated in the right hemisphere of the brain. According to Weinberger & McKenna (1988), "Cells have been found in the auditory cortex that seem likely to process specific harmonic relationships, such as the simultaneous presentation of the second and third harmonics of a note."

In addition to perceiving pitch, cells in the auditory cortex process information about the contour, or shape, of the musical melody. Other cells in the auditory cortex handle rhythmic aspects of the music. This fact was discovered by researchers who studied people with damage to their auditory cortexes, either by surgery or stroke. When there are lesions, or tiny holes, in the brain, the processing of melody or rhythm can be affected. Some people with brain lesions showed difficulty in hearing melody, while having no problem with rhythm. Other people with lesions in other places showed difficulty with rhythm and not melody. Even different sides of the cortex show different processes; for example, damage to the right side can cause a disability in hearing timbre and difficulty feeling the meter, or beat, of the music, while damage to the left hemisphere affects rhythm perception. The varieties of these research findings all point to the specialization of the brain for processing music.

Learning to Sing

A wonderful description of how a young child learns to sing was written by Kathleen Bayless and Marjorie Ramsey in their book *Music: A Way of Life for the Young Child* (1991).

> When Kathleen's two grandsons were babies, the family talked and sang a great deal to them and made up little tunes about what they were doing together with them. Throughout the day nursery rhymes were sung. The boys loved the funny songs. Two of their favorites were "The Peanut Song" and "Ms. Polly." Around the age of two both Matthew and Andrew began to sing these songs in the same way. First, they laughed and clapped when Kathleen would sing the songs to them. Then she began to hear them sing the last word in each phrase or line. For example, when she would sing, "Oh, the peanut sat on the railroad track," they would join in saying the word "track." When she held that note on the word "track" and gave them time to respond, she noticed that they would slide their voices up to the correct pitch for that word. She would do the same with the other words like "flutter," "again," and "butter." When singing the second verse of the song, she did the same for the words "pad," "sky," "in," and "eye." As the boys grew older, they were able to pick up other words and phrases of the song and sing them. To this day they love those songs. (Bayless & Ramsey, 1991)

FRANCES RAUSCHER'S VIEWPOINT

The Power of Music

This article originally appeared in the Sept./Oct. 1996 issue of *Early Childhood News*.

Since the beginning of time, music has been praised by history's greatest human minds. Alexander Pope said, "Music resembles poetry; in each are numerous graces which no methods teach, and which a master hand alone can reach." The Scottish essayist and historian Thomas Carlyle stated, "The meaning of song goes deep. Who is there that, in logical words, can express the effect music has on us?" Shakespeare, Beethoven, Goethe, Plato, Luther, and Einstein, among others, echo these sentiments.

Yet, as a subject in American schools, music is rarely regarded with such esteem. For more than ten years, music programs have been systematically cut or reduced in many US school districts. The rationale given by legislators and school administrators has been starkly pragmatic: In order to revive lapsed academic standards and maintain America's ability to compete globally in business and technology, school curricula must focus on the "basics" of reading, writing, math, and the sciences. Their argument continues that music is a nice activity for children to learn, but, with the tightening of school budget belts, is also expendable.

This trend has continued despite the highly publicized research I spearheaded at the University of California, Irvine, which proved that music plays a crucial role in early childhood development. With the assistance of Gordon Shaw, Ph.D., also of the University of California, Irvine, our team was able to determine unequivocally that music lessons improve a child's performance in school.

In 1993, we completed a pilot study in which ten three year old children were given music training—either singing or keyboard lessons. The scores of every child improved significantly (46 percent) on the Object Assembly Task, a section of the Wechsler Preschool and Primary Scale of Intelligence-Revised (WPPSI-R) that measures spatial reasoning. In a second experiment, we found that the spatial reasoning performance of preschool children who received eight months of music lessons far exceeded that of a demographically comparable group of preschool children who did not receive music lessons.

The link between music and spatial reasoning is significant since spatial reasoning skills are part of the abstract reasoning skills that the brain uses to perform both common, everyday activities—such as walking—and complex functions such as solving problems in mathematics and engineering.

Our research also indicates that music training may most benefit those children for whom maximizing academic and career potential is critically important: the disadvantaged. In our pilot study with preschool children, those from disadvantaged backgrounds displayed a particularly dramatic improvement in spatial reasoning ability after music training.

Unlike many traditional teaching methods, music is nonverbal and does not force children to struggle with language or cultural differences. Music programs in schools can help disadvantaged children to learn on much more equal footing with children from more affluent backgrounds. And unlike children from higher income families who have access to private music lessons, for many of these disadvantaged children, their only opportunity for music instruction is in the school.

In another ongoing study which we have called the *Mozart Effect*, Gordon Shaw, Ph.D., and I concluded that compared to those who simply sat in silence or listened to realization instruction, 36 college students who listened to ten minutes of Mozart's Piano Sonata (K. 448) subsequently experienced a significant increase in their spatial IQ

continued

FRANCES RAUSCHER'S VIEWPOINT *continued*

scores. This study reiterated our conclusion that the relationship between music and spatial reasoning is so strong that simply listening to music can make a difference.

We have now confirmed what teachers have long suspected: Music does more than entertain our children, it also shapes their minds. In fact, *Newsweek* magazine's February 19, 1996, cover story, "How Kids Are Wired for Music, Math, and Emotion," highlighted our studies, proclaiming on their own "if more administrators were tuned into brain research . . . music would be a daily requirement" (Begley).

In light of these findings, eliminating music programs is not acceptable. We believe that our studies, and future work inspired by them, have the potential to revitalize the role of music in education. Rather than be neglected, music should be prized and emphasized as an invaluable way to boost human brain power.

Reprinted with permission from *Early Childhood News.*

This **anecdotal information** is substantiated by the work of Sandra Trehub. In an experiment with infants, she found that a young child responds to the contour of a melody and not the actual pitches of the music. When a song is changed to a new key, the child recognizes it as being the same, but when the relationship of the pitches within the song are changed, the child responds to it as a new event (Trehub, 1990).

Children learn to sing by imitating the adults around them. It helps children learn pitch if adults sing with them in their pitch range (Figure 2–13). It is wonderful if a child can learn pitch in the preschool years. However, even with musical activities and a strong voice to follow, most preschoolers do not sing on pitch. Pitch is learned usually by age eight.

FIGURE 2–13 Children learn to sing more readily when adults match their pitch.

What should I tell parents to do with a musically talented youngster?

With a child under age six, sing, sing, sing. Sing with a tape, sing in the car, sing around the house, sing in the garden, and sing in your spare time. You will not really know if you have a musically talented youngster until your child is about fifteen. If your child's talent has not bloomed by then, he is unlikely to be a child prodigy. Until then, you do not really know for sure, so it is important to encourage the basics, which begin with vocal music.

If you wish to consider some kind of instrument playing, be sure to make it fun. From ages two to five is not the time to start practicing a half hour a day. One child care program for toddlers had a short time to allow each child to experience the piano with supervision. It was called piano lessons, but it was really just exploring the sounds of the piano with fingers, not with fists. The teacher did not allow children to just bang on the piano. The first part of learning began with playing one note with one finger at a time. Then a child graduated to little tunes. "Twinkle, Twinkle Little Star" (Collins, 1990) was the first tune. One child was particularly fascinated with the piano. Within two months she learned to play "Chopsticks" (Various, 1998) on the high notes while the teacher played the accompaniment on the bottom. Even though she was only two and a half years old, the teacher suggested that she take piano lessons. It is not usually a good idea to start music training at such an early age, but she was ready. In preschool music lessons, let the child lead the way.

Instrument training must follow a child's interest and motivation. If a child at age four begs to play the drums, encourage parents to look into appropriate drum classes for four-year-olds. It may be just enough for them to buy a drum (or even a drum set), but it is helpful for the child to have some group lessons, even at this age. If a child is begging for every instrument he sees, wait until the same instrument is requested at least three times. If a child is the shy quiet type, particularly if she is a middle child, pay attention to the first time she expresses interest in the violin. She may not ask again. If you feel a child is ready for an instrument, encourage parents to find a group that teaches that instrument for the child's age group. Urge parents not to get too invested in a preschooler's lessons. He may decide to switch to another instrument next year. However, warn parents not to let a child quit in the middle of the session. Even a preschooler can stick it out for a few months. If a preschool child does not ask to play an instrument, wait until age eight before you try to motivate him.

If a child has musical ability, there is no great harm in waiting until age seven or eight to begin formal music training, especially if he has a lot of musical experience between ages four and seven. If a child is listening to music in the car, singing along with music, and exposed to some classical music, there is plenty of music learning going on. Also, the time lost between ages four and seven is usually made up in the teen years by the motivation of the teen. A motivated teenager can make incredible progress in just a few years. However, a teen who was pushed too hard at too young an age may quit completely.

After children begin instrumental music lessons, parents should find an excellent music teacher and have a regular practice time. It is okay to give rewards for practicing. In one family candy was reserved for practice rewards. In another family, video game time is bought on a daily basis by time spent practicing the piano. One father checked regularly with his sons' piano teacher, and if the teacher said his teenaged children had not been practicing, the father made them pay for their lessons. He had three sons, and he said that each of them had to pay $50.00 for one lesson before learning to practice. There can be problems with negative methods of encouraging practice, but with teenagers, they can work.

Parents can set helpful parameters for the success of a child's musical training, but they cannot do it all. Especially with older teens, parents take on the role of emotional supporter, payer of money, and audience. Teachers can also motivate a child to practice. In a child's

continued

**WHAT SHOULD I TELL PARENTS TO DO
WITH A MUSICALLY TALENTED YOUNGSTER?** *continued*

younger years, parents can motivate him to practice, but in the teen years it gets harder to do. Parents have a delicate balancing act. If they do not make some demands, a child can achieve little. Push too hard, and a child revolts.

If a child is not interested in playing an instrument, consider a children's chorus. Some excellent groups teach singing and music writing in after school programs.

Remember, the window of opportunity is still open at age twelve. The world famous flutist Jean-Pierre Rampal did not begin playing the flute until age twelve. That is pretty late for starting an instrument, but clearly not too late. Lessons can be started even beyond the teen years. Some adults take up vocal training and instrument lessons. They rarely become professionals, but lessons still add a great deal of enjoyment to their lives. Adults who study instruments learn quite quickly, but rarely feel confident in their ability. One group of young adults who took up new instruments in their twenties formed a band and went on the road. An older man started to play violin when he inherited his father's violin. One teacher's mother took up mandolin playing at age forty-one. You never know what talents you might develop. Perhaps playing an instrument yourself could help motivate the children in your class.

The Kodály Method

The **Kodály** (Ko-dah-ee) **method** was developed by Zoltán Kodály (1882–1967), a prominent Hungarian composer and musician. Kodály developed his interest in teaching music education over many years. He first began by composing for children's choruses. Kodály believed that music is meant to develop one's entire being: personality, intellect, and emotions (Figure 2–14). He felt that music is a spiritual food for everyone, so he studied not only the creation of good music, but also how to make good music more

FIGURE 2–14 Musical experience develops the whole child.

ANNE LASKEY

An Expert Opinion

Kodály Specialist; Director, Kodály Music Program, Holy Names College

Anne Laskey's most vivid early memories are of her mother playing the piano, her father singing sentimental songs, and her own piano lessons, which started when she was seven in a tiny attic room in her K–12 country school. Her weekly piano lesson included taps of the ruler on her knuckles when she resorted to looking from the music stand to her hands as she played. She has fond memories of junior and high school choir, church choirs and ensembles, and a highly musical piano teacher during her high school years.

Although Laskey did not have a formal music education in elementary and secondary schools, she was drawn to the opportunity to teach music in her daughters' elementary school in the early '80s. She did not have a teaching credential or any course work in music education, yet she was invited to teach in the private school where her daughters were enrolled. While accompanying her older daughter to a 1981 mini-workshop at Holy Names College, she observed a Kodály class. She proceeded to study in the program at the same time she taught music, learning *solfège*, pedagogy, and materials for teaching in the classroom. After 15 years of elementary school teaching, Laskey became the director of the Kodály program at Holy Names College.

Laskey is hopeful that with the new century, the United States will work towards greater support of the arts in education. The creative arts, by definition, involve learning through experience, rather than through cognition alone. Of the creative arts, music involves the deepest integration of intellectual, emotional, physical, and spiritual processes. She believes that music education will become an essential part of the curriculum when music is taught in such a way that children learn how to think about music as they perform it.

Laskey feels that when children are sung to early, they readily join in music making themselves. Singing games developed by children over centuries are a natural vehicle for combining song and movement. Play is the predominant means of learning for young children and singing games provide the materials towards this end. Games are enjoyed by older children as well.

While numerous rewards result from her work with graduate students, Laskey still prefers teaching children. Their minds and hearts are completely open. Their potential is limitless, their questions are without end, and sharing in shaping of personality is an empowering experience.

accessible to people. He felt that musical training should begin as early as possible, but that training should not be torture but a joy for the pupil and instill in him a thirst for music that will last a lifetime. To this end, Kodály developed a graduated system of teaching young children how to sing and eventually to read music (Kalmar, 1982). It begins with a child's understanding of the relationship of two note songs (such as *so mi*), then progresses to wider and wider ranges. It also begins with differentiating the number and duration of sounds per beat. After rhythm and beat are clearly distinguished and performed, names are attached to the simplest rhythms: eighth notes (*titi*) and quarter notes (*ta*).

If you find this method interests you, some excellent Kodály method training programs are available in the summer that train regular classroom teachers to do the Kodály method with their students.

The Kodály Music Program at Holy Names College. Holy Names College in Oakland, California, has one of the most extensive teacher training programs in Kodály music education in North America. The three week, four unit, summer certification program is especially popular with regular classroom teachers, since it offers a chance for teachers to learn about teaching music while enjoying a stay in the San Francisco Bay Area. Now in its 30th year, the HNC Kodály Program offers the summer certification as well as a specialist certificate and a master's degree in music education. Sister Mary Alice Hein founded the program in 1969, following her observation of Zoltán Kodály when he was at Stanford University in 1966. In cooperation with Erzsebet Szonyi, then the director of music education at the Liszt Academy in Budapest, Sr. Mary Alice planned the first Kodály International Symposium at Holy Names College in 1973. The program, officially begun in 1974, is now one of the few fully accredited Kodály programs in the country.

Learning Pitch Steps

Folk songs are often used as the basis for teaching pitch to children. Singing games are used to provide a connection between movement and song and to help to develop a strong rhythmic sense. As children progress, they continually develop their musical skills via singing, listening, reading, writing, memorization, and improvisation. As new melodic, rhythmic, or harmonic material is introduced, students integrate the new learning with what they already know.

In developing the Kodály and Orff approaches the composers realized that folk music is usually the first exposure children have to music. From it children have already acquired a musical vocabulary, and the composers emphasized using it to teach music. Folk music of central Eastern Europe uses a **pentatonic scale**, which consists of five notes. On the piano these notes are C, D, E, G, and A. Because the Kodály method was developed in Hungary, Hungarian folk music was used for teaching. For this reason, some music educators promote the idea that children should learn songs in the pentatonic scale (Figure 2–15). In the United States most folk songs use a **diatonic scale**. A diatonic major scale is one that has seven notes, with half steps in the scale between steps

FIGURE 2–15 Musical scales and folk songs help teach children about pitch.

three and four and between seven and eight. This is the scale we sing with the *solfa sounds: do, re, mi, fa, sol, la, ti, do.* This scale and the minor scale have become the basic musical building blocks for Western music. The minor scale consists of the same notes but has half steps between steps two and three and between six and seven. Folk music, country music, rock music, and much modern classical music are based on these two scales. As with the Hungarian children, our children are first exposed to music through learning folk songs. However, our folk songs usually do not use the pentatonic scale, so some music educators say children should learn the diatonic major scale and songs based on it rather than using the pentatonic scale. An interesting chapter by John Sloboda in his 1985 book *The Musical Mind* discusses musical development and supports this theory. This is one of those minor philosophical debates that specialists become involved in, but it may be helpful to be aware of some of the controversies that you could run into when teaching music.

In traditional singing methods the standard technique for teaching pitch is the **solfège system** developed in France. The singer uses the sounds *do re mi fa sol la ti do* to designate the steps in the scale. This system is still used extensively in teaching singing by Kodály method teachers. Many students using this method have learned to sight sing, but others have had trouble singing intervals because the solfège sounds do not give an intellectual concept of how the pitches fit together. Sight singing is when you pick up a piece of written music and are able to sing the tune just from looking at the music. It is not an easy accomplishment. Children can learn to sing on pitch using the standard solfège syllables, but a growing number of music teachers use a **number system** for teaching pitch. College music majors are often taught to sight sing using the number system. Some music specialists say the number system is effective with even very young children. Some teachers use both systems. The children sing, "One, two, three, four, five, six, seven, one. One, seven, six, five, four, three, two, one" and follow it with, "Do, re, mi, fa, sol, la, ti, do. Do, ti, la, sol, fa, mi, re, do." This way, children are introduced to both the solfège system and the number system. The beauty of the number system is that when you sing the note one and then five, you sing the pitch range of a fifth. This may sound minor, but the ability to sing an interval correctly is an essential building block of singing. An **interval** is the pitch jump, or pitch step between two notes.

Children as young as four can be taught using the number system to help them understand pitch relationships. The first step is to teach the steps of the scale through imitation and repetition. Next, teach the numbers to a simple, familiar song, such as "Twinkle, Twinkle Little Star" (Collins, 1990). Sing it with the numbers: one, one, five, five, six, six, five—four, four, three, three, two, two, one—five, five, four, four, three, three, two—five, five, four, four, three, three, two—one, one, five, five, six, six, five— four, four, three, three, two, two, one—. Next, begin to identify the sound of the intervals passively. Sing note one, then note five, but sing "one, dah" and have the children guess the number of the pitch for which you sang "dah." This is a fun guessing game, but teachers first have to be able to sing the intervals accurately. The final step is to sing the number one and have children sing the number five for you. If you are brave, you can change to another pitch for number one and have children sing the number five relative to it. This, however, is getting into the territory of music educators and may be hard to do without more training.

Relative and Absolute Pitch

In normal usage, the word *pitch* usually means **relative pitch**. Relative pitch is the ability to sing a note in relation to another note. So, when you begin a song, you sing the song in perfect whole steps or half steps in relationship to the first note of the song. If you are singing with a group of people, you adjust your singing to match their pitch. If the singers are accompanied by instruments, they adjust their pitch to match. Most children learn relative pitch from singing with adults or with other children. When we talk about teaching or learning pitch, we usually mean teaching and learning relative pitch.

Absolute pitch, also called *perfect pitch,* is the ability to produce the exact same sound with the same vibrational level every time. For example, a person with absolute pitch can sing the note A, which has 440 vibrations, every time. The person has internally memorized the sound of that note and can consistently reproduce it (Zatorre, Evans, & Meyer, 1994). Absolute pitch is either developed very early or inherited (Whitfield, 1980).

Teachers can discover young children who have absolute pitch. One kindergarten teacher discovered children with perfect pitch using the following method. Every day she sang a little song before snack time. For the first few weeks, she played a pitch on the piano for the children and then held the pitch before beginning the song. She always began on the same pitch. After the first few weeks, she quietly played the pitch on the piano to herself and remembered it, since she did not have absolute pitch. Then she asked the children, "Can you find the pitch for me?" They sang what they thought might be the beginning pitch. She carefully listened to the children as they sang. Sure enough, one child sang the exact pitch every day. The teacher was thrilled with the discovery of a kindergartner with absolute pitch. The child had not received any particular musical training, and the parents were quite surprised to find their child had this musical talent. It is exciting to discover a child who has this special talent, but, of course, having absolute pitch does not guarantee musical success. That comes only after years of hard work and practice.

Hearing Musical Harmony

Harmony is generally thought of as singing along with the melody and making up a second tune that matches, or harmonizes, with the first tune. Harmony is not something that young children are usually able to hear or do easily. Even a musically talented child will probably not learn how to harmonize until he is at least ten or eleven years old. The first step in learning harmony is to be able to sing a well-known tune while another person sings the harmony. This is called *carrying a tune* and is most easily done as a group. The next step is to learn how to sing a round. Kindergartners usually have not learned how to carry a tune, so teaching them to sing rounds or harmony can be a difficult undertaking. Therefore, with kindergartners and preschoolers, focus on teaching them how to sing melody. Sing along with them on the main melody of the song, and practice it repeatedly. Move your hand up and down, so students can see when the melody goes up or down. Second and third graders are ready to learn rounds if taught in a simple format. Begin with an easy song, such as "Row, Row, Row Your Boat" (Martha, 1995). Practice the song as a group until you are ready to record it. Then, tape record the class singing three times through with no mistakes. When you have made your perfect recording, start the tape and sing the second part with the group while the tape recording sings the first part. Listen to the recording of yourselves and then come in with a repeat of the first line while the tape goes on to the next part.

Another favorite song for teaching rounds is one called "Black Socks." The words are, "Black socks they never get dirty the longer you wear them the blacker they get. Someday, I'll probably launder them something keeps telling me don't do it yet not yet not yet." The last part of the song, "not yet not yet," can be repeated by one group of children while the other groups sings the song.

After the song is finished, the groups switch parts. This is not exactly round singing, because the second group is not singing a tune, but rather repeating a rhythmic pattern.

This repetition is called an ostinato. Carl Orff made extensive use of ostinato patterns with children. Ostinato is an excellent way to begin the process of learning harmony: singing in more than one part at a time.

Musical Expressions

There are many kinds of music expressions. Some are words that determine the loudness of the music, called **dynamic levels**. Others are words that appear in the music as whole words or abbreviations to control the sound. Finally, there are the lines, spaces, spots, dots, and squiggles that make up written music, called **musical notation**.

Dynamic Levels

The loudness or softness of music is called dynamic levels. Teach preschoolers three dynamic levels: soft, medium, and loud. Use real musical words with preschoolers. The correct words are *piano* for soft, *mezzo* for medium, and *forte* for loud. In learning about dynamic levels, the students can practice dancing, singing, tapping, and all varieties of movement using the different words. For example, put on a classical piece of music that is quiet, and dance softly and quietly to the music with your students. Explain that the word *piano* has two meanings. The instrument is called a piano, and the Italian word that means soft is piano. In fact, the instrument got its name from the Italian words *piano* and *forte*. The instrument was originally called a *pianoforte* because it could play both loud and soft. The name was shortened in modern times.

Teach elementary students the standard six dynamic levels: *pianissimo, piano, mezzo piano, mezzo forte, forte,* and *fortissimo* (Figure 2–16). The abbreviations are: *pp, p, mp, mf, f, ff.*

FIGURE 2–16 A child demonstrates fortissimo.

You can do all kinds of activities with these six dynamic levels.

♪ Chant each dynamic level twice, beginning with *pianissimo* (e.g., *pianissimo, pianissimo, piano, piano, mezzo piano, mezzo piano,* etc.). Then have children do it with you.

♪ Sing songs while switching dynamic levels.

♪ Play pieces of music and turn the volume level up and down. Have the children tell you the name of the dynamic level.

♪ Listen to a piece of music that has a variety of dynamic levels and have the children try to identify which level is playing.

♪ Write the six dynamic levels on the board and point to different levels as you or a student reads or recites a poem aloud.

♪ Have a child point to different dynamic levels on the board as you read a passage from a book aloud. Be prepared for classroom giggling with this activity.

♪ A small group of children can have the six dynamic levels on cards and hold a card up while the rest of the class is singing a simple song. Change the dynamic level to that on the card, and continue singing at that level until they hold up another card.

Another aspect of dynamics is the concept of getting louder and softer. The words used are *crescendo,* getting louder, and *diminuendo,* getting softer. *Decrescendo* is a synonym for *diminuendo.* With younger children use the words *crescendo* and *diminuendo,* because the words are different from each other and will not be confused. With older children, ages seven to eight, you can use *crescendo* and *decrescendo,* because children have a better understanding of prefixes and can remember the terms as opposites. Teach older children the abbreviations for these words: *cresc., decresc.,* and *dim.* They are more likely to see the abbreviations rather than the entire words written in music. Also, teach older children the written signs for *crescendo* and *diminuendo* (Figure 2–17).

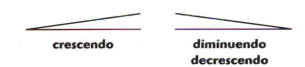

FIGURE 2–17 Musical symbols for crescendo and diminuendo (decrescendo).

After students learn the words and signs for crescendo and diminuendo, do some activities to reinforce the meaning. Movement is an excellent reinforcer for these concepts. Have the kids stand up taller for crescendo and crouch down low for diminuendo. Have them sit on the floor and use just their arms to reach up wide (cresc.) and then curl up small (dim.). They can make sounds with their voices, getting louder when the teacher holds up a crescendo sign, and getting softer when they see the diminuendo sign. A teacher can gradually turn up the volume of a recording for crescendo and turn it down slowly for diminuendo.

Musical Vocabulary

Many words convey ideas about how to make music. For example, at the beginning of a written piece of music, at the top and on the left hand side, there might be one word. Sometimes this word is in English, Italian, German, or occasionally other languages. For example, the word *animato* means to play the piece with animation. The word in this location usually pertains to the whole piece if it is short or to a section of the music for larger works. The section is played in that style until the next major section, which might

allegretto – playfully
animato – animated
larghetto – somewhat slowly
legato – smooth and connected
leggiero – lightly, airily
maestoso – majestically
marcato – mark each note
meno mosso – a little movement
sforzando – suddenly strongly accented
staccato – short and disconnected

FIGURE 2–18 Common musical expressions.

have the word *maestoso*, which means majestically. See Figure 2–18 for a list of other musical terms.

Other words give directions in the middle of a piece of written music as to how to play a few notes or a phrase of the music. These words occur more often. *Legato,* abbreviated *leg.,* means smooth and connected, and is often written as an arc over a group of notes. *Staccato,* abbreviated *stacc.,* almost the opposite of legato, means short and disconnected. It is written as a small dot above a note. Both staccato and legato can be played slow, medium, or fast. *Marcato* is like staccato, but more pronounced in that it means to mark each note. It has the same sign as an accent mark, both of which are written as a sideways V, like this: >. A *sforzando,* abbreviated *sfz.,* means a sudden loud accent on the note, or an abrupt interruption of loud sound, usually pretty short. The descriptive words are easy to teach to a group of young children and a great asset to their later ability to read the cues of music.

Musical Notation

Aa variety of opinions exist among music educators about when to begin to teach children musical notation. As with most other learned skills, it can be introduced over a long developmental period, as young as three and as late as eleven. The earlier you begin, the slower the learning curve. However, if you begin too late, for example, age seventeen, you have lost the motivation and confidence of the younger years and the plasticity of the brain in learning new skills. The best time to teach children to read music is somewhere between ages seven and ten. By then they typically know how to read, so music reading skills can be built on the reading skills they already possess.

If you have a class of second or third graders, you can begin to teach them the elements of music reading. Adults *can* learn to read music, but they often do not have the amount of time necessary to devote to learning such a difficult skill. Learning to read music takes time and repetition. You do not have to know how to read music yourself in order to teach your students basic music reading. It is like knowing the difference between the different letters and knowing how to read fluently. You can teach a group of second graders to look at the five lines and four spaces and begin to learn the names of the lines and spaces in the treble clef.

In Figure 2–19 you see an s-like shape on the left hand side of the lines and spaces. This is called the *treble clef sign.* When this sign occurs at the beginning of the line, the lowest line is called *E.* When the other sign, called the bass clef, which looks like the number nine, occurs at the beginning of the lines and spaces, then the lowest line is called *G.*

Once you know the name of the first line, you can figure out the names of the other lines and spaces. The only letters used to name notes in the musical scale are *A, B, C, D,*

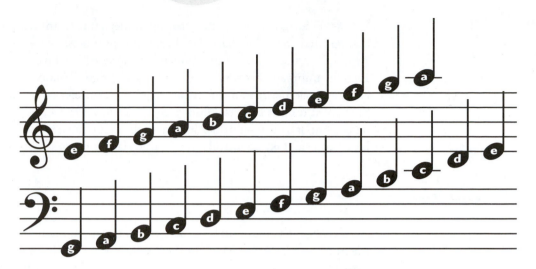

FIGURE 2–19   The musical staff.

E, F, and *G.* If the bottom line is an *E,* then the next space up will be an *F.* The next line up is a *G,* which is the end of the musical alphabet. There is no *H* in music. Therefore, the second space up from the bottom is named *A.* The third line up is a *B.* The next space, third space up from the bottom, is a *C.* The fourth line up from the bottom is *D.* The top space is an *E* and the top line is an *F.* Study Figure 2–19 again, and you will notice that in the treble clef, the lines are named *E, G, B, D,* and *F* and the spaces fall on *F, A, C,* and *E.* As you study Figure 2–19, try to remember that the bass clef lines are *G, B, D, F,* and *A* and the spaces are *A, C, E,* and *G.*

Because of the similarity with reading print, especially the names of the letters and notes, some educators feel that music reading should not begin until children have solid-ified their reading ability. For some children, this may be as early as second grade. For others it may be as late as sixth grade. Other educators start showing musical notation signs to preschoolers.

The other important element in reading music is learning to read the *rhythmic nota-tion.* The lines and spaces are the visual representation for pitch. When the notation on the staff moves upward, the music goes up in pitch. However, the lines and spaces do not tell how long to hold the pitch. This is done by looking at the *spots,* a musical slang word that means the round dots of black with lines attached. Figure 2–20 is a chart with the rhythmic values of different musical notes.

𝅝	**whole note**	**4 beats**
𝅗𝅥	**half note**	**2 beats**
𝅘𝅥	**quarter note**	**1 beat**
𝅘𝅥𝅮	**eighth note** (♫)	**1/2 a beat**
𝅘𝅥𝅯	**sixteenth note** (♬♬)	**1/4 a beat**

FIGURE 2–20   Note values in $\frac{4}{4}$ time.

As discussed earlier in this chapter, understanding musical notation is a little more complicated than the chart. For beginning purposes, the values are given in terms of $\frac{4}{4}$ time. In actual practice, the value of the notes can change according to the *time signature,* the numbers that come right after the clef sign. Practice counting the different notations and see if you can put them together in different variations that add up to four beats. You do not have to know every detail in order to teach some basics to your students, but if you would like information about musical notation beyond these basic ideas, you can take an introductory music class or piano lessons.

Conclusion

Teachers without much musical training can gradually incorporate these ideas into classroom curriculums. Many of these skills are well within the capability of young children. With a little work, you can learn them too. If you have some exposure to music or some experience playing music, you will be surprised how teaching these basic skills will help you in your own musical appreciation and development. One instructor testifies that when she taught middle school band, it greatly helped her own conducting and counting skills, even though she had years of music training. Her own sight reading abilities improved, especially in the area of rhythmic analysis and pitch production.

If you have extensive music training, these skills may seem to basic to you. Remember that your students are young and do not have much exposure to even the basics of music. Repetition of the most basic skills is helpful to young children because it reinforces and coordinates their learning into a consistent whole. Also, the repetition of basic skills helps you, as well as your students, to progress musically, with the focus on musical progress, not perfection.

KEY TERMS

absolute pitch	interval	Orff-Schulwerke
anecdotal information	Kodály method	ostinato
bar	measure	pentatonic scale
beat	musical ability	pitch
beat patterns	musical notation	pitch matching
call and response	musical training	relative pitch
conducting pattern	number system	rhythm
cutoff	off beat	rhythmic patterns
diatonic scale	on beat	solfège system
dynamic levels	Orff instruments	tempo
harmony	Orff music	vocal range

DISCUSSION QUESTIONS

1. Name one great risk to music learning in the preschool years.

2. Is pitch or rhythm learning more highly developed in kindergartners? Why?

3. What is the progression of skills for analyzing the meter or beat of a piece of music?

4. Name 10 tempo words.

5. Write out a five-beat conducting pattern.

6. How will you teach rhythm band activities to young children in the most organized way?

7. Who was Carl Orff and what was his contribution to children's music?

8. Who was Zoltán Kodály and what was his contribution to children's music?

9. Is pitch learned or inherited? When should pitch be taught?

10. When is it best for children to begin learning to sing rounds?

11. How is perfect pitch different from relative pitch?

12. Name the five lines and four spaces of the treble clef.

SUGGESTED LEARNING ACTIVITIES

RHYTHM PRACTICE PATTERNS

Practice the next two examples both ways: 1. Clap and count.
2. Clap and say *ta* and *titi* counting.

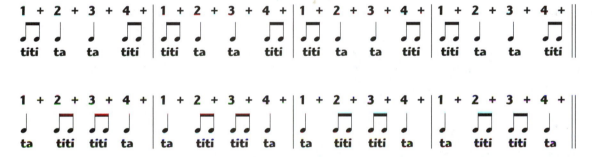

Now, write in your own *ta* and *titi* counting and clap the rhythm.

RHYTHM PRACTICE PATTERNS *continued*

ADVANCED RHYTHM PRACTICE PATTERNS (Note that an eighth rest (𝄾) is equal to *ti* and a quarter rest (𝄽) is equal to *ta*.)

REFERENCES

Bartels, J. (1980). *Sillytime magic* [CD]. Sherman Oaks, CA: Discovery.

Bayless, K. M., & Ramsey, M. E. (1991). *Music: A way of life for the young child.* New York: Macmillan.

Begley, S. (1996, February 19). Your child's brain. *Newsweek.*

Bernstein, L. (1957). *West side story* [CD]. New York: Sony.

Collins, J. (1990). *Baby's bedtime* [cassette]. New York: Lightyear.

Holt, J. C. (1995). *How children fail (classics in child development).* Boulder, CO: Persens.

Kalmar, M. (1982). The effects of music education based on Kodály's directives in nursery school children: From a psychologist's point of view. *Psychology of Music,* Special Issue, 63–68.

Kuskin, K. (1986). *The philharmonic gets dressed.* New York: HarperTrophy.

Martha. (1995). *Songs from the tree house* [CD]. Toronto, ON, Canada: Muffin Music.

Martin, B., Jr. (1994). *The maestro plays.* New York: Henry Holt & Company.

Morley, M., & Ferrante, J. (1999). *Carmina burana* [CD]. New York: Vanguard Classics.

Neill, A. S. (1995). *Summerhill school: A new view of childhood.* New York: St. Martin's Press.

Orff, C., & Keetman, G. (1959). *Music for children* [record]. New York: Angel Records.

Sloboda, J. (1985). *The musical mind.* Oxford, England: Clarendon Press.

Trehub, S. E. (1990). The perception of musical patterns by human infants: The provision of similar patterns by their parents. In M. A. Berkley & W. C. Stebbins (Eds.), *Comparative perception.* New York: John Wiley and Sons.

Various artists. (1998). *Learn to play piano* [CD]. New York: Koala.

Weinberger, N. M. (1994, Fall). *Musica research newsletter.* [Retrieved from http://www.musica.uci.edu, October, 2001.]

Weinberger, N. M., & McKenna, T. M. (1988). Sensitivity of single neurons in auditory cortex to contour: Toward a neurophysiology of music perception. *Music Perception, 5,* 355–390.

Whitfield, I. C. (1980). Auditory cortex and the pitch of complex tones. *Journal of the Acoustical Society of America, 67*(2), 644–647.

Zatorre, R. J., Evans, A. C., & Meyer, E. (1994). Neural mechanisms underlying melodic perception and memory for pitch. *The Journal of Neuroscience, 14,* 1908–1919.

ADDITIONAL RESOURCES

Goodkin, D. (1999). *The Orff Approach, A Short History.* Unpublished manuscript.

Rauscher, F. (1996, Sept./Oct.). The power of music. *Early Childhood News.*

Trehub, S. E., Bull, D., & Thorpe, L. A. (1984). Infants' perception of melodies: The role of melodic contour. *Child Development, 55,* 821–830.

CHAPTER 3

Growing Up the Musical Child

This chapter focuses on the development of young children and how it affects music learning. To understand this relationship, you need to know about the windows of opportunity for teaching certain skills. If a skill is presented too *early,* a child can feel overwhelmed and reject learning the skill altogether. If a skill is presented too *late,* the optimal years for learning the skill may be over and a child's ability to learn it greatly reduced. Fortunately, the *window* is wide for learning important skills, such as music and language. For example, young children typically begin speaking between the ages of eleven months and three years. Many stories have been told of the younger child in a family who does not talk and then begins to speak in complete sentences at age three. However, the **window of opportunity** for learning to speak does not remain open indefinitely. A child who has not learned to speak by age six has a severe disadvantage. Learning may not be impossible, since the brain is flexible and continually learning, but it is much more difficult at this later age.

Music learning, like language learning, also has windows of opportunity. In fact, early language learning is, in a sense, early music learning, since children learn both skills simultaneously. Learning to speak has certain **developmental steps**, including hearing sound, imitating the sound patterns of language, approximating language, and the ability to speak and use language. Learning to sing has the same developmental steps: hearing sound, imitating the rise and fall of the melody—called the *contour* in musical terms—approximating the pitches, and the ability to sing a tune with the correct pitches and rhythms. This final step usually occurs by about age eight.

The window of opportunity for learning to sing opens at age one and closes somewhere around age eleven or twelve. It is the same window as the one for learning to speak another language with a native accent. Similarly, the window of opportunity for learning to play an instrument begins when a child is able to hold an instrument and produce sounds and closes when a child has no time to devote to the intensive study of an instrument. Starting an instrument as young as three is not unreasonable in some cases, if a child has the necessary physical development and especially the attention span. However, this is an early opening of the window of opportunity. If the child is interested and motivated to learn to play the instrument, if playing the instrument is fun, and the teacher is inspiring and nonpressuring, three years of age may not necessarily be too young. The same child can learn to play the same instrument in half the time if she waits to start until age five. A five-year-old child has much better physical coordination and an increased attention span over a three-year-old. Ten years later, it is very difficult to detect a difference between children who started an instrument at age three and children who started at five. However, if a child waits until age fifteen to start playing instruments, it would certainly be pushing the limits on the window of opportunity for instrument learning. Research shows that people over the age of fifteen can learn to play instruments, but the window of opportunity has been missed, and it may be much more difficult to find the time and motivation to begin. In extremely unusual cases, adults can learn a totally new instrument and develop to professional levels. Certainly, adults can learn to play instruments, but they often have less confidence and facility than children or adolescents. The brain has the flexibility to allocate undeveloped brain cells for additional storage space for complex instrument fingering before the age of twelve that it simply will not have in adulthood (Elbert, Pantev, Weinbruch, & Rockstroh, 1995).

As you can see, some skills are best taught at particular ages. The following discussion of the chronological sequence of children's development outlines developmentally appropriate periods for teaching musical skills. Then you can present the right skill to the right children at the right time, which is called **developmentally appropriate practices (DAP)** in teaching.

In the past few years, new research has shown the connection between music learning and other aspects of brain development. The difference between **correlation** and **causality**, two concepts in research that are related but often confused, is an important distinction to understand before discussing the various new areas of research on cognitive development and music. Correlation means a relationship between two happenings. For example, a correlation probably exists between music learning and mathematical ability.

Many educators have remarked that students who are good in music tend to do well in mathematics, and vice versa. These remarks are called *anecdotal information.* Researchers often begin with anecdotal information. A theory is formulated, then a researcher looks for a correlation. One such correlation was found when preschoolers who were given extra musical training did better on tests of spatial relationships in mathematics. These two events can now be linked, but does this actually prove that the extra music training caused better mathematical performance? Until many studies have been done showing that treatment A *causes* outcome B, one cannot really say that the relationship is causal. This is the stage that has been achieved in music research. Further studies will begin to show actual causes, but at this point, most research is establishing correlations and not causality. However, this establishment of correlations is an important step in determining what research *can* and *should* be done to show cause and effect.

Music and Brain Development

Marian Diamond is a well-known researcher who is a pioneer in the field of neurobiology of the brain. In her book *Magic Trees of the Mind* (1998), she discusses her research and gives excellent, comprehensible descriptions of how the brain works. The title of the book gives an insight into the structure of the brain: it is a forest of neurons and dendritic fibers that make the magic of human behavior come alive. She has studied the behavior of rats in enriched and deprived environments, and her conclusions are striking. Rats in enriched environments—spacious areas with toys and other rats—have anatomically larger brains than rats raised alone in cages with no toys or company. This small fact has stunning implications for educators and parents. It means that learning has a physical impact on the brain. The brain actually grows in response to environmental stimulation (Figure 3–1). The converse is also true; the lack of stimulation causes the brain to shrink. This fact is not only true for rats, but for other animals as well. Diamond's research group went on to study the effects of enriched environments in a variety of rat situations.

FIGURE 3–1 Music is important for brain development.

Their findings were many and varied.

1. The impact of a stimulating or boring environment affected the regions of the brain involved in both learning and remembering. Different parts of the brain can grow new dendritic branches and spines, not just the cortex.
2. Enriching the environment of a pregnant rat resulted in the newborn having an enlarged cerebral cortex.
3. Newborn enriched rats' brains grew 16 percent thicker in two weeks, the biggest increase in any brain region at any age.
4. Teenage rats had a more startling result. The impact of a boring, unenriched environment had a more powerful thinning effect on the cortex than an exciting environment had on cortex thickening. Shrinkage of the brains showed up after just four days in the boring environment, but shrinkage could be reversed by four days of enrichment.
5. Young adult, middle-aged, and elderly rats had brain changes due to environmental enrichment or impoverishment. As Diamond says, "Use it or lose it is clearly a lifelong prospect for both rats and people" (1998).
6. A thicker cortex actually *does* mean a smarter animal. This means that an animal's brain can grow in size when environmental stimulation demands a smarter animal.

What are the implications of these findings for music learning? Certainly rats are not people, but both do grow brain structures in similar ways. It means that at any time we can develop our musical ability, but that the brain is apt to grow faster and respond better to environmental stimulation at certain times. These times include pregnancy, early childhood, and the teen years.

The Infant

The period of infancy is considered to be from birth to age one. The development of a child in the first year is astounding (Figure 3–2). The rate of change is the fastest it will ever be in a child's life. So much change occurs in one year, this section is broken up into three developmental periods for music.

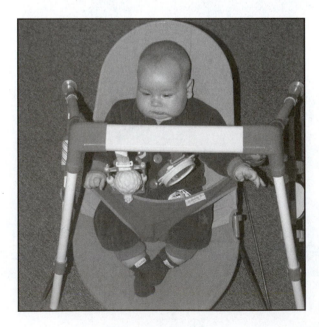

FIGURE 3–2 Infant development occurs rapidly.

Birth to Four Months

Awareness of music begins before a child is even born. Studies show that babies in the womb respond to music with movement. Researchers theorize that **neural development** can be positively influenced by the presence of music *piped in* to the infant through external players or through the sound of the mother's voice singing. Mothers who sang a particular lullaby to their infants during pregnancy had infants who recognized and preferred that lullaby after birth. Infants indicate their awareness by responding differently to different kinds of music, becoming quiet when listening to a soothing lullaby and becoming more active when lively music is played (Lafuente, Grifol, Segarra, Soriano, Gorba, & Montesinos, 1997).

Typical infants also respond to sounds beginning at birth, especially high-pitched human voices. After a few months, a typical infant listens to a voice for 30 seconds, and some children listen even longer. The ability to sustain attention to the voice and face of a caregiver begins in these first few months. Adults help children develop this attention by looking at and talking to them (Trehub, Bull, & Thorpe, 1984).

Language acquisition and early music learning operate in tandem during the first few years of life. Researchers have noticed that adults speak to newborns in high-pitched, singsong voices. It is developmentally appropriate at this phase to talk to infants this way, not because children can only hear in the higher ranges, but because they attend better to higher, singsong sounds.

Infant cries express needs and feelings. A baby's cry can vary in pitch, volume, and rhythm, showing rudimentary musical patterns. Gradually, a child adds new sounds: coos, gurgles, squeals, and then **babbling**: long strings of sound such as "da, da, da, da." All of these sounds are early speaking, but they are also early singing. The "ba ba ba" of an infant later becomes the "ba ba black sheep" of a preschooler.

Four to Eight Months

Musical awareness becomes more active at the age of four months. Infants enjoy listening to all types of sounds in the environment. Active awareness of music is shown when an infant turns her head toward the source of a sound. However, even at this very early age, personality traits of introversion (shyness) and extroversion (outgoingness) begin to appear. Some children bounce along to the music, and others listen with awestruck attention.

Four-month-olds awaken or quiet to sounds of their mothers' voices and soon become more attuned to the particular voices of caregivers. An infant can look for the source of a sound and show interest in it. She begins to respond to the sound of her own name and will look intently at a caregiver and vocalize sounds in response to her name. Even at this young age, a child begins to babble with inflection similar to adult speech.

By six months a child plays peekaboo, and her babbling increases in pitch range, tone, and vocal flexibility. Imitation of sound is typical of this period (Figure 3–3). Whatever sound a child makes, an adult imitates and repeats it. This, in turn, leads to a child imitating adult sounds. This early form of conversation is also the beginning of call and response singing.

Early instrumental learning begins when a child reaches for objects that make a noise. Rattles and spoons to bang are the first percussive instruments. Banging and hitting objects come naturally to very young children.

Eight to Twelve Months

An eight-month-old moves to music. Many children this age can rock to music, although usually not in time to the beat. At this age, every movement is whole body

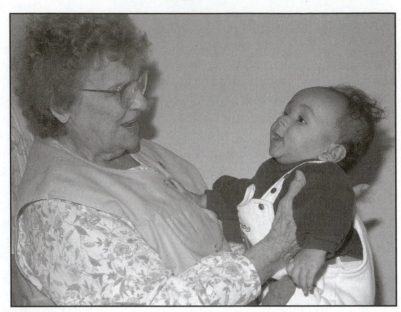

FIGURE 3–3 A six-month-old can imitate musical sounds in his environment.

movement, although adults introduce isolated movement by teaching a child to clap or raise her arms and hands. This kind of movement training is usually done to some kind of song. *Patty-cake* is a perfect example of this activity.

By this stage, babbling is a pastime. Children babble even when left alone. Caretakers can often hear children lying in their cribs, practicing the newest learned sounds.

Many parents play a familiar recording for their children as they fall asleep. Sandra Trehub found in her studies that at this age, children can already recognize the contour of a melody in the same way that adults learn to remember melodic patterns (Trehub, Bull, & Thorpe, 1984).

Toward the end of the first year, a child begins to manipulate objects to make sound (Figure 3–4). Tapping, kicking, and hitting are all newly acquired skills that are applied to objects in order to experiment with sound. At this age, a child also begins to express musical preferences. She may indicate that she likes a particular kind of music, particularly vocal music, by smiling and attempting to sing along. She may also indicate her preferences by rocking or swaying to the music, although often not in time to the music. She also shows displeasure at music she does not like. This dislike is often shown by screaming or attempting to interrupt the music with vocal or physical activity.

Many babies are very interested in music when they watch older children sing or dance. Some babies are so interested in the music that they will jiggle as they sit there, while other babies, probably equally interested, will sit there and look stunned. As a wise preschool music teacher said, "Don't jump to conclusions; the child who sits there and looks stunned can be 'mister music' the next year."

The Musical Infant

Discovering what exactly is going on in the heads of infants is difficult. They cannot yet do much to show that they know something. They cannot tell us anything in words, although they do communicate by crying or not crying. However, making babies cry is not something researchers or parents want to do in their studies. Infants also cannot move around much until they get to be six to nine months, when they can crawl pretty fast. One of the few ways that researchers can get a *yes* or *no* from infants is through

FIGURE 3–4   A one-year-old begins to manipulate objects to make sound.

movement. Two forms of movement have been used by researchers in studies: beginning around two to four months, babies turn their heads in response to sound and they like to kick at things (Figure 3–5).

Sheila Trehub and her research group used babies' action of turning their heads toward sounds to study behavior. In the research, babies sat on their mothers' laps with speakers on either side. Each speaker had a box next to it with a toy that could light up. Sheila and her cohorts first trained the babies to turn to a speaker when a new sound was presented, then they measured if babies noticed very small differences in music. The research group reported that babies heard the difference between musical sounds as close as a half step (semitone), the closest musical steps used in Western music (Trehub, Bull, & Thorpe, 1984).

Infants hear melodies the same way adults do. They remember the tune, not the key in which the tune is played. This is called the **melodic contour**. Infants also divide the sound into chunks called *melodic phrases* (Thorpe & Trehub, 1989). The first part of "Twinkle, Twinkle Little Star" (Collins, 1990) is a phrase. "How I wonder what you are" is another phrase. Babies know how to listen for musical phrases. If you play the same tune faster or slower, infants still recognize it as the same melody. Finally, they also notice that *titi ta* is not the same rhythm as *ta titi* (Trehub & Thorpe, 1989).

Another way that researchers study babies is through their kicking. Fagen, Prigot, Carroll, and Pioli (1997) studied three-month-old infants by comparing their kick rate on a musical mobile that played one of two tunes. The infants' feet were attached to the mobile by a ribbon, and the kick rate went way up when babies found they could make the music happen by kicking more often. The babies remembered this fact one day later. Seven days later, they remembered that kicking made the music happen after they heard the same music that was played during the learning. This result probably indicates that infants used the music to help them remember, the same way that music helps memory recall in adults.

FIGURE 3–5 Infants show musical preferences by turning their heads.

One other way that researchers can get information from infants is to measure their **developmental milestones**. However, not all babies do exactly the same thing on the same day. Babies turn their heads toward sounds between two and four months. Baby books do not say, "On the 65th day after birth, the baby will turn his head toward sounds." All babies are different. Early or late development does not necessarily mean a baby is smart or has a disability, which is why all typical behaviors are given in ranges.

Therefore, when doing an experiment with babies using early developmental behaviors for measurement, researchers need a large group of babies so that the results are not based on the atypical development of a few babies. These kinds of studies are less often done because it is hard to get a large enough group to test. One such study was done on a group of pregnant women (Lafuente et al., 1997). One hundred and seventy-two expecting mothers were divided into two groups. One group wore waistband speakers that played violin music for the babies from week 28 of the pregnancy to the end. The other group did not. After birth, the mothers measured the babies' developmental progress, using the Observational Scale of Development. The experimental group were developmentally advanced over the control group. This experiment, however, is seriously flawed. First, the control group of mothers did not wear speakers around their waists or have any special treatment. Second, the mothers who did wear speakers must have figured out that their babies were getting special treatment. Then, those same mothers rated their own babies on development. If you had made the effort to put on a speaker every day for twelve weeks while struggling through the last three months of pregnancy, would you not expect your baby to do better? Even if the babies did develop faster, does that mean they will be smarter later?

Is it worthwhile to play music to an unborn baby? Probably, but it might be just as effective for mothers to sing some lullabies during the last few months of pregnancy. Given what is known about pregnant rats in enriched environments, it may be just as effective to have mothers lay down and listen to that violin music every day themselves. Those mothers would probably be grateful for the chance!

The Toddler

Toddlers are one to two years of age. This is a period devoted to language acquisition and motor skills. Because growth and change are so marked during this period, this section is broken up into two six-month periods.

Twelve to Eighteen Months

Junior percussionists begin their training at this age, playing instruments by banging, hitting, pounding, and slamming (Figure 3–6). A child now has enough mobility to travel to the kitchen, open the cabinet with pots and pans, and proceed to explore early instrumental learning. Some parents encourage this learning and others tolerate it. Try to encourage the parents of your students to be the first kind. Children learn more quickly if an adult participates in their play. A parent can occasionally enter into early instrument learning by showing a child how to hit pots with different spoons. Wooden spoons make a particularly pleasing sound to adult ears. They can also show a child how to bang along with music. Empty cardboard canisters, such as oatmeal containers, are also preferred by adults' sensitive ears. When adults get to a point when they cannot stand the banging and crashing anymore, they can interest a child in new explorations: presenting a new toy or new task without directly pulling the ear-splitting bangers out of a screaming child's hands. Distraction is the key to changing to a new venue of play at this age. Some adults use direct confrontation. It may work short term, but it is sure to fail in the long run. Even the most patient adults occasionally make the mistake of yelling "I can't stand this any more," and ripping the offending plaything from the child's grip.

Children of this age are very interested in animals and their sounds. Many of the first words learned during this time period are names and sounds of animals. In one word

FIGURE 3–6 Junior percussionists make music by banging, hitting, and pounding objects.

game, a teacher can ask, "What does the dog say?" and a child might answer with "ruff, ruff." The game continues with cats, cows, pigs, chickens, etc. Songs with animal sounds are popular with this age group because children are just starting to sing and are interested in animals. Since they are interested in both singing and animal sounds, the combination is doubly inviting. Mind you, they don't sing much yet, but they are certainly interested.

Another **developmentally appropriate activity** for this age is to match sounds to pictures of animals. A wonderful book by Peter Spier, *Gobble, Growl, Grunt: A Book of Animal Sounds* (1988), has pages full of animal pictures with sounds next to the pictures. It comes in board book format so that children can look at the book on their own without parents fearing they will damage it. However, a special book for this purpose is not necessary. You can use magazines with pictures of animals, point to them, and say or sing the sound.

Eighteen to Twenty-Four Months

A one-and-a-half-year-old jabbers tunefully at play, imitates environmental sounds, attempts to sing with words, enjoys nursery rhymes, and loves to sing songs with motions. Full body motion is best, but finger play will also do. This is the time when a child will run to watch a favorite commercial on TV. *Sesame Street*® studied this age group to find that short segments with catchy music and fast-paced visuals are the appealing format for children's programming. They developed the whole series around the discovery that children love to watch commercials. So, if you watch *Sesame Street*® with an educator's eye, you will notice plenty of commercials, except that *Sesame Street*® sells letters and numbers, rather than toys and cereal.

Eighteen months is an appropriate time for a child to watch regular preschool programs about music. Some people feel that television is inherently bad for children, but excellent programs exist for very young children. Teachers need to encourage parents of children ages three and older to be vigilant in selecting appropriate programming and not allowing their children to watch violent television. With children under age three, parents usually turn the television on and off. Some programs made for this age group, like *Barney & Friends*®, are excellent in introducing children to the standard repertoire of songs, while others, like *Mister Rogers' Neighborhood*®, teach values and emotional understanding.

At this age sounds in the environment captivate toddlers. Besides running to the TV for commercials, children run to the window to watch a dog barking outside or a recycling truck banging the bins. Children also begin to try to have control over sounds, seeking out ones that provide pleasure. The exploration of musical sounds increases (Figure 3–7). Developing language skills and increasing mobility allow children to explore more possible sounds. For these reasons, children make efforts to locate particular objects—pots and pans, cups, bowls, and other utensils—for sound-making activities. An eighteen-month-old is a little more sophisticated in her choice of instruments than a twelve-month-old. A child may find a favorite instrument, either at home or preschool, and begin to play with it more regularly. A child may also begin to show interest in a CD or tape player, even if only to watch it play. An eighteen-month-old child may watch with fascination as a parent, friend, or teacher plays an instrument.

Between ages one and two, singing begins. A child's tuneful jabbering during play sounds more like real songs, even though the songs often only have two pitches. This is the age of the two-pitch song, often *sol* and *mi,* or pitches five and three in the numbering system. The two-pitch song can go on for quite a long time, with small variations in the

FIGURE 3–7 Toddlers try new musical sounds.

rhythm but the same notes. This can wear on the nerves of an adult who spends a lot of time with a toddler. The same two-pitch song can easily transform into whining, which becomes prevalent at ages three to five, and can be later recognized as a teenager's refrain "Why can't I?" that has an almost musical quality in its complaining tones.

Toddlers also try to sing along with adults or other family members. However, children tend to follow the general pattern and not the exact pitches of a melody at this time. When a tune goes up, a child sings higher sounds, and when it goes down, a child picks some low notes to vocalize. This **singing around the pitch** is a style used by children from ages two to nine. By age nine, if a child has not learned to sing closer to actual pitches, she will usually stop singing and say, "I can't sing."

Some adults feel that singing for this age group should be slow. This opinion can be true if you want a child to understand the words. However, children of this age also love to hear fast, exciting music. Include both fast and slow songs in a program of music for children of this age.

The Two-Year-Old

At age two, dance begins. Think of it as whole body singing. A two-year-old dances by bending her knees, bouncing up and down, turning in circles, swaying to the beat, swinging her arms, and nodding her head (Figure 3–8). Sometimes it is hard to get two-year-olds to do more than jump up and down and run around the room in groups. Add jazzy music, and this dancing becomes falling on the floor with shrieks of laughter. A popular two-year-old dance is the "turn around and fall down" dance. You guessed it, the dance consists only of turning around and falling down.

FIGURE 3–8 At age two, dance begins.

Two-year-olds respond especially well to rhythmic music: band marches, light rock 'n' roll, and catchy TV jingles. They are interested in almost any music that you play for them, but only for about two minutes. If you want to play music longer, then choose a piece that has a regular, obvious beat so that they can dance.

Two- to four-year-olds also enjoy repetition. A child of this age would happily watch the same episode of *Barney & Friends*® every day, possibly twice a day, if her caregiver would let her. Repetition is not bad; children need it to learn skills. It is adults who can't stand the repetition enjoyed by toddlers. In the age of video and tape recorders, we do not have to sing the same song fifty times; we can replay it on the cassette. However, children may still beg for more, no matter how many times we play it.

A two-year-old can begin to pay attention for longer periods. She can now lie down quietly and listen to music for a few minutes at a time. Teachers can work with children in small groups to lengthen their attention span. Younger children in larger groups have shorter attention spans because one lively child can distract the entire group. But if you limit the group to three or four children, the group may listen for three to four minutes. That period may seem short, but for two-year-olds, it is an accomplishment. If a group has many older children, the younger children will imitate the older ones and some will sit still, fascinated. In some schools, two-year-olds are expected to sit with older children and attend to the musical activities. In other schools, two-year-olds have their own directed musical play time, which includes movement and music. Still other schools have no group time for younger children until about age three. A general agreement does not exist about how much sitting and listening is important for children under three. Depending on a child's **readiness**, training her to stay with a task and pay attention can begin at age two or three.

Two-year-olds can sing the ends of song phrases. If you start a line, they can say the last word of it. If you focus on pitch, some of them can sing the last word on pitch. This is how children later learn to sing songs, first by completing the end of the line and later singing more of each line until they can sing the whole song.

Stefani Okasaki
Development of a Young Artist

At age two, Stefani Okasaki ran to the piano when her music teacher arrived. Just before turning three, she could play the top part of "Chopsticks" (Various, 1998) while the teacher played the bass part. Early music lessons are not always productive, but Okasaki was so motivated that the teacher encouraged her parents to consider starting her on piano. Later, when she was in elementary school, she was a good singer and had a lovely voice, but it was her piano skills that wowed everyone. By age six, she played piano in the Junior Bach Festival.

Okasaki is now a graduate of MIT and wrote this reminiscence of her musical education:

For as long as I can remember, music has been a significant part of my life. My mother has always told me stories of my fascination with the piano at the age of three, maybe even earlier. I know that I officially began taking piano lessons at the age of four, but the earliest memories I have are not labeled with a date, or even a year for that matter. I can remember chorus in my elementary school, playing the flute at a young age, always being fairly good with rhythm in my gymnastics and ballet classes, and having a particular aversion to math and other patterned subject matters. I would assume that all of these have a direct connection with my early musical involvement, although I cannot be sure because I have no basis for comparison.

Knowing rhythm and basic musical patterns made me able to carry a simple melody and identify a harmony. It gave me confidence in rhythmic motions, and so I was able to pick up gymnastics and dance quite easily. Its tendencies toward consistent patterns led me to create memory devices that helped in areas of mathematics. It also sharpened my ability to play a melody on a piano by ear, so that I could play "Happy Birthday" (Countdown Kids, 1998) for a birthday party or simple Christmas carols for family singing. As a child, it gave me something to be proud of, something to show off. Music, like athletics or performing arts, is a talent that a child can excel in and feel good about possessing. It is an area of study that is praised at every simple advancement and a skill in which frequent advancement is imminent. It is a starting point for self-esteem, not only in performance in front of an audience, but also in the mathematical classroom where patterns may come easier. Confidence at a young age is a crucial step toward academic excellence; children need confidence in order to push themselves further.

In retrospect, it is quite obvious to me that my musical training from a very young age has made a big difference, but I cannot imagine a young child understanding that fully. I know that I never could understand why I had to go to piano lessons every week, or why I was in the chorus. All I knew, and really all that matters to a small child, was that it was fun. It was something that I could do well and something that always allowed for improvement, for another sticker in my music book, or another chorus performance, or even just another "good job, Stefani" from one of my instructors.

Her mother, Nancy Okasaki, comments on her parenting experiences:

For children of all ages, I have always sensed that exposure to music through rhythm and song provided another way for them to socialize. I remember some of the occasions when the music specialist came to Stefani's preschool to provide that exposure to the kids, and I marveled at their focused attention, at that early age, and genuine interest in participating: clapping, ringing bells, tambourines, hitting drums, etc. I recall these activities when Stef was two to three years old. We had a piano at home, and sometimes Stef would pretend she was playing a song. She kept the rhythm, but did not necessarily strike the correct keys. Seeing this

continued

STEFANI OKASAKI *continued*

curiosity and interest led me to eventually look into piano lessons which she began at age four.

The routine of mimicking the teacher's notes and rhythm at each lesson was boring to me, but I soon realized that repetition was what children enjoyed at that age, kind of like wanting parents to read them the same story over and over again. Also, the repetition taught them to pay close attention and listen to the notes so that when they played the same tune, they could tell right away whether they were striking the correct notes themselves. During ages four to five, the ability to play simple songs gave Stef a sense of real accomplishment; i.e., it allowed her to develop self-confidence and pride, which transferred to other activity areas besides music. In school, she was able to quickly master mathematical concepts: addition, subtraction, fractions, etc., and she was able to read by age four. She was the only reader in her kindergarten class when she began school. With piano recitals, she was taught to prepare for the program by practicing, to be attentive to other performers and the audience, and to accept the fact that feeling nervous was okay. All these experiences helped her develop her *own unique style* and allowed her to develop her own *performance personality*. Obviously, the support and encouragement she received throughout her many performances further enabled her to grow and mature. Aside from the regimen of daily piano practice, Stef had to learn to organize her personal daily routine in order to make sure she had practice time. She became a time manager, and consequently developed strong organizational skills and daily habits. Today, these practices continue to help her in her college studies and activities. I believe that Stef now relaxes through playing and listening to music whenever she can find time to do so. In short, the exposure to music in early childhood produces lasting impressions that can only help a person as she develops in every way—physically, emotionally, and spiritually.

The Three-Year-Old

Three-year-olds are beginning to understand the words that are used in songs and can appreciate the silliness of nonsense rhymes. Singing songs that have many repeating words at this age is important because children can better understand the meaning of words if they are repeated. Songs that are virtually the same from verse to verse, with only a single word change per verse, are perfect for this age group. Pete Seeger named this kind of song the **zipper song**. You just zip out one word and zip in a new one.

At three, a child can sing along with a group. However, the entire group does not usually match pitch; rather, at this age, children approximate a tune. They often can tell when the music goes up or down in pitch, but they typically cannot communicate this in words. If you ask them to sing a high note, they can do that. If you ask them to sing a low note, they can do that as well. But if you ask them whether the next note is higher or lower, it is nearly impossible for them to identify the answer in words. However, if you ask them to sing along with you, they can follow the contour of the melody, going generally up and down when you do. They sing tunes in the same general direction, but they often do not get larger intervals right. They can come close to matching small, stepwise pitches, but for a jump of four, five, or six notes, they do a lot of vocal guessing. This *singing around the pitch* gradually improves to closer pitch matching, so that by age eight, a child is usually able to sing simple songs entirely on pitch.

FIGURE 3–9 Three-year-olds have difficulty following a beat.

Children progress in their pitch learning ability at different paces. Some children can sing a familiar song like "Twinkle, Twinkle Little Star" (Collins, 1990) on pitch as early as three. Others do not match pitch well until age seven or eight. The early years are too soon to tell whether a child has unusual musical ability. Too many factors can affect musical development both positively and negatively in the first three years of life. However, by age three, indications of musical *interest* are apparent in some children. If by age three a child can sing a few simple songs on exactly the right pitches, especially the jumps of larger intervals like fourths and fifths, then she probably has focused hearing and good pitch matching ability. This ability should be nurtured and trained in order for her to achieve musical capability. Raw talent without training can rarely create musical competence. However, if a child cannot sing on pitch by age three, then she is fairly typical in development and may later become quite musical. This is true of boys, who typically cannot sing on pitch by age five but develop a good ear for pitch by age eight if given training.

Most three-year-olds cannot follow a beat exactly (Figure 3–9). They can march or clap to a beat with some accuracy, but they have a tendency to speed up or get behind. After the music stops, a rare three-year-old can remember the speed of the beat and clap to it without the music.

The Four-Year-Old

By four years of age, the differentiation of sexes becomes a more pronounced issue in choosing music. Boys begin to show preferences for loud, jumpy music, with a marked preference for rock 'n' roll. Girls enjoy this music as well, but many girls have also discovered ballet and respond well to some classical music. These generalizations are not true of all boys and all girls, but as a teacher, be aware that boys and girls are different in their preferences. Be sensitive to gender differences beginning in late preschool and continuing into the upper grades. This recognition is important because you must be aware of children's interests when you choose music. If you choose only quiet, relaxing, classical music, children who are bored by it may begin to act out. At this age, impulse control is not high.

Both boys and girls respond well to songs that have a humorous twist, with the types of humor varying according to the age of a child. With four-year-olds, humor in music consists of singing a well-known song in a high-pitched voice, singing the same song in a very low voice, singing faster and faster, singing it very slow, or doing some silly hand motions to accompany the song. Four-year-olds greatly appreciate repetition and will laugh at the same silly tactics repeatedly. Repetition becomes less interesting as a child grows older.

Toilet and bodily function songs are regarded by most four-year-olds as hilariously funny. This interest continues through the junior high school years, especially in boys. Most teachers do not encourage this type of humor because the silliness can quickly escalate to uncontrollable levels. Try to choose songs that satisfy children's interests without going over the edge of sensitivity. Other avenues of humor are available. One humorous topic is squeezing large objects into small spaces. Another is retelling a familiar story with a surprising new ending. Finally, great silliness is evoked by anthropomorphizing animals, such as having an alligator drinking Gatorade or a pet rhinoceros eating doughnuts.

By four, children can understand the words of a song and the meaning of the words, so content becomes more important. Contrary to popular belief, songs like "The Fox (went out on a chilly night)" (Peter, Paul & Mary, 1993) and "I Know an Old Lady (who swallowed a fly)" (Peter, Paul & Mary, 1993) are not best for this age. The fox song goes so fast the children hardly hear a word. The words they do understand may be about the little ones chewing on the bones. This can lead to discussions of things that eat bones in the forest, which frightens some four-year-olds. Also, the values in the song about the fox may suggest that it is okay to steal.

"I Know an Old Lady" is problematic for other reasons. Four-year-olds do not really understand size and volume, and they are often fearful of going down the drain or being eaten. After singing this song, one little girl began to cry. She said that her grandma had just died and she was worried that her grandma had swallowed a fly.

Consider the meaning of words when you choose songs for children who vaguely understand the vocabulary. You must match the vocabulary and content level of a song with the age of a child. Those same two songs are excellent for third graders, who enjoy the pronunciation gymnastics of singing the fox song very fast and enjoy the silliness of an old lady who would consider swallowing larger animals to catch the ones supposedly flying around her insides.

Four-year-olds are very active, even during music time. They enjoy activities that require good balance, such as standing on one foot or walking on a line on the floor. So, include movement in a four-year-old's music program (Figure 3–10).

Children this age often find new ways to resist adult direction. Rather than confronting adults like two-year-olds in the "no" phase, four-year-olds have learned how to passively avoid doing what an adult asks or expects. You will know right away if children this age are bored with a music activity because they will wander off, roll on the floor, or begin to play with a nearby toy. Occasionally, they will tell you if they do not like the music, but more often they will just drift away.

Four-year-olds have also learned how to ask questions, and they can take up your entire music time with a variety of meandering questions that can easily spill over into telling you about the family dog and grandma. Unfortunately, while you listen to one child, the rest lose interest and become bored. For this reason, stay focused on the songs or dances that you want to do with a group. Four-year-olds are old enough to wait until the end of music time for you to answer their questions.

FIGURE 3–10 Four-year-olds enjoy balance and movement activities to music.

Children this age love to talk. They have learned language, and now they use it, use it, use it. They love nonsense words, silly language, poems, stories, rhymes, and songs. However, they have trouble separating fantasy from reality. A child can begin to tell you about her dog, and soon she is telling you about a dog she saw on the street who broke his leg when he was a baby. She does not actually know this dog, but the fantasy seems to weave itself. Keep this in mind when singing songs with four-year-olds. Very absurd songs can be easily distinguished as fantasy. If a song's story line is too close to reality, children this age can be confused.

Four-year-olds love to dance, sing, do drama, and hear poems and stories. They love to make up songs, but adults usually find the songs to be like disconnected, run-on sentences. A typical four-year-old's composed song goes like, "I went down to the grocery store with my Mom and then I said I wanted some candy but my Mom said she couldn't buy any so then I went out the door and we saw Santa and he said do you want some candy and I got a piece of candy from him and then we went to the swimming pool." All of this is usually sung on a four-note repeating melodic phrase.

Four-year-olds are competent in many areas, and music helps them be more competent. They typically know their phone numbers and have learned their last names. They may be able to learn their street addresses and perhaps even the names of their cities. Putting this information into a song format can greatly aid their memory. They are also just learning the days of the week and the months of the year, which can best be learned in song format. Choose a simple tune, like "Mary Had a Little Lamb" (Jenkins, 1993), and change the words to naming the days and months.

Another area of language that four-year-olds learn to master is prepositions such as on, over, under, around, through, into, below, and above. A song like "Ten in the Bed" (Arnold, 1995) that includes a variety of prepositional words can help teach four-year-olds about the meanings of these numerous small words. They can also follow simple directions with two steps. Songs that include directions like "Put Your Finger on

Jane Timberlake
Preschool Teacher and Children's Songwriter

Jane Timberlake started writing songs in 1975 when her youngest child was in nursery school. She said, "I couldn't find enough songs that I liked for little kids." Twenty-three years later, with 18 years of experience as a preschool educator, Jane is still writing songs for young children. She explained, "I like singing with kids. Little songs find me, flying to me. I whistle hundreds of tunes a week and some of them stick around and become songs." She is always trying out new songs and changing songs based on children she knows. She hates having no control over the songwriting process. "When a song is in rough form it sometimes takes a lot of tedium to find out what it will be. Sometimes it wakes me up in the middle of the night and won't go away."

Jane feels humor is probably more important for preschoolers than anything else, but preschool humor may not take the same form as adult comedy. Some topics, like bathroom humor, are more appealing to preschoolers than adults. She has found many topics that interest preschoolers: frightening monsters and scary animals, magical powers, allusions (however tactful) to any kind of excretory function, and daily woes (like missing your mommy, waking up with gum in your hair, or getting an *owie*).

Jane involves kids in her music by writing songs she knows will interest them and tunes they can remember. She writes songs with easy to learn choruses and other repetitive or additive elements. She does songs that let children play rhythm instruments and move to the music, either with their hands or their whole bodies.

Jane has some great stories. She said, "My niece Stella used to put her portable tape recorder down beside her newborn baby brother, Rex, and play for him, over and over, a song about Tyrannosaurus Rex. I'm relieved to report that Rex is four now, a great kid, apparently unaffected by early imprinting." A five-year-old told Jane, "Your brain tells your nerves to tell the heart to pump blood as hard as it can. When the motor of the heart is hot enough, then it pumps the blood up and fills your head. PS, I love your songs."

Jane chose to work with children rather than adults because "I love to be around young children. They're extremely entertaining, and they're far cuter than a busload of them will be in fifty years." When asked if there is something important to her about music, she said, "Since I spend so much time wandering around aimlessly, whistling my tunes, I guess there must be."

Your Nose" (Various, 2000) or "Head, Shoulders, Knees and Toes" (Bartels, 1992) can help children practice this important skill.

Four-year-olds are often ready to try real instruments. The Suzuki violin method starts children at four. Some children do well beginning an instrument at this age, but for others the progress is very slow and a child can become frustrated by comparison to older, better players. If a child is begging to play an instrument, follow her lead. However, there is no harm in waiting a few more years to start instrument lessons.

A set of rhythm instruments can be useful with this age group, but it can be hard on adult nerves. Remember, four-year-olds only follow two steps of directions, so it is easy for them to *start* but hard for them to *stop* playing instruments. See the section in Chapter 2 on teaching rhythm band if you want to try this with four-year-olds. They can identify the sounds of familiar instruments like a piano or guitar, so encourage this ability by playing pieces of music that include instruments that each have a different tone quality, or **timbre**. They are willing to listen to short pieces of music, so encourage this as a way to slow them down during transition times. They can also accurately identify the feeling of the music, so play music with different emotions, such as happy, sad, and scary music. In this way you can develop a variety of musical skills with equipment as simple as a tape recorder.

An interesting study was done on the attention spans of four-year-old children. A child sat at a table with one marshmallow on a plate. The researcher said that she had to go on an errand but that she would come back in a few minutes. If the child could wait to eat the marshmallow until she got back, then she would give the child another marshmallow. The study followed up on the same children 14 years later. Children who were able to wait seven minutes until the researcher returned scored on average 210 points higher on their SAT scores (Goleman, 1997)! Learning how to attend to a task and delay impulsive gratification could have great benefits for a child. Music is one of the best ways to help four-year-olds develop attention.

The Five-Year-Old

Five-year-olds have the new world of kindergarten expanding their interests (Figure 3–11). Though a child may have attended preschool, kindergarten is a new challenge. There are more children and fewer adults, so a child must learn to wait for adult attention. Older children are in the school for kindergartners to watch and imitate. Waiting and imitating are important skills for kindergarten children. Music is an excellent way to minimize waiting and a vehicle for learning appropriate imitation.

Five-year-olds are musically between younger children who love to repeat the same songs and older children who are intrigued with complex words of new songs. Children of this age do well with zipper songs, which are great for them because these songs combine the repetitive qualities of favorite preschool songs with the added interest of new

FIGURE 3–11   Five-year-olds enjoy trying new music.

words in new combinations. Often, in a well-crafted zipper song, the new combination of words creates silly sounds or concepts that tickle the funny bone of a five-year-old.

Remember that humor helps children engage with an activity and retain instructional material. At five, the concept of telling jokes has just begun. However, a five-year-old's joke is probably only funny to others in her own age group. A typical five-year-old joke starts with a repetition of a joke formula, such as, "What did one hat say to the other hat?" The real answer is, "You stay here, I'm going on a head." However, a five-year-old's version of this joke is, "What did one hat say to the other hat? You stay here, I'm going to go buy a dog." Five-year-olds will roll on the floor, laughing at a joke like this and are the masters of non sequiturs. The first part of the joke has absolutely no relationship to the second half. These important points about humor apply to songs for five-year-olds as well.

Songs for this age group are successful when they appeal to the emerging vocabulary of children and their growing ability to make sense of language. These children are interested in the natural world, family relationships, and bodily functions. These topics are the foundation of hundreds of songs written for kindergartners.

Most five-year-olds can already sing familiar tunes. Favorites are "Twinkle, Twinkle Little Star" (Collins, 1990) (which has the same tune as the "Alphabet Song" [Bartels, 1980] and "Ba Ba Black Sheep" [Jenkins, 1993]), the chorus of "Jingle Bells" (Bartels, 1990), "Mary Had a Little Lamb" (Jenkins, 1993), and "This Old Man" (Raffi, 1980). All these standard songs are tunes that encompass only a six note range, from about middle C to the A six notes above it. Sandra Shelly (1976) found that the preferred singing range of young children is the same as the range in these songs. They prefer to sing in a six note range even though they can sing in a wider range. Young children are able to sing much higher than middle C. Many can sing or squeak notes two and a half octaves above middle C, but children ages five and younger are not able to sing lower than middle C. Children's actual singing voices widen in their range to almost three octaves by age thirteen, when they can sing from a G below middle C to a G three octaves above that.

At this age it is important to challenge a child's vocal range and begin to build it up. At least one octave and perhaps even an octave and a half can be reached. Songs like "I'm a Little Teapot" (Wonder Kids Choir, 1998), "The Itsy Bitsy Spider" (Monet, 1989), and "Somewhere Over the Rainbow" (Arlen, 1939) all have a vocal range of about one octave. Emphasize that boys can sing high, because boys of this age begin to think that they ought to sing low, like men. When they know their voices will not change until ages twelve to fifteen, and that they will know when it happens, boys are more willing to sing high.

This is also the age to introduce different classical instruments and their various sounds. This activity is useful for both its musical value and also for the vocabulary development that it promotes. Five-year-olds can play simple percussion instruments in time with a rhythm, both in memorized patterns and in response to nonverbal directions, such as hand motions or beat cues given by a conductor. For kindergarten instrumental music ideas, consult the rhythm learning section of Chapter 2.

With assistance from a teacher, kindergartners can create simple accompaniments to songs. After some practice, a group can read from a large chart with words to songs printed on it and play along with the music. At this age, children can also make up their own melodies and words; they can write songs as a group activity. They can also illustrate songs on paper.

Kindergarten is the time to introduce simple dance steps to music. This is not as easy as it would seem. Remember that children this age do not know right from left. Therefore, they have no idea which way to turn and can end up just wandering around. A song called "Hands" (Fink, 1986) is helpful with this. Children put their left hands behind their backs and walk around shaking right hands with everyone while the music plays. Additional dance activities are suggested in Chapter 9.

The Six-Year-Old

Six-year-olds have conquered kindergarten and now are ready to enter the world of the *big kids*. At this age most children begin to put together their early word recognition and basic phonemic skills to master the printed word. First graders come to school in the fall reading a handful of words and graduate from this grade reading whole books. Math skills move beyond counting to number groups. The concepts of time—today, tomorrow, and yesterday—really take hold.

Unfortunately, this is the year when music is left behind for most children, just at the point when they are solidifying the ability to really sing on pitch and in rhythm (Figure 3–12). At this time, extra practice discriminating sounds and pitches is helpful in learning to read. Finally, this is the point at which the concentration developed in music learning can be a serious benefit in mathematics ability and standardized testing. Unfortunately, most schools no longer have music teachers, so regular classroom teachers are the only resources children have for music. If teachers put on a recording and encourage children to sing along, children can still get some musical experience.

Six-year-olds who receive some musical training can coalesce their **pitch development** and music reading. They can understand high and low pitches and relate these sounds to notes that are higher and lower on the musical scale. They can understand pitch relationships when learning how to sing intervals more accurately. They can learn to hear the difference between an interval of a whole step and an octave. They can begin to identify more difficult pitch discriminations, such as the difference between a fourth and a fifth. Finally, they can understand basic rhythmic patterns consisting of eighth and

FIGURE 3–12 At age six, music learning really begins.

DEBORAH MOORE

Children's Music Journalist

Deborah Moore writes a weekly syndicated column, *Music and Moore,* that is distributed by Tribune Media Services, Chicago. She also writes articles for regional and national parenting publications.

Moore started taking piano lessons at age five, and she composed her first song when she was a first grader. She later studied cello and classical guitar. She was exposed to classical music in her lessons, but she also heard a lot of '40s and '50s popular songs.

Moore's interest in children's music peaked after her daughter was born. She began working with preschool children in 1990, doing musical entertainment and education. She started writing children's music features and review columns in 1995.

When Moore hears first graders singing Britney Spears songs, she is determined to teach parents and teachers about age-appropriate alternatives to current pop music through her columns. She is inspired by talking with school age kids about appropriate music. She loves having kids' eyes light up when they hear examples of music made for their age group. She said, "Well-crafted, quality, age-appropriate music has as much potential for influencing positive behavior as violent, sexually oriented music has the potential for influencing negative behavior." Moore has a great story that illustrates the assistance she can give to parents and teachers. After speaking to a group of parents at a school open house, one mom approached her and told her she was glad she had come that night and listened to Moore talk. Her son had tried to convince her to buy a CD by a shock rock group; he had told her it was a new kind of Christian group, Christian shock rock. Moore was able to give this parent the information she needed to tune in to her child's musical pretenses.

Moore enjoys all kinds of music. However, her favorite songs for children have a respect for and an awareness of the emotional and physical developmental needs of young listeners. She advocates creative, clever, respectful songs with a good marriage between lyrics and music. Deborah favors children's music composed by children's musicians because the intentions of children's performers are generally more child-centered and less egocentric than mainstream performers'. If this music is not as well-produced, it is not because it lacks care; rather, it lacks a production budget. Children's music is also usually more varied than pop music. Moore said, "After you've listened to the variety on a good children's album, adult mainstream albums can get boring quickly."

Moore's favorite music is Bach's Brandenburg Concertos (Boston Baroque, 1996), but she listens to all different kinds of music: nonviolent rock, folk, blues, contemporary, gospel, and sometimes even a little swing. She finds rhythmic patterns fascinating. She believes that "music has an emotional impact on human beings, from the very young to the very old. It can calm you down, pick you up, make you laugh, or move you to tears. Music is also an excellent cultural and societal mirror. It's a great way to learn more about other cultures."

Moore is happy to talk with anyone who has a genuine interest in music for children, either in the classroom or at home.

Reprinted with permission from Deborah L. Moore.

quarter notes. Much of the rhythmic learning described in Chapter 2 can be done with first through third graders.

Six-year-olds have a good **sense of rhythm**. They can follow a beat, and, with a little training, they can feel out the downbeat. This is the time to teach beginning conducting. First graders can learn not to rush or drag behind the beat. Time permitting, they are able to learn most of the musical concepts and vocabulary presented in Chapter 2.

The Seven-Year-Old

Seven-year-olds are real kids. No longer do they stand on the sidelines while older children run the games. Second graders run the show themselves. They are old enough to know the school grounds and classroom layouts. They have been in school long enough to know how the system works and how to work the system. They read quite well and are beginning to choose the areas of interest they will have for the rest of their lives.

This is the perfect time to introduce a child to formal instrument lessons, so they need to have some exposure to the different instruments they can learn to play (Figure 3–13). Some music educators feel that children should start on an instrument within a particular family of instruments. For example, a child may start on the trumpet and later move to the baritone horn or tuba. Other educators start children on the instrument of choice. If tenor sax is the child's interest, then they begin with that instrument. Remember that a child often does not have enough exposure to the possibilities and varieties of instruments at this young age. A classroom teacher can help her students learn the different names of instruments and the sounds they make. It is wonderful when second grade teachers instruct children about the families of instruments and about how instruments are related to each other.

If children choose instruments later, in the fourth grade, they are often influenced by the sexism of their peers. Boys are encouraged to play trumpets, drums, and saxophones. Girls are encouraged to play violins, flutes, and clarinets. Any band or orchestra teacher will tell you the children have somehow absorbed these prejudices from their peers by age ten.

Seven is the age of performance. Second graders are still young enough to be relaxed on stage and yet old enough to remember songs and lines. The excitement of doing a musical performance attracts their interest and motivates children to work hard in order to perform well. They still find rehearsing for these performances fun, although

FIGURE 3–13 Seven is the perfect age to introduce a child to formal instrument lessons. *(Courtesy of Anthony M. Riservato, Cambridge Photo, Clifton Park, NY)*

At what age should a child begin to study a musical instrument?

The current cultural agreement is that in the fourth grade, at age nine, children all over the United States are given an option to start to play an instrument in school music programs. Some school districts delay this opportunity until fifth grade. This cultural notion has been around for probably fifty to seventy years. Parents are advised that fourth grade is a good time to start lessons because by then children have learned to read and are independent enough to practice on their own.

This notion was challenged in the 1950s by Deisetz Suzuki, who invented the Suzuki violin method. He taught two- and three-year-olds in Japan to play violin on tiny, child-sized instruments. By the time the children were fifteen, they played amazingly complicated violin pieces. The children became world famous, and the method was adopted by violin teachers around the world. Many Suzuki programs exist in the United States. He revolutionized the whole notion of when to start children on instrument lessons.

These are the two ends of the spectrum. If a child begins playing at age three, it is very slow going. A three-year-old takes six months just to learn how to hold a violin properly and another year to learn how to play "Twinkle, Twinkle Little Star" (Collins, 1990) on the strings with her fingers. A child at age eight can learn how to hold the instrument and play with her fingers in about six months. A twelve-year-old can learn it in a month. However, if you begin at age three, by the time the child is eight, she can really play tunes well, and by age twelve she will be well on her way to concert violinist status. A child who begins at age eight will probably catch up to a child who began at three somewhere around age fifteen. A child who begins at age twelve may never catch up and will probably not become a professional violinist unless she is highly motivated and musically talented.

This progression can be influenced by a number of factors. When a child is started between two and four, parents must invest much time and energy, taking her to lessons, practicing with her, and motivating her to continue. Suzuki's program succeeded because he had dedicated mothers, not dedicated children. He also had compliant children. The great risk in starting a child so young is that she may not succeed as quickly as she expects because of her age, and she may decide that playing the instrument is not worth the effort to continue because it is difficult and her progress is slow. This is especially true if she is exposed to older children who play better and progress more quickly. It may also become a battle between parent and child if she does not like to practice and feels discouraged by the sound of the instrument. A musically sensitive child may find the out of tune sounds and scratchy bow frustrating to hear. At this age, the motivation of the parent keeps violin lessons going. After a year or two, a child will either take over the motivation and begin to practice to please the teacher, the parent, and herself, or she will quit complying. If she has some musical talent and perceives herself to play well, she will probably continue. If she has little musical ability, a short attention span, difficulty with fine motor coordination, or feels discouraged in comparison to others, she will most likely want to quit. If parents have paid attention to the cues given by a resistant child, the violin lessons will end without a fight. If not, a child will probably harbor resentment against parents for making her play violin and quit as soon as she can figure out how to passively resist (ages eight to ten).

After many years of gathering parental and teacher opinions, experts have concluded that age seven, second grade, is a particularly good time to begin lessons. A child this age understands that making a commitment requires follow-through. Preschoolers do not have the time sense that second graders have, but by second grade children have learned how to do homework, follow through on assignments, and read. These abilities help a lot with instrument learning. In second grade, a child is still young enough to be influenced by a parent's motivation, a parent's praise still means something, and a parent's encouragement

continued

AT WHAT AGE SHOULD A CHILD BEGIN
TO STUDY A MUSICAL INSTRUMENT? *continued*

can still motivate a child. This can help a child succeed in playing an instrument. Some piano teachers feel that first graders, age six, are at the best age for beginning music lessons. However, others feel that the first grade year is already an intense year for the child. She is learning to read, to achieve, and to become a real grade schooler; they think it is better not to add the pressure of learning a new instrument.

By second grade, a child can also have some real input about what kind of instrument she would like to play. An excellent musical recording for assisting this choice is narrated by Peter Ustinov and called *The Orchestra* (1987). This album has recordings of all the various classical instruments; it plays the sound of each instrument and a short piece of music featuring each instrument.

Starting instrumental music in the fourth or fifth grade is not outmoded, however. Children progress much faster in instrument learning in fourth grade than they do in second grade. Fourth graders are much better readers and can read instructions in music training books. Fourth graders are also physically bigger and can hold larger, almost adult-sized, instruments. However, we know that the brain at the younger age can be greatly benefited by early stimulation of the neural pathways. The younger the child, the more flexible the brain is in determining how it will organize the information. Elbert, Pantev, Weinbruch, and Rockstroh (1995) reported that string players who began at age seven have a larger portion of their brains dedicated to left-handed fingering. Fourth graders have certainly not missed the developmental window of opportunity, but the brain is more organized and less flexible by age nine than it was at age seven. Finally, fourth graders have more focused attention and higher motivation, especially if they, rather than their parents, are the ones who choose to play the instrument.

If a child starts at age twelve or thirteen, her motivation must make up for the four crucial years missed between ages eight and twelve. It takes a great deal of intense practice to make up for those missed years. If a child is highly motivated and musically talented, the intensity and focus of the early teen years can be a great benefit in instrumental learning. For example, one student did not start playing violin until age thirteen, although she played piano from ages ten to fourteen. She was highly motivated because she had an excellent and beloved violin teacher. By age sixteen, she had surpassed some other students who began playing violin in fourth grade. Only one other violin prodigy in her high school orchestra was better. That person started young and had many years of practice behind her. She now plays both the violin and the viola professionally.

instructors will sometimes meet resistance when suggesting that it is time to practice. The problem is the *idea* of practicing and the transition to a new activity. Once children are actually on the stage or the practicing has begun, they enjoy it and often do not want to stop.

In terms of pitch development, most second graders should be able to sing a song on pitch, especially in a group led by an adult with a strong voice singing in the correct pitch range. Occasionally, a strong singer in second grade can sing an entire song on pitch as a solo. However, it is best not to begin having children solo at this age because children who do not get the solo parts will assume they are no good at singing. This is too young an age to make that assumption.

Most second graders cannot yet sing rounds, but a simple technique can be used to help teach round singing. Have a class learn the round, practicing it well. Then record the class singing the round three times. After this, start the tape and have students sing the second part of the round against the tape as it plays. This way, teachers can sing with students both times, and children have the support of a large group singing each part. This technique can also be used to create a lovely performance for parents.

Children at this age can begin to learn complex rhythms. Second graders can imitate rhythmic patterns four to eight beats in length, or equivalent to one or two bars of music. Second graders can reproduce rhythms that include quarter notes, eighth notes, half notes, whole notes, and sixteenth notes. However, the concept of dotted eighth notes and tied notes are still difficult for this age group to understand. With a good music teacher, students can learn these concepts, but only after learning the foundations of easier rhythmic patterns. Second grade is the perfect time to practice being a conductor and working together as a group.

The Eight-Year-Old

Eight-year-olds enter third grade as young children and leave as competent young people. This is the year when talents and interests begin to take hold. Up until now, a child has not known enough about the outside world to develop a wide range of interests. By the end of third grade, she has begun to discover interests and issues independently. Teachers and parents may only have a vague knowledge about these interests. She is also developing her own areas of expertise. This knowledge base will broaden until she begins to specialize in the teen years.

An eight-year-old can usually **carry a tune**, though some children can sing better than others (Figure 3–14). Girls tend to be more interested in singing and music, but this may be because the kinds of songs chosen for music may not interest an eight-year-old boy. One problem with boys can be that they try to sing in the low register, like a man. This is hard on a young voice and may contribute to a boy's decision to stop singing. Also, boys take just a little longer to learn to sing on pitch than girls. Some children will stop singing altogether, especially if they are criticized for not being able to sing. Many,

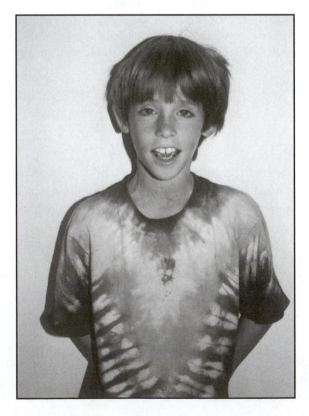

FIGURE 3–14 Eight-year-olds can usually carry a tune.

DEVELOPMENTALLY APPROPRIATE MUSIC

An Article by Deborah Moore

When you look on the racks of the kids' music section in most local stores, it would seem that children's music is a pretty much *one size fits all* business. The truth of the matter is, there are certain kinds of music that are more developmentally appropriate for specific age groups than others. There is a widely held myth, as well, that once a child passes preschool age, children's music no longer applies. There is life after Big Bird®, really!

Here are guidelines to help you choose age-appropriate music for that special little person in your life:

♪ Infants: Babies love melodious sounds, all kinds of sounds. The sound of your voice, birds singing, a cat meowing. Sounds are stimulating and aid in the development of verbal skills. The best music for babies is any style that is not too loud. (Heavy metal might be a bit too much.) If you like reggae, pop, classical or do-wop, folk, jazz, country or soft rock, then play it and sing with it to your baby. Your voice, regardless of pitch or timbre, will get your infant's interest and direct it to the musical sound. By the time a little one is old enough to sit up on his own, she will be able to bounce to a good beat.

♪ Toddlers: Once your child begins walking, she will start moving to the music. Kids this age are not developmentally ready to follow interactive songs with directions like "touch your nose, touch your head," but they will delight in watching you do these moves when you share songs like "Head, Shoulders, Knees and Toes" (Bartels, 1992) and "The Itsy Bitsy Spider" (Monet, 1989). It is important that you sing and move with your toddlers. This helps them make the connection between music and movement and aids in gross motor and verbal skill development. Music with a strong rhythm will have toddlers bouncing on their bottoms, waving their arms in the air, and squealing with glee. If you enjoy musical moments with your child, your child will enjoy them, too. Keep this focused time short, though, because this age has an attention span of about 2 minutes.

♪ Two- to three-year-olds: By the time your little one reaches this age, she will be able to follow directions, learn simple lyrics and, as she moves into her third year, be able to *act out* songs. Finger plays such as "The Itsy Bitsy Spider," which she watched as a toddler, now become a favorite pastime. Two- and three-year-olds are becoming aware of their bodies, so songs that point to different body parts or encourage shaking a hand, foot, leg, or head are great fun. Kids this age also will find a favorite song or finger play and repeat it. A favorite song becomes *my song*. At times, children get very possessive of the tune and do not like to share it with others. Tapes that use lots of interactive music and invite the child to participate are best for this age. Use caution in playing adult, mainstream music with this age group, because as their verbal skills increase, they will parrot the lyrics they hear. This is excellent practice for little kids, but it can prove embarrassing to parents if they sing an inappropriate song in the middle of class. Focused attention span is maxed out at about 10 minutes, so keep it short and fun.

♪ Pre-K through first grade: As your child becomes more communicative, verbal skills and movement are becoming more refined. Pre-K and kindergartners adore interactive songs and enjoy the challenge of trying to keep up with directions. Children this age are capable of learning relatively complicated lyrics, following a tune, and keeping basic rhythm by clapping, stomping, or tapping a pencil or drum stick to the beat. As your child becomes more communicative, verbal skills and movement are becoming more refined. Pre-K through first graders adore interactive songs and enjoy the challenge of trying to keep up with directions. Kids this age

continued

DEVELOPMENTALLY APPROPRIATE MUSIC *continued*

have two priorities: move and have fun. This is a perfect age to begin teaching simple foreign language songs. Kids can even enjoy learning American Sign Language used in conjunction with song lyrics. They also enjoy classical music, as long as there is movement to accompany it. So feel free to dance around the room with your favorite classics and build a great memory for you and your child. Focused attention span has increased to 30 minutes.

♪ Grades two through five: Although your child's taste in music will largely be influenced by your likes and dislikes, kids begin picking particular sounds and styles that especially appeal to them. Word play, puns, cleverness, and quirkiness are appreciated. Lyrics and content of songs are now easily understood, so use caution in what you listen to on the radio or the CD player when your children are within earshot. Positive messages with a good beat, excellent production, and a Top 40 sound can have a good influence on kids this age. Children this age are also old enough to pursue interests in musical instruments. If the child has been asking about piano, violin, saxophone, or drum lessons, this is an excellent time to explore opportunities.

The most important element in laying a good musical foundation for your child is you. If you like music, your child will like it. Share your music with your child. Sing with her, dance with her. Your vocal talent does not matter. It is the time that you spend sharing that makes the difference, that creates the memory, and teaches the child an appreciation for good music.

Reprinted with permission from Deborah L. Moore.

many a child has been damaged when another student tells her, "You can't sing." Worse than that is a teacher who tells a child to just mouth the words while everyone else sings. Eight years of age is just too young to decide that a child cannot learn to sing.

Instrument learning begins to diverge from singing at this age. Many instrumentalists cannot sing very well. This makes it difficult for a talented instrumentalist to learn how to sight sing, to pick up a piece of music and sing just by reading the melody without any help from playing the tune on an instrument. This is a necessary skill in college musical programs. Well-trained musicians who can both sing and play an instrument can tell you that the skills are different. Reading music while playing an instrument uses hand-eye coordination. Sight reading music uses eye-ear and voice coordination. Because of this difference, children who have good hand-eye coordination will begin to excel in instrument playing at the third grade level, whereas children with good ear-voice coordination will excel at singing. These latter children will also do well in the theater arts, which also require ear-voice skills.

By the third grade, some children are already beginning to show talent in certain areas of music. However, the ability of a child to stay focused on the activity, not innate talent, will determine how well she will progress in musical competence. The ability to stay focused on instrument learning and to practice regularly is influenced greatly at this age by music teachers and parents.

Practice Makes Perfect

A great debate in music research is taking place about the issue of talent versus practice. This is similar to the nature versus nurture debate in parenting. Is musical ability inherited, a biological given, or is it trained and developed by parents and teachers? Is it mostly talent—nature—or mostly practice—nurture? This debate is discussed in great detail in the August 1994 issue of the British journal *The Psychologist*. This excellent set of articles presents the views of one research group, John Sloboda, Jane Davidson, and Michael Howe and their critics David Hargreaves and Bruce Torff and Ellen Winner.

The first research group supported the theory that talent is a developed trait, mostly created by hours and hours of practice. They hotly contested the belief that some people are naturally more musical than others. Their research showed that in some other cultures, particularly the Anang Ibibo people of Nigeria, everyone is expected to be musical, so children learn hundreds of songs before the age of five and play several percussion instruments. Even in U.S. culture, nonmusical people have many musical skills, mostly of a receptive nature; that is, they can listen to music and hear important musical differences. Early childhood indicators of later musical fame are hard to find. It is hard to predict which student studying piano will become a concert pianist. If talent were an inherited trait, they said, surely it would surface by that age. Furthermore, they argued that there is no such thing as effortless progress. The best violinists at age twenty-one had accumulated over 10,000 hours of practice, whereas the less able violinists had accumulated only half. Although musical ability runs in families, it seemed to be the interest in music and the support of music by these families, such as paying for lessons and encouraging practice, that made the difference, not the biological inheritance. In one school, 40 percent of outstanding music pupils had nonmusician parents. Studies of high achieving young musicians found that their parents sang to them daily, encouraged song games, and danced and sang to music. Musical ability does not seem to be only one trait, but a combination of a number of different skills.

Of course, people who become musicians must be motivated to do all that practicing (Figure 3–15). This motivation can be divided into intrinsic and extrinsic motivation. *Intrinsic motivation* is the drive that comes from within the individual: the love of the sound of the instrument or the enjoyment of the experience of singing with a large group. *Extrinsic motivation* is that which comes from outside the individual: others tell them they are talented, give them praise for their achievement, or they win prizes in competitions. It

FIGURE 3–15 Practice makes perfect.

seems that too early an emphasis on extrinsic motivation can inhibit the intrinsic motivation of the child. This emphasis on achievement and identifying early talent, on picking a winner, is damaging to the majority of children who are not chosen. More children would have greater musical ability and achievement if we emphasized the nurture concept rather than emphasizing inherited talent.

Arguing in opposition to the research group, David Hargreaves (1994) contended that Sloboda, Davidson, and Howe had too narrow a definition of achievement. Hargreaves pointed out that great musical achievements have been made outside of classical music, such as the success of the Beatles. He also pointed out that new music standards have been set in British schools of which Sloboda's group seemed unaware. The British are way ahead of the United States in setting a national curriculum. It was implemented in 1988 and requires music as one of the 10 subjects that must be taught at all age levels. Not only that, but children are required to compose music at all levels and submit a portfolio of those compositions when they take the General Certificate in Secondary Education at age sixteen.

The other rebuttal, by Torff and Winner (1994), cogently suggested that though talent may not be totally inherited, some children learn music with more ease than others and that children differ not only in musical ability, but in their ability to learn mathematics, dance, or throw balls. The fact that some children teach themselves to read while others work at it for years does not mean that all children are equally talented in reading. They agreed that some environmental conditions, especially early musical stimulation, may well promote musical skill, but pointed out that not all children respond to that stimulation in the same way. If you gave all children the exact same hours of lessons and practice at age five, they would probably not all achieve the same level of performance by age six.

This set of articles is certainly interesting. Both sides in the debate of talent versus practice made good points. No matter which viewpoint you take, all would agree that practice makes perfect. The question is, how do you get children to practice?

Music and Cognitive Development

New research is beginning to show a relationship between music instruction and benefits to children in other educational areas. These benefits are found in a child's motor development, intellectual skills, and social abilities. Taken together, these add up to a child's cognitive development. The body of research in the area of music and cognitive development has greatly increased over the past five years. Before that, the studies done were not well publicized. Many studies were unpublished dissertations done by doctoral students but never widely read by experts in the field. As a result, wide interest in the effect of music on cognitive development has only begun to attract attention in the past few years.

A significant area of research has been the effect of music on spatial reasoning. The concepts of spatial reasoning and spatial intelligence can be confused. Spatial *intelligence* is the ability to visualize objects—like houses, bodies, or footballs—moving through space. Spatial *reasoning* is a specific area of mathematics that studies putting together puzzles, matching patterns, recognizing duplicate visual patterns, and rotating objects mentally. It examines the mental visualization of shapes and the recognition of matching patterns. Spatial reasoning is an important indicator of later mathematical ability (Figure 3–16). For example, a child who can put together a 20-piece puzzle at age two displays many characteristics of a mathematical genius.

Why are researchers trying to show a relationship between music lessons and their effect on spatial reasoning in children? Because they suspect that music trains more than just a child's ear for pitch. In an important study on preschoolers, a group of researchers

FIGURE 3–16   Musical counting and repetition help strengthen children's intelligence.

first did a pilot study in which inner city three-year-olds had nine months of individual piano keyboard lessons. They had a second group of inner city three-year-olds who received 30 minutes of singing lessons a day, also for nine months. Both groups showed significant improvement on tests given after the specialized lessons to measure spatial temporal reasoning ability (Rauscher, Shaw, Levine, Wright, Dennis, & Newcomb, 1997).

In a larger study following the preliminary study that Rauscher and her colleagues did on preschoolers, preschool children were given either keyboard lessons, computer training, or singing lessons. Prior to training, the research group tested all the children using the spatial reasoning tasks from the WPPSI-R, a standardized preschool intelligence test.

The researchers found that the keyboard group did significantly better than the other groups on these particular intellectual tasks. They were actually surprised that the singing group did not do significantly better. The researchers theorized that either a more structured singing program or one with a visual component showing the pitch relationships was needed to show an effect. They suspected that the improvement found in the pilot study with inner city children may have been due to the low socioeconomic level of the school. A little extra training for these students added up to a lot of improvement.

In the past, researchers found significant influence on research results when one group received extra attention and special treatment. Children responded to the extra attention and not to the particular training. In this research, all of the children received extra attention and special training, but only the piano keyboard group actually did significantly better in spatial reasoning. They concluded that the improvement was not an effect of extra attention.

This was a landmark study because it showed that music lessons can affect a child's ability in other areas of intellectual development. This is called an **extramusical positive effect**; that is, the music has a positive effect on skills that are not thought to be related to music. So it seems that studying music not only has good effects on a child's music skills, but it also has beneficial *side effects* on cognitive development. We still do not know how powerful the effect is or how pervasive it is.

Music and Mathematics Achievement

In a 1996 study by Gardiner, Fox, Knolls, and Jeffrey, 96 first graders, ages five to seven, received specialized music and visual arts training that emphasized sequenced skill development for seven months. This group was compared to matched classrooms that had a standard arts curriculum, the school system's standard visual arts and music training. The study compared the standardized test scores of 80 students who had scores from their kindergarten year. The results showed that the children in the musical and visual arts treatment group started behind the control group in their scores on mathematics and reading, but after seven months they had caught up to statistical equality on reading and were ahead on learning mathematics. The study continued for another year at the second grade level, and again, the music and visual arts treatment students were ahead on mathematics. This time, the greatest gains were shown in mathematics comprehension by those students who had two years of arts, less in those with only one year, and lowest in those with no arts treatment (Gardiner et al., 1996).

In another study done in 1999 by Graziano, Peterson, and Shaw, second graders were given one of three special trainings. The first group played a specially developed spatial temporal math video game. The second group played the video games and received four months of musical keyboard lessons as well. The third group received English language training. The students were later tested on their ability to solve problems involving fractions and ratios. Both math game groups scored higher on these tests than those who received no special instruction; however, the students who had the keyboard lessons did the best of all (Graziano et al., 1999).

Conclusion

Beginning as newborns, children develop through the crucial years of early music development, then can begin to play instruments and put on entire musical productions. The crucial years for music learning are ages five to eight. This is the time when a lack of music training can seriously impede later development.

KEY TERMS

babbling
carry a tune
causality
correlation
developmental milestones
developmental steps
developmentally appropriate activity

developmentally appropriate practices (DAP)
extramusical positive effect
language acquisition
melodic contour
neural development
pitch development

readiness
sense of rhythm
singing around the pitch
timbre
window of opportunity
zipper song

DISCUSSION QUESTIONS

1. What is a developmentally appropriate practice? Define and give an example.
2. How are language learning and music learning alike and different?
3. Describe the musical behavior of a normal two-year-old.
4. Name four favorite musical activities of a four-year-old.
5. What are the pros and cons of starting children on musical instruments at different ages?
6. Describe the components of a developmentally appropriate kindergarten musical program.
7. Briefly describe some of Marion Diamond's findings.
8. Do you believe that talent or practice is more important in developing musical ability? Support your choice with arguments.
9. Name two findings researchers have learned about infants and music.
10. What is the significance of research findings for you as a teacher?

SUGGESTED LEARNING ACTIVITY

Choose an age group with which you intend to work. Select 10 songs to sing with this age group. List the song title, writer, recording artist, and album title for each song. Describe how you will use each song in your classroom. Be sure to include a variety of musical styles in your selection.

REFERENCES

Arlen, H. (1939). *The Wizard of Oz* [cassette]. New York: Sony.

Arnold, L. (1995). *Sing along stew* [cassette]. Canton, MI: A&M.

Bartels, J. (1980). *Sillytime magic* [CD]. Sherman Oaks, CA: Discovery.

Bartels, J. (1990). *Christmas magic* [cassette]. Sherman Oaks, CA: Discovery.

Bartels, J. (1992). *Bathtime magic* [cassette]. Sherman Oaks, CA: Discovery.

Boston Baroque. (1996). *Bach—The complete Brandenburg concertos* [CD]. Cleveland, OH: Telarc.

Collins, J. (1990). *Baby's bedtime* [cassette]. New York: Lightyear.

Countdown Kids. (1998). *Old MacDonald had a farm.* New York: Excelsior.

Diamond, M. (1998). *Magic trees of the mind.* New York: Dutton.

Elbert, T., Pantev, C., Weinbruch, C., & Rockstroh, B. (1995). Increased cortical representation of the fingers of the left hand in string players. *Science, 270,* 305–307.

Fagen, J., Prigot, J., Carroll, M., & Pioli, L. (1997). Auditory context and memory retrieval in young infants. *Child Development, 68,* 1057–1066.

Fink, C. (1986). *Air guitar* [cassette]. Cambridge, MA: Rounder Records.

Gardiner, M. F., Fox, A., Knolls, F., & Jeffrey, D. (1996, May). Learning improved by arts training. *Nature, 381,* 284.

Goleman, D. (1997). *Emotional intelligence.* New York: Doubleday.

Graziano, A. B., Peterson, M., & Shaw, G. L. (1999). Enhanced learning of proportional mathematics through musical training and spatial temporal training. *Neurological Research, 21,* 139–152.

Hargreaves, D. (1994, August). Music education for all. *The Psychologist*, 357–358.

Jenkins, E. (1993). *Early childhood songs* [cassette]. Washington, DC: Smithsonian/Folkways.

Lafuente, M. J., Grifol, R., Segarra, J., Soriano, J., Gorba, M. A., & Montesinos, A. (1997). Effects of the firstart method of prenatal stimulation on psychomotor development: The first six months. *Pre- and Perinatal Psychology Journal, 11,* 151–162.

Monet, L. (1989). *Circle time: Songs and rhymes for the very young* [cassette]. New York: Warner Brothers.

Peter, Paul & Mary. (1993). *Peter, Paul & Mommy too* [CD]. New York: Warner Brothers.

Raffi. (1980). *Baby beluga* [cassette]. Cambridge, MA: Rounder Records.

Rauscher, F. H., Shaw, G. L., Levine, L. J., Wright, E. L., Dennis, W. R., & Newcomb, R. L. (1997). Music training causes long term enhancement of preschool children's spatial-temporal reasoning. *Neurological Research, 19,*1, 2–8.

Shelly, S. J. (1976). Music. In C. Seefeldt (Ed.), *Curriculum for the preschool primary child—A review of the research.* Columbus, OH: Merrill.

Sloboda, J., Davidson, J., & Howe, M. (1994, August). Is everyone musical? *The Psychologist*, 349–353.

Spier, P. (1988). *Gobble, growl, grunt: A book of animal sounds.* New York: Doubleday.

Thorpe, L. A., & Trehub, S. E. (1989). Duration illusion and auditory grouping in infancy. *Developmental Psychology, 25,* 122–127.

Torff, B., & Winner, E. (1994, August). Don't throw out the baby with the bath water. *The Psychologist,* 361–362.

Trehub, S. E., Bull, D., & Thorpe, L. A. (1984). Infants' perception of melodies: The role of melodic contour. *Child Development, 55,* 821–830.

Trehub, S. E., & Thorpe, L. A. (1989). Infants' perception of rhythm: Categorization of auditory sequences by temporal structure. *Canadian Journal of Psychology, 43,* 217–229.

Ustinov, P. (1987). *The orchestra* [cassette]. Toronto, ON, Canada: Mark Rubin Productions.

Various artists. (1998). *Learn to play piano* [CD]. New York: Koala.

Various artists. (2000). *Tunes for tots* [cassette]. New York: Legacy.

Wonder Kids Choir. (1998). *Mother Goose songs* [cassette]. Toronto, ON, Canada: Madacy.

ADDITIONAL RESOURCES

Bayliss, K., & Ramsey, M. (1991). *Music: A way of life for the young child.* Englewood Cliffs, NJ: Prentice Hall.

Haines, B. J., & Gerber, L. L. (1996). *Leading young children to music.* Englewood Cliffs, NJ: Prentice Hall.

Wolff, K. L. (1979). The effects of general music education on the academic achievement, perceptual motor development, creative thinking, and school attendance of first grade children. *Dissertation Abstracts, 40,* 5359A.

CHAPTER 4

Music and Children with Special Needs

This chapter discusses different kinds of children who have special needs. It shows how a classroom teacher can integrate children with special needs into music learning in the classroom. These needs can be divided into certain categories, but remember that categories overlap and each child is unique.

Some children have special *physical* needs. Physical difficulties can range from a child with a minor problem with delay in the development of gross motor skills to a child who is completely immobilized by muscular dystrophy. Other children have special *learning* needs. Some children may have severe mental development problems, while others may be intellectually gifted. Some children have special *social and emotional* needs. These range from children from abusive backgrounds to children who are young for their grade levels and socially behind. Children with special needs come in all sizes and styles. Many appear normal until you get to know them well in your classroom. The more experienced you become as a teacher, the faster you are able to identify the special needs of individuals in your classroom.

Most special needs are viewed in comparison to **normal development** of children. Of course, there is really no *normal* child. Every child has a combination of abilities and strengths. One could therefore argue that every child has special needs. However, in working with children, you will become accustomed to working with children who are **normal** for your school. Remember that you will begin to consider as normal the typical child who attends your school. If you teach in a wealthy area or in a private school, you will get a different idea of normal than if you teach in a low income neighborhood. Keep this in mind when you identify students' special needs. In California, wealthier high schools identified more students with special needs who required extra time on the SAT exams than the lower economic high schools in the state did. Perhaps this indicates that special needs are less often identified in populations of children from low economic status. Particularly if you teach in a low socioeconomic area, try to notice small clues that may indicate a developmental delay or an attention disorder that may have been overlooked. These clues show up not only during reading and math time, but they can also be evident during music and dance activities (Figure 4–1).

Hundreds of reasons exist for **developmental delays** in children. Some are due to organic syndromes, some are inherited disorders, and some are caused by child abuse, Fetal Alcohol Syndrome, or distress due to emotional conflicts in the home. A child's developmental delay is usually measured in terms of normal developmental milestones. This means that a delay is often measured in months or years behind the time when the behaviors usually develop. For example, a child entering kindergarten who does not speak can be considered at the three-year-old level, approximately two years behind normal development of speech. Developmental delays may include physical abilities, language

FIGURE 4–1 Musical activities can influence a child's development in language skills and other areas.

development, social relationships, and verbal and mathematical ability. Generally, a child's development in music is not measured.

A child's development in other areas can be influenced by musical activities. For example, if development in language skills is delayed, intensive training in singing may help a child develop better speaking abilities because singing uses different locations in the brain than language acquisition. Although some skills, such as hearing pitch and words, are closely located in certain areas of the brain, each uses a different pattern of brain activity. For example, hearing pitch for language and for music both utilize the auditory cortex. However, language uses the tongue muscles to produce sound, while playing music relies heavily on the use of hands and fingers. A different brain pattern is seen on an electroencephalogram for the different activities. Just as a child with motor deficits can be trained to use other areas of the brain for walking and muscle control, children with disorders such as autism, impaired language acquisition, and impaired social skills can be helped by music learning. Music therapy is a specialized area of training that uses music to assist people to retrain impaired areas of their brains. If a child in your class has a specific severe disorder, try to get a consultation with a **music therapist** to develop a music program that is specialized to the child's needs.

Music and Memory

Information about music and memory can be useful in dealing with all children but especially children with special needs. This is because many children with special needs have memory deficits.

Information is transferred into the memory in two ways. One way is to link the remembered information to an emotional event. We remember happy, fun, novel, and frightening events. All of us have had experiences that we never forget. Perhaps it was a school play, helping a favorite teacher after school, a great field trip, or a week at outdoor education school. These are the kinds of events that teachers create that children will remember their whole lives.

The second way to remember is by repetition and practice. We learn to write our names, add sums of numbers, and read words on a page. This kind of memory is called **procedural memory**. It becomes automatic, like typing, riding a bicycle, playing piano, and doing gymnastic tumbles. Procedural memories learned well early in life remain in our storage of skills. For example, if you practiced violin for ten years, from age seven to seventeen, and then put the instrument away and did not play it at all for 20 years, you could still play pretty well at age thirty-seven. These two kinds of memory, emotional memory and procedural memory, are stored in different parts of the brain, and are thus somewhat independent of each other.

Educational researchers have learned that repetition learning needs to include as many sensorial approaches as possible in order to be effective. To practice spelling, you should include writing sentences, saying the letters out loud, writing the letters with your finger in the air, and singing the words to a jingle.

What does all this have to do with music? There are two kinds of musical memory. The first is the memory of music itself. The second is the effect that the presence of music has on the ability to memorize unrelated information. Music has both kinds of memory components. Each kind of learning interacts with the other. Emotional events occur in music learning, such as the first time you meet your piano teacher or the first time you sing in a concert. Then there is procedural learning, such as practicing the piano or singing every day. In order to have successful music learning, both kinds of learning have to be positive and effective. If every time you go to a music lesson, the teacher hits your hands or tells you to stop singing off key, you will remember this because it is emotionally charged. It may not be effective in promoting your music learning, but it will be remembered. On the other hand, if your experience is positive and rewarding—for example, your teacher tells you how well you are doing—then the positive emotional memories will help you to keep practicing. The more you practice, the better you will get, and the more a teacher will give you positive feedback. For a further discussion of the topic of talent and practice, please see *Practice Makes Perfect* in Chapter 3.

Music also helps with learning facts and information. The scientific term for this is **context dependent memory**. People remember information better if recalled in the same context in which they learned it (Godden & Baddeley, 1975). For example, people remember terms for basketball better when they are learned on the court rather than if they learn them in a classroom and are then expected to use them on a basketball court.

Music can be part of the context of learning. If a student hears the same music in the recall situation as in the learning situation, then he can recall more of the information. In a study done by Steven Smith (1979), people viewed a list of words, one at a time, while listening to one of three music contexts: a Mozart piano concerto (K. 491) (Haskil, 1998), a jazz piece by Milt Jackson, "People Make the World Go Round" (1972), or silence. Two days later they were asked to recall as many of the learned words as possible. During the recall, they had either the same music condition or a different one. They recalled the most words when the music was the same, and they performed the worst when the music was changed to other music. Having quiet for both times did not seem to help in remembering the words.

William Balch, Kelly Bowman, and Lauri Mohler (1992) researched the effects of tone quality and tempo on memory recall. They divided their subjects into four groups: slow jazz, fast jazz, slow classical, and fast classical music. Their groups also learned words while the music played. They were tested for recall while either listening to the same music or a different music situation; for example, slow jazz listeners listened to fast classical for the recall situation. As expected, they had better recall when the music was the same, worse when it was different.

The group performed a second experiment for some of the subjects. The music switched from slow jazz to fast jazz or from slow classical to fast classical. For other subjects, the switch was from slow jazz to slow classical or from fast classical to fast jazz. The group that had two speeds of the same kind of music, or genre, had poorer recall than the group that kept the same tempo and changed genres of music. It was surprising to the researchers to find that the change in tempo made such a difference.

In 1996 Balch and Lewis did a follow-up experiment that tested tempo of the music. This time they played the exact same pieces of music with the same or different speed. They found the same results as the other group; recall was better with the same tempo, worse with a change in tempo.

What implications does this have for classroom learning? If we play a certain music in the classroom while students learn something like spelling, do you think that they will have better recall of the spelling if we play the same music during the spelling test? If we play background music while children take a pretest for upcoming standardized tests, will they do better on the standardized test if the same music were played? This study has not yet been done. Perhaps you will be the pioneer teacher researcher to show the effects of background music in a classroom.

These findings on music and memory have implications for all students, but students with special needs could benefit the most from the application of learning practices based on some of these findings. Many of these students have some kind of physical damage in the brain. Even when the cause of a disability is emotional or social in nature, such as child abuse, there is often a physical reaction in the brain. This, in turn, affects how a

FIGURE 4–2 Musical experiences give children a sense of accomplishment.

child learns to do a task or remember something. We know that the brain is flexible enough in childhood to compensate for some physical damage. Music can be used to help children develop new neural pathways that can compensate for injury or deficits in the brain. Music can be played in the background while a child is learning a new skill. Certain kinds of music motivate the child. For example, children with autism are more willing to dance to music with a strong beat. A child can be encouraged to continue a physically difficult exercise until the end of a piece of music. Music performance can be an opportunity for a child to be proud of an accomplishment (Figure 4–2).

The Varieties of Special Needs

This chapter on special needs is not meant to be a definitive discussion of children with special needs, their diagnosis, and treatment. It is offered as a general overview of how music can assist these children. Keep in mind that you, as a child's regular teacher, can make a difference in how he feels about his role in classroom social life. You *do* want to give each child special attention, and yet you *do not* want to single out one child for continuous special treatment. This is the difficult balance you have to maintain. For example, you do not want to have a child with a wheelchair always be the one who gets to play the big drum because that is the only instrument he can play. Rather, you need to figure out how to give different children turns on the big drum while allowing for the special needs of your child with a wheelchair. You may even find that a child with special needs can play other instruments.

Another area of caution for a classroom teacher is how you speak about the special needs of a child. Many parents are upset about labels being applied to their children. Professionals in the field change their language in defining the needs of children. The language used 20 years ago to define categories is now improper. For example, we now refer to a child *not* as autistic but as a child with autism. Children are not blind or deaf, but

Do children benefit musically when taught by their regular teachers rather than by specialists in music education?

Neurobiologist Norman Weinberger (1995) said, "Yes, without doubt. The vast majority of students who study music were introduced to musical activities, such as group singing and the use of percussive *rhythm instruments* in preschool, kindergarten, or early grades." Specialists in music can help children achieve more musical progress. But this fact does not eliminate the essential influence of regular teachers. A recent study showed that preschool students learn a good deal about music and increase their attentiveness in class when their nonmusical teachers are given more musical training (Nichols & Honig, 1995). Therefore, regular classroom teachers should be encouraged to introduce or increase music in the classroom.

Many educators agree that a regular teacher should provide some music. Fifty years ago, *all* elementary school teachers had to take a class in music to get a credential. Many states still require teachers to take a music course for their credential. However, some states such as California do not require teachers to take *any* music classes at all. Fortunately, even without any special training, a great number of teachers incorporate music into their curriculum plans. These teachers make a difference for children in their intellectual and musical development.

they are called children with visual or hearing disabilities. We try to consider a whole child and not just treat a child as equivalent to his diagnosis. When we say a child has a disorder, that is different than categorizing the child as the autistic one, or the Down syndrome child.

In the following section, different special needs will be discussed by category.

Children with Physical Disabilities

Children with **physical disabilities** have difficulty getting some part of the body to work properly. You may have a child with a disability as minor as breaking an arm playing on the monkey bars. You may someday have a student with a deformed limb. A child could have a disease that interferes with his walking. A student could be in a wheelchair due to muscular dystrophy, or one of your children may be in a wheelchair due to a car accident. The range of difficulties is great, lasting from a few weeks to a lifetime. When one of your students has a physical disability, try to consider musical intervention as a way of helping him feel successful.

Musical interventions for physical disabilities include the whole range of musical activities: listening to music, singing along with music, and playing music. If one of your students is in a wheelchair, plan a music activity for the class where that child can sing a solo for one of the verses to the song. Other children can also have a solo turn, so that the child with special needs is not singled out for a solo. Your solo singers do not have to sing on pitch. Over the years, music teachers have selected many students for solos who could only speak a verse instead of sing, so that they would have an opportunity to be soloists.

Listening to music is an option for children of all types. Suggestions for this are given in the following sections, specific to the disability. Keep in mind that a child with a disability such as Attention Deficit Disorder (ADD) may seem to be inattentive at times but often hears things we do not even notice. If you have a child who is temporarily homebound or in the hospital for an extended time, your students can choose some music to record for him to listen to at home. Have each student record a short personal message to the child that precedes the pieces of music he has selected. When given a greater purpose for accomplishing a task, such as selecting classical music pieces for a child with special needs from their class, children are more willing to spend time listening to alternative music styles than usual.

All children need to have experiences making music (Figure 4–3). Children with special needs have to do this even more. Playing music develops small muscle coordination, encourages positive group interaction, and helps the brain create new patterns of interaction.

Motor Deficits. Motor deficits can come in many different forms, from mild to severe. They are usually due to an injury or disease in the brain of the fetus or newborn. The mild forms affect only one small part of the brain and may seem hardly noticeable by age eight. More severe forms affect children who are completely wheelchair bound and have difficulty speaking.

Children with motor deficits usually respond well to listening to music. You can make a tape of classical music for a child, and he will often spend time listening to it, particularly if he listens to it with headphones. Many children with this diagnosis are intelligent and enjoy the intricacies of classical music. If the disability is severe, they have trouble singing because of the muscle control needed for the face. However, singing by himself is helpful to a child who needs practice with pronunciation of words and the formation of speech. Activities like clapping and tapping are quite frustrating, and should not be used for these children. Encourage them to feel the beat by some gross motor activity, such as nodding their heads.

Visually Disabled. Many people think that children who are born with visual disabilities are more talented than others in music because they must rely on their hearing. Ray Charles and Stevie Wonder are examples that come to mind. However, this is not necessarily the case. Children and adults with blindness do not seem to be automatically more musically talented than the rest of the population. Just because a child is **visually disabled** does not mean he can hear better than others. However, teachers should train

FIGURE 4–3 All children benefit from having musical experiences.

113

the hearing of a child with a sight loss because he will have to rely on hearing for environmental clues. Therefore, training in music appreciation and singing is as important in the curriculum for a child with blindness as reading and math. Music also can give many children with visual disabilities something they can do *well* for the rest of their lives. It may become their livelihoods.

Many children with visual disabilities have other complicating factors, such as learning disabilities, developmental delays, and attention disorders. Extra attention should be given to training a child to play an instrument, particularly the piano. Piano lessons have been shown to develop spatial reasoning (Rauscher, Shaw, Levine, Wright, Dennis, & Newcomb, 1997). Because of the visual disability, a child will have less opportunity to develop spatial reasoning using visual cues. Therefore, piano training will substitute for some of the visual loss. Piano training will also help develop the finger skills necessary for a child to use a computer keyboard and a brailer, the machine used by people with visual disabilities to write in Braille. In addition, musical ear training will help to develop auditory acuity that can support a child's mobility skills.

Teachers are sometimes distracted by the continual head movements and body rocking of children who have visual disabilities. Be aware that these movements, such as swaying the head side to side, are an effort to substitute for depth perception. Lacking visual cues, one can perceive depth by turning the head this way. If our eyes were on either side of our heads, we would turn our heads to take in the depth of the visual field. Because our ears are on the side of our heads, we can get a better idea of where things are using sound if we turn our heads side to side. Close your eyes and try it sometime.

Hearing Disabled. Just as many people consider that all children with blindness should be musically gifted, they also tend to assume that children who are **hearing disabled** cannot experience any music at all (Figure 4–4). Not so. This type of child needs rhythmic training as much or more than a child with typical hearing. A child with a hear-

FIGURE 4–4 Adults can help children feel the rhythm by playing along with them.

ing loss lacks two parts of the hearing connection. First, most sound is not loud enough for a child to hear; he cannot *physically* hear the sound. Second, because a child cannot hear the sound, the brain fails to develop the necessary auditory nerve connections that must be formed in childhood. This is why most children with a hearing loss wear hearing aids. It may not make speech and hearing available to them, but it does keep the neural pathways forming and the auditory centers alive.

Most children with hearing disabilities have some residual hearing. For those with a hearing loss, the development of rhythmic ability is crucial to keeping the neural pathways alive. Do activities with this child that include tapping, hitting, and clapping the body. Use rhythm instruments: maracas, cymbals, cowbell, claves, triangles, and drums; the louder the better. This type of child responds really well to rock 'n' roll music or any kind of music with a really strong beat. Be sure to get up and dance to the beat of the music. Hand motions and sign language used with songs, as suggested in Chapter 9, are a great choice for these children, especially if the signing matches the rhythm of the song. Dance and music help to organize the nerve pathways in the brain and aid the child with a hearing disability to develop Visual-Spatial intelligence, one of the multiple intelligences, in reference to body orientation and movement through space.

Learning Disabilities

Most **learning disabilities** are caused by some kind of physical problem in the brain. Because of this, most problems with learning are considered organic, rather than emotional, in nature.

Learning Differences

Learning differences, often shortened to LD when referring to students in elementary school, can include dyslexia, memory problems, auditory and visual processing, and attention disorders. Attention deficits will be discussed in the following section, since the musical issues can be different with these children than for those with other learning difficulties. Be aware that the topic of learning disabilities can be an issue of sensitive feelings and sometimes heated arguments. Educators disagree on the definitions (should it be learning disabilities or learning differences?) and have widely varying suggestions for treatments. Parents often become defensive when someone suggests that their child might have a learning difference. Learning problems are often not identified until a child is in second or third grade. This is fairly late in the child's development. Parents have had eight years in which they have considered their child as normal. Suddenly, they have to adjust to the thought that their child does not learn as easily and as efficiently as other children. Some parent have trouble with this, while others are relieved to find that their child has a learning problem and are glad to find a reason for their child's struggles in school.

Songs about valuing ourselves and individual differences are excellent for children with LDs. In Chapter 7, the section about valuing our differences includes a number of suggested songs for use with both normal and learning challenged children. These children will learn the songs better if given a multifaceted approach to delivering the music. A child needs to see, sing, act out, dance, and tap the rhythm of the words.

A new auditory intervention, though not musical, has helped some children with dyslexia. For children who are having difficulty with the phonemic phase of learning to read, researchers have found that dramatically slowing down the sound of the letters so that the child can hear the differences in sound can help a dyslexic child overcome reading problems in a much shorter time.

Attention Deficit Disorder. Attention Deficit Disorder (ADD) comes in two forms, with and without hyperactivity. Children without hyperactivity often go undiagnosed because their deficit is not recognized. These children are often termed lazy or inefficient. Recent research indicates that the brain activity of people with ADD can be shown by positron emission tomography (PET) scans to have decreased brain activity, specifically decreased glucose uptake, than brains without ADD. This indicates that ADD is a chemical brain disorder, not just a made-up catchall term (Amen, 1995).

Children with hyperactivity are often challenging for teachers to deal with. Children with Attention Deficit Hyperactivity Disorder (ADHD) often cannot sit and sing with the rest of the group. They get up, wander around the room, and clown around at the back of the class. Teachers have been seating these children in chairs away from the rest of the group for years. Music time is often one of the most difficult challenges for children with ADHD. The best way to help them focus during music time is to have a special, defined location for them and to continually acknowledge them positively for doing a good job of staying in that spot.

Music with these children is best done with headphones on in front of a computer. Children with ADD are often intelligent and have an affinity for computer operations. They are able to hyperfocus: concentrate on only one task and tune out everything else if the task is appealing to them. Therefore, music delivered to them on an individual basis with visual accompaniment of computer animation is the best way to develop musical awareness for them. Listening to music with headphones while looking at a book is also an excellent way of helping these children attend to the music (Figure 4–5).

Developmental Delays. We no longer refer to children as mentally retarded, since that term has been acquired by the general population as a synonym for stupid. Currently, children who have difficulty with mathematical concepts or vocabulary acquisition are designated as developmentally delayed. There can be many reasons for the delay, often related to birth trauma or early problems in development. Two specific syndromes of developmental delay are discussed in the next two sections.

One of the biggest issues with children with developmental delays is helping them to experience themselves as normal. Many of these children are three to four years delayed

FIGURE 4–5 Headphones often help children with ADD focus their attention.

and often in separate, special education classes. Music is an excellent time for a child to be integrated into a group of typically developing children. When in a large group, children with special needs are less obvious and can participate in normal childhood activities without being singled out as special. A child with a developmental delay can participate in many kinds of musical activities. Singing, rhythm band, finger plays, and dancing to varieties of music are just a few of the many choices. If you are a teacher of students with developmental delays in a special education class, find another class with which you can regularly share musical activities.

Down syndrome. **Down syndrome** is a chromosomal abnormality resulting in specific developmental delays in muscle coordination and in understanding mathematical concepts and spatial reasoning. As with other disorders, Down syndrome has a range from low to high functioning children.

A child with Down syndrome needs special training in singing to help with the pronunciation of words. One of the features of this disorder is a larger tongue. Because of this, speaking is more difficult. Singing, particularly repetitive songs, is helpful in developing the tongue muscles and thus assisting pronunciation.

Because they also have developmental delays in muscle coordination, children with Down syndrome need more work on keeping the beat and rocking to the pulse of music. Dancing to music is an easy way to do this. These children need to develop clapping and stomping skills in order to train the large muscle groups (Figure 4–6). They often have difficulty with balance and jumping. Piano playing with one finger can help not only muscle coordination of the small muscle group, but also can assist spatial reasoning skills.

Autism. Thirty years ago, **autism** was thought to result from problems with poor parenting and parental difficulties with forming close emotional bonds with a child. Parents were blamed for their children's lack of responsiveness to social stimuli. Research has confirmed the fact that autism is a physiological disorder with genetic inheritance as a major factor.

The hallmark of a child with autism is the lack of language development, social interaction difficulties, and a preference for routines and rigid structure. At about age

FIGURE 4–6 *Musical activities that help develop muscle groups are essential for a child with Down syndrome.*

three, teachers and parents begin to notice the striking lack of language skills. These children focus on things, not people. Many children with this disorder are absolutely fascinated by machines, particularly computers. At age five, children with autism are still grunting, yelling, withdrawing, or whacking other children to make their wishes known, much like a two-year-old who lacks language skills.

Musical activities are very important in the education of children with autism. Begin with rhythm to capture the interest of these children. An electronic piano or a QChord will fascinate them. Both instruments can be used with headphones. At first, a child will experiment with the instrument. Soon you will find him rocking in time with the beat. This fascination with rhythm and beat can be transferred into the group experience through dance. A child with autism responds well to music with a good beat. One of the first effective interventions with these children is to dance along with them by imitating their dance patterns. This connects a child with an adult in the first steps of social interaction.

Once a child with autism is accustomed to being in a group for dancing, you can introduce songs into the dance repertoire. Repetitive songs with clearly pronounced words will help these children begin to use language in connection with music. Emphasize the word at the end of the musical line. Soon, a child will begin to shout that particular word. Accept the shouting at first, since you want to encourage participation in language production. Gradually, help the child, through positive reinforcement, to soften the sound to singing.

If you can develop singing in these children, you have made great progress. Once a child can sing, he can listen to music on his own tape recorder, using headphones if you wish to do other activities with the rest of the class. Songs about animals are a good first choice. Again, choose music with a strong beat. Progress to songs that develop language, such as repetitive zipper songs. A child with autism will benefit greatly from learning rote information, such as the alphabet, from songs. Music will ultimately be the vehicle you can use to help these children interact in a group situation.

Fetal Alcohol Syndrome and Crack Cocaine Babies. Children whose mothers abused alcohol or used drugs during pregnancy fall into the category of **Fetal Alcohol Syndrome (FAS)**. The use of drugs during pregnancy can cause severe and permanent brain damage. Although this is a syndrome caused by emotional, physical, and social factors, the damage to the child's brain is physical and permanent. Children with this disorder are similar to those with ADHD, only the hyperactivity is often more pronounced.

Like children with ADHD, children with FAS can be very disruptive during group music activities; therefore, teachers should structure this child's energy by having him sit in the same location each time. Listening to music with headphones also is an excellent activity for him.

Social and Emotional Disabilities

Children with **social disabilities** or **emotional disabilities** who live through difficult emotional situations are best served by choosing music that can help them both in words and feeling. The sound of the music should be soothing and comforting (Figure 4–7). The words of the music should be positive, helpful, and happy. Because music can actually induce a mood, the kind of music chosen for children with emotional difficulties can set a tone for their entire day. Finding a piece of music that a child enjoys and playing it every day can be extremely comforting. One special education teacher had a student who came from a very deprived home situation. He became attached to the *Masquerade Suite* by Khachaturian (1994). This is lively and uplifting music, so the child

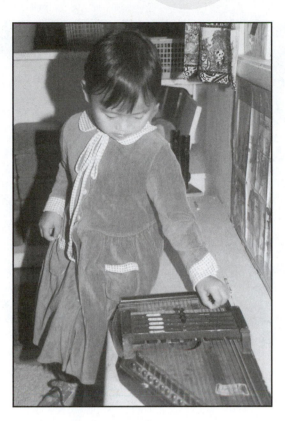

FIGURE 4–7 Music that is soothing and comforting can help children express their emotions.

listened to it every day. At the end of the year, the teacher gave him the record. He wrote to her a few years later to tell her how much that music meant to him.

Children from Abusive Situations. Children who are currently in abusive situations are often unwilling to talk about the difficulties they are experiencing at home. In a classroom setting, there is not usually a time when a child can talk to a teacher alone. Through the use of songs, a teacher can bring up the topic of abuse. Peter Alsop is a particularly good children's musician for this purpose. Chapter 7 cites songs of his that help children express their emotions.

The Child with Depression. Children with depression are not usually noticed in the classroom, except they often have more stomachaches and headaches than other children. They are usually quiet with occasional angry outbursts. Depression is most noticeable during music time, when these children do not seem as interested in singing as other children. They do not want to play instruments. They would rather sit and watch than dance.

Be aware that depression in young children is often due to an emotional climate in the home. Divorced parents may be very angry with an ex-spouse. A child will focus the attention on himself in an effort to distract a parent from his anger. Thus, the child prevents the parent from being angry because the parent becomes focused on the child's depression.

In general, musical interventions are helpful but not effective in dealing with the underlying problems of children with depression. One musical intervention can be songs about anger and its appropriate expression. Depression in both adults and children is usually due to an inability to appropriately express anger.

Children with Mood Swings. Much like a child with ADHD, a child with mood swings has good and bad days. Unlike a child with ADHD, this child's behavior is usually triggered by events at home. The difference is determined by consulting with a

FIGURE 4–8 Music helps children transition to new activities.

parent of this child. If the parent is well balanced and tries to provide a structured home environment, the child more likely has ADHD. A child with mood swings has irregular meal times, no structured bed time, and watches a lot of television. One home visit, especially done early in the school year, will help a teacher understand the difference.

Music can be used to help these children transition from the home to the structured classroom (Figure 4–8). A piece of music that calms them can be put on a continuous loop tape. They can then spend time at the beginning of the day listening with headphones to the piece of music for a specified period of time, set on a timer. This music should help calm them and organize their day so they can deal with the classroom structure.

The Child with Severe Illness. Children who have life threatening illness are in particular need of music that helps them make sense of their lives and uplift their spirits during times of difficult treatments. One teacher received a letter from a family describing how much it meant to a child to listen to her tape of songs about nature and the environment while going through painful medical procedures. Because the songs were cheerful and uplifting as well as humorous, the child was able to get through the treatments with less pain.

Children of Divorce. Children from divorced families need songs to help them deal with their living situations. Many children from divorced families live in two homes. Each home usually has its own set of rules, different from the other. When doing songs in the classroom, be aware of the family structures portrayed in the song. Songs that help children identify their feelings can help children of divorced families. Songs dealing with anger and frustration can also help children work out the feelings engendered by the divorce. Peter Alsop has many of these kinds of songs on his albums.

Multiple Disabilities

The disabilities described in the previous sections often do not occur in the classroom as a single difficulty in an individual child. Often, one child has **multiple disabilities**. Sometimes, one problem is compounded by other problems. In the following section, individual children with multiple problems are described in order to give you a sense of

Peter Alsop
Children's Musician, Teacher, Trainer in Self-Esteem and Humor

As a boy Peter Alsop sang in choir at church. But when he was a teen, he went to a dance and found the love of his life: performing. Seeing that those rock 'n' roll guys were the object of screaming teenage girls inspired him to take up the baritone ukulele. He tuned it like a bass and started to play in bands. Alsop heard that bands always needed a bass player, so he bought a real electric bass and played in rock bands throughout high school and college. After college, he went to graduate school at Columbia University, pursuing a Master's degree in educational psychology. After he finished his degree, he taught second and third grade emotionally disturbed children for a year. During that time he played with a band and recorded with other musicians on their albums.

At one point, his friend Dan Crow called him and said, "Let's make an album of kids' songs." Alsop replied, "I'm not a songwriter for kids." Crow argued that some of Alsop's songs would be great for kids. From this conversation, the compilation album with songs from a variety of artists, *Silly Songs and Modern Lullabies* (Alsop, Crow, Phillips, & Traum, 1980), was born. Later, when Alsop made an adult album, therapists started buying it. He was surprised, but thoughtfully remarked, "So many of the scars we have as adults came from injuries we sustained as children. Wouldn't it be great for kids to have some skills to cope with some of these issues themselves?" Bringing up issues for kids was his motivation for making more albums for children. That is why he made his first solo children's album, *Wha'd'ya Wanna Do?* (Alsop, 1983).

According to Alsop, a great song has to be accessible as it goes by, so it can be understood as it is happening. A great song has truth that seems simple when you hear it but is profound when you think about it. Music can access feelings and ideas at the same time.

Currently, Alsop trains teachers and adults who work with children and sings to adults about children.

the kinds of difficulties that can be encountered and helped through the use of music. Each child described is an actual student who was integrated into a group of typically functioning children. Names have been changed for confidentiality.

Annabelle: Premature Baby with Visual Impairments. Annabelle was born three months early. Today, it is not unusual for children as young as 26 weeks to be saved by the wonders of modern medicine.

Annabelle was such a child. Her eyesight was severely damaged, and her lack of brain development caused a fairly severe developmental delay. By age twelve, she functioned at about the first grade level in language and understanding. She attended a school for children with blindness and used a cane to get around. She could see some light but had severe visual impairments.

Annabelle was larger and older than most of the typically functioning children in her group. She enjoyed group singing time and sang along softly. She rocked while she sang. Sometimes she continued singing after the group had finished. She learned some of the songs that the group was practicing, and she performed in the concert given by the children for their parents.

She was not able to play an instrument, but she liked to sit at the piano and play random notes. Teachers encouraged her to play with one finger on each hand so that she could begin to find tunes on the piano and so she would not bang on the keys, which irritated other children. She was allowed to use the QChord by herself so that she could experience making her own music. She loved playing the QChord and would play it for 20 minutes at a time. She did not have much of an idea of how it worked, so she just randomly hit chord buttons and played on the sonic strings. She also loved to change the rhythms.

Annabelle had difficulties relating socially to the other children. She had a tendency to request adult approval 10 to 15 times an hour, unless she was preoccupied by an activity like playing the QChord. When not requesting attention, she sat alone and rocked back and forth. The singing period gave Annabelle a structure in which to relate to other children and to be successful in a group activity.

Kintami: Child with Developmental Delays and Divorced Parents. Kintami was born with hydrocephaly, a condition which caused his head to be small. At age eleven, he functioned at about kindergarten level. Physically, he was normal size and had typical coordination, but mentally and emotionally he was quite delayed. His parents divorced during the stressful period of adjusting to a child with special needs.

Kintami could not sing very well, but he could speak fairly normally. He loved to pretend to play the drums to rock 'n' roll music. Kintami developed a method of interacting with other children that teachers felt was inappropriate to encourage. He liked to pretend to be a wild animal and chase other children. Younger children, ages six and seven, enjoyed this game with him, but teachers felt that it reinforced behaviors that would be ultimately problematic for him. Songs about animals became the primary intervention for transforming his interest in animal behavior into a more manageable form. In the songs he was allowed to briefly make animal sounds, so this attracted his interest, but the songs were sung in a more controlled setting with a more manageable outcome. Through the group activity, he began to see himself as more normal and less of a wild animal. Best of all, when he sang in the concert, both of his parents came to hear him sing.

Singing also helped during another activity, swimming. Kintami had never learned to swim. He was tall enough to walk around in the four foot area of the pool, but he had never learned how to float. He overcame his fear of putting his face in the water by learning to hum into the water.

Sarafina: Child with Down Syndrome. Sarafina was a high functioning child with Down syndrome. She was integrated into a normal kindergarten class. Sarafina had the typical speech pattern of a child with this diagnosis, so she needed to learn songs that had the particular sounds that she needed to develop. In Chapter 6, songs for learning pronunciation in English are suggested. Songs like these were used in Sarafina's class. Even though the songs chosen were particularly selected for Sarafina's speech development, they were taught to the group as a whole, without singling Sarafina out of the group as the reason for the choice of songs.

Jordan: Child with Speech, Hearing, and Learning Impairments. Jordan had difficulties that became evident in the first year of preschool at age three. He was the youngest child in a family of four children, so no one took his language delay seriously until age three. At that point he spoke only a few words.

Jordan liked to play the electric piano. He spent hours discovering the different features of the piano, listening with headphones. He particularly liked some of the programmed tunes that could be played with a press of a button. After he attained some skill on the electric piano, two of his favorite tunes on it were chosen as dance music for the class. In a small group setting, Jordan and a few other children danced to the music on his electric piano. Jordan started the music for the group by pressing the button. During dance time, the teacher made a special effort to imitate Jordan's dance movements. The dance activities progressed to dancing to songs played on a record. His favorite was "The Rooster" (Miché, 1988) a traditional song that he liked because of the roar of the lion and the hissing of the snake. To encourage Jordan's speech, repetitive zipper songs were chosen at that point. He usually said the words at the end of lines. He particularly liked songs about wild animals. During that year, Jordan's music participation progressed from isolated play with the piano to group participation and vocalizing single words in repetitive songs.

Kincade: Child with ADHD and Dyslexia. Kincade was an energetic and intelligent second grader who could not sit on the rug with the rest of the children, even though he loved music. Both his parents were professional singers, so he learned to be on stage at an early age. It was difficult to get him off the stage in the classroom. He also had difficulty with the visual discrimination needed for reading. He reversed letters and had difficulty with tracking print.

One of the best interventions for him was having him listen to sing-along books with headphones. He would "read" the book while listening to the words sung to him on the audio.

When he exhausted the supply of books with audio tapes, he would choose a favorite song on tape and then make a book to accompany it. Instructions for making this kind of read-along book are in Chapter 8. Working alone was the best solution for Jordan and the classroom. The greatest difficulty of this method was generating enough material to keep him focused and busy. Teachers were relieved of the burden of trying to stay ahead of this energetic child when they discovered that he could make his own sing-along books by typing the words into the computer.

Music and Gender Differences

A special need that divides children into two groups is gender. Though no special prescriptions exist for doing music differently with girls and boys, teachers should understand that there are differences in how males and females hear and respond to music (Figure 4–9).

In a study of brain waves using an electroencephalogram, Johnson, Petsche, Richter, and von Stein (1996) analyzed brain wave patterns for men and women and musicians and nonmusicians. They found that women have more coherence, probably caused by more connections across the two halves of the brain, called interhemispheric coherence. This finding was not surprising, since studies of males and females have shown differences in the past. According to Diamond and Hops (1998), females have a larger corpus

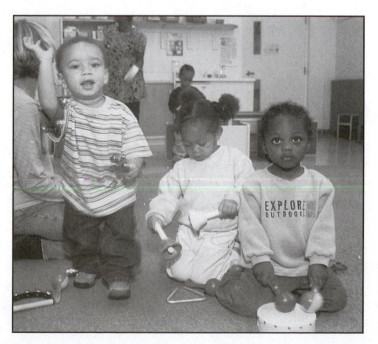

FIGURE 4–9 Boys and girls hear and respond to music in different ways.

callosum and a larger anterior commissure. Both are brain structures that connect the two sides of the brain. In his book *The Wonder of Boys,* Michael Gurian (1996) discusses the fact that boys have fewer connections across the hemispheres of the brain. This is due to the testosterone surge that occurs in fetal development during the second trimester of pregnancy. Because of this surge, the development of neural connections across the brain are slowed. Some people think this is why men have more difficulty than women in accessing their feelings. All of this information points to the possibility that women hear music differently than men. Especially interesting about the brain wave study was the fact that *musicians,* whether male or female, had significantly more coherence than non-musicians, both across the hemispheres of the brain and within each hemisphere. Although this has implications greater than just how music is heard, it clearly indicates that musicians hear music more intensely than the rest of us. More connections across the brain caused by music training could be helpful to both men and women, not only in listening to music but in understanding the feelings of others and their own feelings. It may also affect intellectual performance in other areas, particularly those which require creativity or intuitive thought, which draws from both sides of the brain's hemispheres.

Conclusion

Special needs come in all shapes and sizes. This chapter comprises an overview of the variety of difficulties you might encounter. Consider how music can help to inspire and educate a child with special needs. Most teachers never think of music as an option. You can be the one teacher who makes a difference for that child through your use of music.

KEY TERMS

Attention Deficit Disorder (ADD)	Fetal Alcohol Syndrome (FAS)	normal
autism	hearing disabled	normal development
context dependent memory	learning differences	physical disabilities
developmental delays	learning disabilities	procedural memory
Down syndrome	multiple disabilities	social disabilities
emotional disabilities	music therapist	visually disabled

DISCUSSION QUESTIONS

1. What is procedural memory? What sensorial approaches should be included to promote procedural memory?
2. Why should regular classroom teachers do some music with their students?
3. Name three kinds of physical disabilities in children.
4. Why is it important for a student with a visual disability to have some piano training?
5. What should you do with a child with a hearing disability while other students are playing music?
6. How can music help the development of a child with Down syndrome?
7. Give suggestions for musical activities for children with autism.
8. Discuss how you would do music with a child with ADHD.

9. Fetal Alcohol Syndrome is like what other disorder? How should music be presented to this child?
10. Do men or women have more connections across the two halves of the brain? Discuss how this affects music.

SUGGESTED LEARNING ACTIVITY

Design a series of five music lessons for a child with a visual disability child, age six. This child has normal intelligence and visits your class for a half hour once a week. Describe the songs or instruments you would choose for this child and your class. If you do a song with the group, give the name of the song, the name of the album, and the artist who recorded it.

REFERENCES

Alsop, P. (1983). *Wha'd'ya wanna do?* [cassette]. Santa Cruz, CA: Flying Fish Records.

Alsop, P., Crow, D., Phillips, B., & Traum, H. (1980). *Silly songs and modern lullabies* [record]. Los Angeles: Sweet Briar Records.

Amen, D. (1995). *Windows into the ADD mind.* Fairfield, CA: Mindworks.

Balch, W. R., Bowman, K., & Mohler, L. (1992). Music-dependent memory in immediate and delayed word recall. *Memory & Cognition, 20,* 21–28.

Balch, W. R., & Lewis, B. S. (1996). Music-dependent memory: The roles of tempo change and mood mediation. *Journal of Experimental Psychology, Learning, Memory & Cognition, 22,* 1354–1363.

Diamond, M., & Hops, J. (1998). *Magic trees of the mind.* New York: Dutton.

Godden, D. R., & Baddeley, A. D. (1975). Context-dependent memory in two natural environments: On land and underwater. *British Journal of Psychology, 66,* 325–331.

Gurian, M. (1996). *The wonder of boys.* New York: Tarcher/Putnam.

Haskil, C. (1998). *Mozart* [CD]. New York: Uni/Philips.

Jackson, M. (1972). *Sunflower* [CD]. New York: Columbia/Legacy.

Johnson, J., Petsche, H., Richter, P., & von Stein, A. (1996). The dependence of coherence of estimates of spontaneous EEG on gender and music training. *Music Perception, 13,* 563–582.

Khachaturian, A. (1994). *Masquerade suite* [CD]. Atlanta, GA: Audiophile Classics.

Miché, M. (1988). *Animal crackers* [cassette]. Berkeley, CA: Song Trek Music.

Nichols, B. L., & Honig, A. S. (1995). The influence of an inservice music education program on young children's responses to music. *Early Child Development, 113,* 19–29.

Rauscher, F. H., Shaw, G. L., Levine, L. J., Wright, E. L., Dennis, W. R., & Newcomb, R. L. (1997). Music training causes long term enhancement of preschool children's spatial-temporal reasoning. *Neurological Research, 19* (1), 2–8.

Smith, S. M. (1979). Remembering in and out of context. *Journal of Experimental Psychology: Human Learning & Memory, 5,* 460–471.

Weinberger, N. M. (1995, Spring). Musica research newsletter. [Retrieved from http://www.musica.uci.edu, October, 2001.]

Integrating Science and Music

Most teachers consider each subject area a separate part of the curriculum. Activities for students are put in time slots: art projects, science activities, circle time, outside playtime, music time. Some teachers think in terms of themes for the month or season, but they tend to apply those themes only to art projects and read-aloud books. Many teachers would like to coordinate their programs to fit together, so the science projects, art activities, books, outside playtime, and even songs fit into one synthesized theme for the month, season, or year. The difficulty is finding materials to put together into a coordinated whole. Over time, new pieces are added to the curriculum. Experienced teachers sometimes need moving vans and storage sheds to house their treasured materials.

This chapter covers ideas for coordinating music and songs with science activities. If you are new to the educational field, it will give you curriculum design ideas that you can use for activities with your students. If you are already an experienced teacher, it will provide some new ideas for reinforcing **science concepts** with science-related songs or using songs as a springboard for introducing science concepts.

Teaching Science Concepts through Song

Many songs are available for teaching young children about science. The trick is to find the song you need to fit the curriculum area you want. In searching for good science songs, it is best to start with artists who are well known for focusing on science and nature songs. A list of these artists follows. Another method is asking other teachers if they know of a song that fits your subject. Parents sometimes know of songs they use for recreational listening. Finally, you could write a song yourself, combining some clever rhymes with a catchy tune and, if possible, a funny twist that will interest your students.

Instead of looking for a song that teaches the concept you want to reinforce, you can build some of your activities around the songs that you find. This reduces the cost and the time and energy of finding songs.

More artists than you might expect create nature and science music for children. Working with children in science or music education seems to encourage the development of music that teaches children information, concern, and love for our world.

♪ Banana Slug String Band is probably the best known. Three albums by this Santa Cruz, California, group are: *Dirt Made My Lunch* (1987a), *Adventures on the Air Cycle* (1989), and *Slugs at Sea* (1991). They have fantastic songs written by a member of the band and former kindergarten teacher, Steve Van Zandt. He has an unusual ability to explain the natural world in clever lyrics. The band performs their own songs, wears crazy hats, and gets their audience involved by teaching them to shout about nature.

♪ Another group, Tickle Tune Typhoon from Seattle, Washington, have an album entitled *Hug the Earth* (1985) with an outstanding recycling song by a great songwriter, Dennis Westphall. This choral/instrumental group creates a sound that is both musically appealing and fun for classroom listening.

♪ Jeff Moran is a scientist turned musician. His songs about science processes and information are great for elementary school–age children. His albums have particularly good lyrics that are a little advanced for most preschoolers but a wonderful challenge to older children. For more information, visit his Web site at http://www.tranquility.net/~scimusic.

♪ Bungie Jumping Cows is another environmental music group. They formed at the Lawrence Hall of Science in Berkeley, California. They have a rock 'n' roll sound with some wild songs that are great for dancing. Some favorites are the songs about arachnids, "Have an ArachniDay," and cockroaches, "We're Gonna Rule the World" (1994).

♪ Doug Wood worked with the Science Museum of Minnesota. He has a lovely solo voice and a good guitar sound. He is the author of the beautiful book and matching recording, *Old Turtle* (1992).

♪ Bill Brennan of Washington, D.C., has written great songs about the natural world. He has two nature albums, entitled *Billy B. Sings Tree Songs* (1982) and *Romp in the Swamp* (1984). Bill has some of the catchiest tunes and cleverest lyrics around.

♪ Another wonderful performer is Gail Lynne Dreifus, who began her natural science music career as a naturalist in Yosemite National Park. She has created a country music style group called The Recycled String Band and has written delightful songs. She has several natural science albums, including *Yosemite by Song* (1987) and *National Parks by Song* (1996).

♪ Finally there is the author, Mary Miché, with two environmental education albums entitled *Earthy Tunes* (1987) and *Nature Nuts* (1990) with science songs from several different songwriters selected to help teachers find great science songs for the classroom.

The following sections discuss how to build curriculum units focusing on a particular theme, such as teaching respect for nature, around a group of songs.

Songs That Teach Respect for Nature

Much preschool and early elementary science teaching focuses on learning about animals because children identify easily with them (Figure 5–1). That is why animals are featured in many children's books and movies. When you teach young children science, you can use songs to capitalize on this interest and teach them accurate and useful information.

Factual songs are accurate in science information and yet funny enough to catch the children's attention. One favorite is a song called "Banana Slug" by Steve Van Zandt (Banana Slug String Band, 1987a; Miché, 1987). In this song, the children sing, "Banana slug, banana slug, when some people see you they say ugh! Banana slug, banana slug, when I see you I'll give you a hug!" The verses describe what banana slugs look like and their function in nature: to eat dead material, turning it into soil for trees and plants to use in making oxygen. The song has a catchy tune and is fun to sing, but the important lesson for young children is that even unattractive creatures have a place and function in nature. This is summed up in the final verse, "So, when you're walkin' down the path and

FIGURE 5–1 Children learn about science through singing songs about animals.

you see a slug, you can bend over and give it a hug. You can pick it up. It won't bite or hiss. Show that you love it and give it a kiss!" Many times kids want to squish or destroy slugs, worms, roly-polys, or other **decomposers**. Learning to respect unappealing animals in nature is an important part of living in harmony with the natural world.

Another song along the same theme of **nature appreciation** is "Spiders and Snakes" (Axlerod, 1980; Miché, 1987). This song combines love of unappealing creatures, "Spiders and snakes, spiders and snakes, I'm gonna learn to love them no matter how long it takes," with verses full of information about spiders and snakes. This song can be accompanied by sign language for "spider," "snake," "love them," and "no matter" (Figure 5–2).

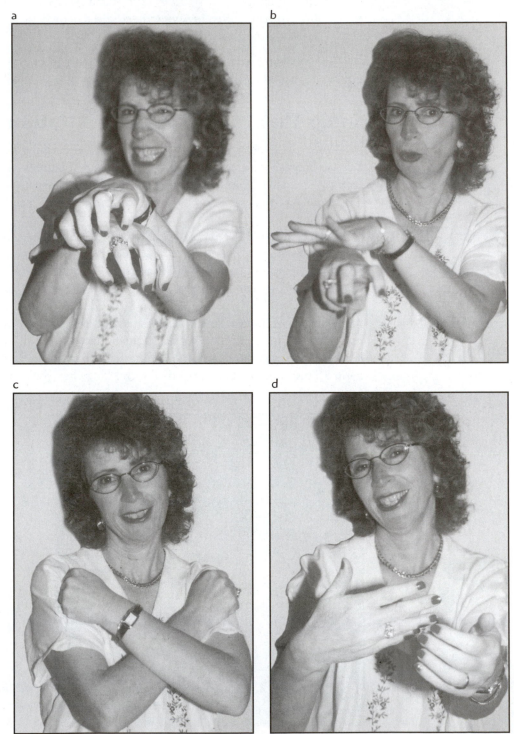

FIGURE 5–2 Sign language can be used with songs to teach children about animals a) "spider," b) "snake," c) "love them," d) "no matter."

For preschoolers it is important to emphasize safety with spiders and snakes, but for early elementary-age children, focus on the vocabulary and concepts in the verses, such as "what is a **rodent**?" to extend the song into science learning.

Bill Brennan's music makes children aware of the fragile **environment** of swamps in his song "Romp in the Swamp" (1984; Miché, 1990). The message of concern comes across as they tiptoe through the grass and pretend they are holding baby muskrats. The kids love the humor of a mother telling her kid to get back in the swamp and the song is just plain fun for dancing. You can pretend you are going to visit a swamp before you sing this song by putting on make-believe boots, raincoats, and hats. This song is great preparation for actually visiting a swamp.

In his song "Ranger Rick" (Wood, 1992), Doug Wood sings, "Ranger Rick I want to help if I can, Ranger Rick giving nature a hand." Students can open *Ranger Rick* magazine, look at pictures of nature, and talk about how to give nature a helping hand.

Kids have a lot of fun singing the silly lyrics to Linda Arnold's song, "Ms. Spider" (1986), "a spider on my knee and she's crawling over me, oh what, oh what should I do? Should I brush her on the floor and sweep her out the door? Should I shake hands and say 'How do you do'?" Teachers can talk about how spiders are living things that we need to respect. At that point, you can explain how to capture spiders in a jar and put them outside so they will eat lots of bugs. In the process, students can look at the eight legs and find out if this spider will spin a strand when released out of the jar.

On one memorable field trip with a group of preschoolers to a nature center, a four-year-old girl stood in front of the turtle cage singing, "You can't make a turtle come out . . . So you'll have to patiently wait." This sweet song, "You Can't Make a Turtle Come Out," by Malvina Reynolds (1972; Miché, 1987), helps young children understand that animals are not always interested in doing what we want them to do and that respect for animals means allowing them to live without our controlling them.

Many songs about animals can teach respect. Teachers should talk about the information given in a song, especially if some of it is accurate and some is not. Young children need help distinguishing between fact and fancy. Even if a song is not completely accurate in its information, like "Ms. Spider" (Arnold, 1986), children can still learn care, concern, and respect for the natural world. They can also learn a great deal of information about the natural world through the coordination of books and magazines with pictures showing the correct information, while enjoying making music. They do not realize that they are also simultaneously practicing pitch, keeping the beat, and group cooperation.

Fanciful Songs about Animals

Many songs about animals do not teach accurate information. These **fanciful songs** can be a great asset in teaching science, but teachers should remember to give children the correct information about animals. Many of these songs are written to be humorous, and it is the juxtaposition of real science and fanciful information that makes them funny. For example, in the song "Al the Alligator" by Jane Timberlake (1989), Al needs a refrigerator to keep his Gatorade® nice and cool while living in the swamp. This song can be confusing for a three-year-old, since it is difficult for a child to understand which information is correct. For a seven-year-old, however, this song is funny because she already knows that alligators cannot walk into department stores or travel on elevators and escalators, that alligators live in swamps but there are no plugs for refrigerators there, and she has possibly heard of Gatorade®. If a teacher decides to use this song, the children should learn which facts are accurate and which are not. The humor of mismatched facts motivates the imagination of the child and children can differentiate fact from fancy once given an explanation.

Even for preschoolers, a well-crafted fanciful animal song can teach a great deal and still be funny. In the song, "Oh Me, Oh My" (Raffi, 1984), the child is presented with some funny images of animals: "Oh me, oh my, what'll I do? I don't have an elephant to tie my shoe. But I know what and so do you, you don't need an elephant to tie your shoe. No, you don't need an elephant to tie your shoe." The message that elephants do not tie shoes is an example of a wonderful combination of fanciful information combined with real facts. In this case, the song itself teaches the child which information is accurate and which is not.

Jill Jarbo wrote a great song with a rock 'n' roll sound called "I'm a Reptile" (Forest & Schimmel, 1990). "I'm a reptile, Whoa!, so shiver and shake, 'Cause I'm a reptile, Whoa! my cousin's a snake, and, I'm a reptile, Whoa, I'll eat you for lunch, so back off baby, we're a cold-blooded bunch." The verses are about a turtle cruisin' down the road with a heavy load and an alligator who is makin' a movie. Here is an example of a fanciful song with some facts included. This is a popular song with seven- to eight-year-olds because they enjoy acting out the chorus and the verses. The song is appealing to preschoolers because of the catchy tune and rock 'n' roll sound. Still, teachers should take the time to teach children the facts about reptiles. Many children have had experience with reptiles and know some information. Yes, reptiles are cold-blooded, yes they are cousin to a snake, but they do not eat children for lunch. Turtles, lizards, iguanas, crocodiles, and alligators are all reptiles, but they do not carry heavy loads and make movies.

Bill Staines is not known for his science and nature songwriting, but his song "All God's Critters" (McCutcheon, 1983; Miché, 1990) is one of the best fanciful animal songs around. "All God's critters got a place in the choir. Some sing lower, some sing higher. Some sing out loud on the telephone wire. Some just clap their hands or paws or anything they've got now." Just imagine singing this song around the campfire with children and adults all clapping their hands. Each verse describes a group of animals and ends with an animal sound. The coyote howling is a popular sound; sometimes it is a little difficult to get the coyotes to stop howling and sing the rest of the song. This song makes the point with children that we are all different, like the animals, and yet we all have a place in nature.

A great favorite of second and third graders is "Old Mr. Mackle Hackle" by Gunnar Madsen (1999; Miché, 1988). Most chickens do not lose their cackle and most chicken owners would not bother to try to get it back. Every time someone tries to cure Mr. Mackle Hackle's chicken, she starts to squeak, quack, talk, and do everything but *bok* like a chicken. So, at the end of the song, the only way he can get her back to normal is to tell chicken jokes, which of course the children have to do. Children do not tell real jokes until they are about seven or eight years old. So, if you teach preschool, be prepared for jokes that only tickle the funny bones of four-year-olds. However, Mr. Mackle Hackle is a great lead into barnyard fun and discussions about chickens.

Songs That Teach about Animal Habits

Some songs present accurate information throughout the song. Some exceptional songs can teach accurate information and still retain the interest of the children. One example is "Newts, Salamanders & Frogs" by Steve Van Zandt (Banana Slug String Band, 1987a; Miché, 1990). In this song the children learn from the chorus that "newts, salamanders, and frogs are amphibians" and that they live in ponds and under logs. From the verses children learn that amphibians have "legs and lungs and sticky tongues." They munch bugs by catching them on the tip of their tongues. They have pores on their skin and like to swim. Some favorite activities with this song include having the children

♪ pretend they are breaststroking like frogs.

♪ swim while they sing, "newts, salamanders, and frogs, oh yeah!" and throw their hands up in the air when they yell, "Oh yeah!"

♪ make the pond with their arms when they sing, "Livin' in ponds, on lily pads and logs."

♪ act out the verses by pointing to their legs, lungs, and sticky tongues where they catch the bugs.

♪ act afraid of the big snake that might catch them.

To prepare for this song, check out a few amphibian books from the library so that the children can see photos of newts, frogs, and salamanders.

Steve Van Zandt has written more than one excellent song that teaches true nature facts. In "Bats Eat Bugs" (Banana Slug String Band, 1987a; Miché, 1990), he addresses a common fear of children that animals will eat them (Figure 5–3). "Bats eat bugs," he sings, "They don't eat people. Bats eat bugs, they don't fly in your hair. Bats eat bugs, they eat insects for dinner. That's why they're flyin' up there." That's just the first verse! In the chorus he reassures us that "Nothing out there eats people for dinner 'cause they know how sick they would feel." At that point everyone can put their hands on their stomachs and pretend to throw up. Of course throwing up is one of the best parts of the song, being almost universally funny to children. The verses help kids realize that snakes eat mice, coyotes eat rabbits, and bears eat berries. A thoughtful child will occasionally realize that of all animals, only mosquitoes are *really* interested in eating people.

Steve Van Zandt's "Nocturnal Animals" (Banana Slug String Band, 1987a) is a wonderful source of information about **nocturnal animals**. "Nocturnal animals, they come out at night. Shh. Nocturnal animals, on the ground and some in flight." This is a very rhythmic song and really lends itself to being accompanied by rhythm band.

"Niche in Nature" (Miché, 1990) is a way to communicate to young children what a biological **niche** is. "Do you know what a niche is? It's when something fits just right.

FIGURE 5–3
Songs about insects help children overcome their fears.

Steve Van Zandt
Natural Science Songwriter, Banana Slug String Band

Steve Van Zandt wrote his first environmental children's song in the late '70s while sitting on the porch of the house where he grew up in West Los Angeles. He was strumming his mother's 1954 Martin Guitar and looking at the orange tree that was planted when he was eight years old. Its branches and green leaves were now higher than the roof, and it was filled with sweet oranges. It was the perfect setting for writing "I'm a Tree" (Banana Slug String Band, 1987a).

That fall, when Van Zandt returned to college, he heard about an internship teaching outdoor education. The following fall he took a year away from college to teach fifth and sixth graders at a camp in La Honda, California. This experience provided just the inspiration he needed to write educational, environmental, natural history songs.

Van Zandt continued as an environmental educator and formed the Banana Slug String Band in 1983. He gives workshops for teachers on how to use music to teach science. Creativity, joy, silliness, the light in children's eyes, crazy groupie adult fans, the sense that they are doing something right, and a purity of purpose are all factors that keep him going. He loves to perform with the Slugs. He says, "It's great to see a full room of kindergarten teachers shaking out the water cycle boogie."

Van Zandt involves the children through singing, dancing, hand motions, body motions, costumes, puppets, and humor. A long time ago, he found that the more a song called for participation, the better the learning.

He commented about the importance of music, "Let it fill our lives—our world—and unite us as one people and one planet."

Reprinted with permission from Banana Slug String Band, P.O. Box 2262, Santa Cruz, CA 95063, (888) 327–5847, http://www.bananaslugstringband.com.

Well, nature has niches so that everything fits tight. We each have a place in nature, whether we're big or small. If niches are protected, there's room enough for all." Animals, plants, and even people occupy an environmental space. Humans are beginning to use up all the available space and are crowding out other plants and animals. After singing this song, talk about niches and take a walk around the school yard to look for places where animals live in niches: under rocks, in weeds, and in bushes (Figure 5–4).

FIGURE 5–4   Children search for insects hidden in their niche habitats.

Songs about Plants and Plant Processes

In almost every preschool and often in early elementary grades, students plant seeds and watch them grow. There are numerous methods, such as planting a seed in a cup of potting soil, putting a seed in a jar with paper towels, and putting cotton and water in plastic baggies taped to a window. In preschool, the idea is still novel to children, but jaded second graders will tell you "we did that in preschool." Teachers can add other dimensions to retain the interest of elementary students. Songs, books, stories, and videos can help do that. The class can even take a trip to a vegetable farm. Make sure preschoolers understand the larger concept, that seeds also grow in soil and in fields. For example, one teacher planted seeds in a jar with the seed between the side of the jar and a wet paper towel rolled up. For years her students thought that was how seeds were supposed to be planted. The teacher probably thought it was a great activity for the children to actually see the roots and the stems, but the children never made the connection between those seeds and actual plants in the soil until years later.

Songs can enhance the comprehension of students in observing and remembering **plant processes** (Figure 5–5). A good example is "The Sprout Song" (Brennan, 1982; Miché, 1987). In this song, especially well suited to preschoolers and kindergartners, each child curls up on the floor to begin life as a seed. You can either sing the song or play the recording, doing the body motions that the music suggests.

> Wet ground, warm sun, my life as a tree has just begun.
> [Nod head "yes."]
> I'm so sure, I have no doubt, 'cause my shell is cracked and I have a sprout.
> [Clap hands together and keep them together forming the "sprout."]
> It's growing up and growing out and growing up and growing out.
> [Stand up slowly and let the hands grow up.]

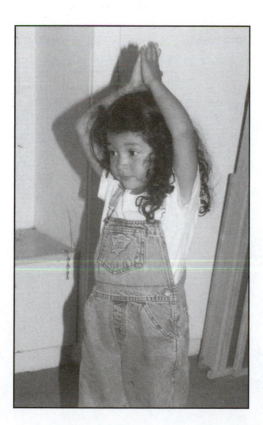

FIGURE 5–5 Music can teach children how a sprout becomes a tree.

Yippee, Hooray, I am a sprout, Yippee, Hooray, I am a sprout!
[Pull the hands apart for the calm version, jump and yell, "Yippee" while pulling the hands apart for the wild version. Once you have taught the wild version, you can never go back to the calm one.]
Hey I'm a seed too.
[Go back down to the floor to be a seed again.]

It is especially helpful to plant bean seeds in conjunction with this song because they grow up and open up just like students' hands opening over their heads. With elementary age students, you can grow a variety of seeds to see that seedlings look different even when they are just sprouts. This concept can be used to promote multicultural awareness with students, helping them to realize that varieties of people are much like varieties of seeds.

A second song that goes well with planting seeds is one by Tom Hunter, "Lotta Seeds Grow" (1985; Miché, 1987). As mentioned in Chapter 3, Pete Seeger calls this kind of song a zipper song. Zipper songs are excellent for preschoolers because they have a lot of repetition, something that preschoolers enjoy and need in their musical development. This song says, "Lotta trees start from seeds so small you gotta look close or you can't see them at all. It's hard to believe that trees grow so tall from seeds that start so small." In the next verse, he replaces the word "trees" with another one like "flowers." You can take suggestions from the children for the different kinds of seeds to plant. Discuss all different sizes of seeds; some groups of children are really interested in comparing the size of a seed with the grown size of its plant (Figure 5–6).

After you decide what kind of seeds to plant and have started the sprouts, you can sing or play the "Song of the Young Tree" (Brennan, 1982; Miché, 1987).

In the forest a young tree grows so small and so alive,
it sings a song if you want to know just how hard it tries.
Now listen, it's singing in the wind and the song is making the big trees grin.
"Hey you big guys, let me have some sun, yeah, the sun is for everyone.
Hey what's the matter, you act like you can't hear, oh, forget it I'll grow over here.
Gonna grow over here, with sunshine energy, sunshine energy."

FIGURE 5–6
Exploring pinecones
reveals tiny seeds.

Talk about how the sun's energy is needed to help plants grow big and strong. Then have kids pretend they are little trees growing in the forest. They have to lean over sideways, like some small trees do, to reach around the edge of a big tree so they can get some sun too. Occasionally, they fall over when they lean too far, but that is part of the fun.

Bill Brennan's "Bugs in Your Bark" (1982; Miché, 1987) helps teach that one of the problems that trees have is bugs. "This bark on me is my skin, it keeps diseases out and tree juices in. It protects me from bugs, dust, and wind, even though, sometimes, the bugs get in."

Talk about the vocabulary in songs even if you think students understand the words. Most first graders would understand all the words in this song, but the concept of bark being a skin for the tree is usually new. Depending on your class, you can spend time talking about what diseases trees can get. Take a short walk around the neighborhood and find trees with brown edges on their leaves. You might find rust (an insect pest), aphids, or other diseases on trees or plants. Surprisingly, kids easily get the idea that plants get sick too.

Bill Brennan sums up his lessons on trees with "What Is a Tree?" (1982; Miché, 1987). This song helps teach the usefulness of trees; not only the uses that people have for trees, but also how trees meet the needs of animals and birds.

> What is a tree, does anybody really know, just what they are, just how they really grow?
> What do they need, and what do they do? What are they used for and by whom?
> Oh I tried to find out, went down to the library and I took a book out.

With a group of young children, teachers can make a class list of as many uses for trees as possible.

David Mallet has written one of the most popular and singable children's songs about the garden, appropriately named "Garden Song" (1997; Miché, 1987).

> Inch by inch, row by row, gonna help this garden grow,
> gonna mulch it deep below, gonna make it fertile ground.
> Inch by inch, row by row, please help these seeds I sow
> and warm them from below 'til the rain comes a tumblin' down.
> Plant your rows straight and long, temper them with prayer and song.
> Mother Earth will make you strong if you give her love and care.
> Day by day, seed to sprout, this is what life's all about
> from the garden reaching out with food for many to share.

This song has a particularly beautiful melody and is great for singing. It also has the added bonus of teaching a lot about how to plant a garden. Adults are also fond of this melodic and gently rocking song. You can use a song like this to help children calm down after singing some of the more rowdy songs like "Romp in the Swamp" (Brennan, 1984).

"Root, stems, leaves, flowers, fruits, and seeds, that's six parts, six parts, six plant parts that plants and people need." These lyrics are from "Roots, Stems, Leaves" by Steve Van Zandt (Banana Slug String Band, 1987b; Miché, 1987). It is an all-time favorite for teaching children about **plant parts**. This is when rote learning through music really pays off. Many classes have gone on six plant part hikes around the neighborhood, in the playground, on the school grounds, and in parks that they visited on field trips. Classes stay engaged in finding parts of different plants and wondering, "Now which plant part is this?" You can even do scavenger hunts where each child has to find one root, two stems, three leaves, etc. (Figure 5–7). The song's verses are excellent explanations of the function of each plant part. "The root holds the stem into the ground, it gathers up the water that

FIGURE 5–7 Children collect leaves to learn about the parts of a tree.

falls around. And there's a root inside of me 'cause carrot is a root that I eat." Children can try to think of other roots that people eat. The first time you sing this song, do not stop on every verse, but stop on the verse about fruits and name as many different kinds of fruits as possible. So far, the most named in any class was 52 fruits.

Songs about Dirt, Mud, and Pollution

Dirt is a favorite topic, appealing to lots of children. There are silly preschool songs like "Mud, Mud, Mud" (Miché, 1990). Experiment making different kinds of mud pies. You can be scientific about making different kinds of mud with different amounts of water. Gooshy mud has more water in it, is very fun to squish, but takes a long time to dry out.

"Dirt Made My Lunch," another Steve Van Zandt original (Banana Slug String Band, 1987a; Miché, 1987), is a favorite. Most of the food we eat comes from dirt. Most children have not realized this until they sing this song. "Dirt made my lunch, dirt made my lunch, thank you dirt, thanks a bunch for my salad, my sandwich, my milk and my munch cause dirt, you made my lunch. Dirt is a word we often use when we talk about the earth beneath our shoes. It's a place where plants can sink their toes and in a little while a garden grows." Whenever you sing or play this song with a group of children, ask them if they can think of anything they eat for lunch that is not made from dirt. Most children start with hamburgers or candy. You can explain that hamburgers are made from beef, which comes from a cow, which eats grass, which grows in the . . . The children will yell "dirt!" Then sing "Dirt made my lunch . . ." It takes a while for children to figure out something we eat for lunch that does not grow in dirt. For the answer, think of animals in salt water. You can then discuss how plants bloom in the ocean without any dirt.

Speaking of dirt, you can also sing "Dirt!" by Jon Gailmor (1983; Miché, 1990). This song is much more fanciful than "Dirt Made My Lunch." "Dirt, I can rock and roll around in it. Dirt, mud pie à la mode, Dirt, all covered by sundown, I'm a day crawler."

FIGURE 5–8 Children can sing while they dig in the sand.

Children mostly like this song because it is fun to yell "dirt!" at the beginning of each line of the song (Figure 5–8).

Pollution is closely related to dirt: they can both be disgusting. There are two really good songs about pollution. Pollution is a difficult topic for preschoolers, so neither of these songs is appropriate for younger children, but they are good for third graders.

The first is a song by Tom Lehrer, "Pollution" (1965; Miché, 1990). Though written in 1965, the song is still timely in its message. "Pollution, pollution, we've got smog and sewage and mud, turn on your tap and get hot and cold running crud." The vocabulary of this song is very clever and well worth the time it takes to explain it to your students. "See the halibut and the sturgeon being wiped out by detergent. Fish gotta swim and birds gotta fly, but they don't last long if they try." You can spend time going over the meaning of each verse, and it is fun to see students begin to understand the jokes. A great activity in conjunction with this song is to draw pictures of different kinds of pollution and make posters about cleaning up the environment.

The second song, "All Across the USA" (Brennan, 1984), is another sharp-witted commentary on the state of the environment. "All across the USA you can hear the people say, 'Aw there's so much algae in this lake that when I swim I bring a rake. And when it stinks to high heaven, well it ain't for heaven's sake, P.U.'" Children really get interested when they start singing about yucky topics. They are usually also interested in finding out what they can do to help clean up the environment. A fun book that helps answer this question is *50 Simple Things Kids Can Do to Save the Earth* (The Earth Works Group, 1990). A particularly beautiful book that complements this theme is *A River Ran Wild,* written by Lynne Cherry (1992). It tells how concerned adults and children helped to clean up the Nashua River in Massachusetts.

Songs about Recycling

The disposal of all the waste created in our throw-away society is intimately connected with the problem of pollution. Hundreds of teachers across the country are involved in teaching their students about **recycling**. Teachers have an impressive level of

Gail Dreifus
Children's Musician, The Recycled String Band Touring National Parks

As a child, Gail Dreifus took piano and cello lessons and taught herself to play guitar. As an adult she taught choral music, music theory, and piano in a private alternative school. She started giving concerts, playing original folk music in coffeehouses. Dreifus was also a park naturalist at one time. Now, she works in Yosemite National Park performing shows about nature, science, and the environment, both solo and with the Recycled String Band, a group of women who play a variety of instruments.

Dreifus travels with the band all over the United States to perform at schools, festivals, concerts, museums, and libraries. She enjoys performing, and said of her work, "I hope that I'm teaching students about our planet. I also hope they have a good time at our show." Dreifus and the Recycled String Band involve kids in their shows by having them participate with masks, sound effects, lines to songs, sign language, and playing instruments. She enjoys working with children and families because "I guess the kid in me has a chance to come out."

concern for the environment, and hundreds of small efforts by children across the country add up to an enormous difference in helping to improve the environment. Songs about recycling are a great way to communicate information about preserving the environment (Figure 5–9).

Tom Hunter's "Garbage" (1985; Miché, 1990) is great for teaching about reuse and recycling. He sings, "We just call it garbage when we don't know what to do with it." Then, during the verses, children find out that people have made puppets and invented art projects from what was called garbage. Garbage art (creations from leftover stuff) is a great follow-up activity lesson to this song. So what things can be collected instead of throwing them away to make more garbage? Go right on to the next song.

FIGURE 5–9 Many songs help promote recycling and taking care of Mother Earth.

Dennis Westphall
Children's Musician, Tickle Tune Typhoon, Children's Music Band

Tickle Tune Typhoon started as a group of musicians doing street and cafe performances. They decided to put on a show geared to children and families, so they rented a hall, made some posters, and performed. The show's success led to the first Tickle Tune Typhoon concert five months later.

Lorraine Bayes and Dennis Westphall are the founders and directors of the Tickle Tune Typhoon. Bayes was an early childhood teacher. Other musicians joined them, and they have been a group for over 20 years. They provide songs on many topics for children. They love music and are committed to providing a quality musical experience for families. Not only do they entertain, but they also teach others and bring communities together through music.

Westphall does most of the songwriting for the group. He said, "A song should be able to draw a child in, to inspire his or her imagination, to entertain, to make a child laugh or enable a child to feel the emotion. A song can teach and it can motivate. Most importantly, a song [can] create a safe haven and allow people to enjoy one another without prejudice or boundary, just for the sheer pleasure of being together." Westphall's favorite kind of songs are those about science.

Tickle Tune Typhoon involves children in music through singing, sign language, creative movement and dance, call and response, drama, costumes, and characters. They also teach others through their workshop programs. They feel that all musical expression is viable and important and that their group cannot be categorized into any particular musical style. Children should be exposed to as many musical styles and varieties of instrumentation as possible, so they can experience the full spectrum of music and the cultures to which they belong. This way, children can intelligently choose for themselves what they prefer by knowing all the options.

One of Westphall's favorite funny stories is about the time when they were recording the song "Bear Hunt" (Tickle Tune Typhoon, 1984) on their first album. To get the slogging through the mud sound effect, Westphall had to be shut into a small bathroom in the dark, so the fan would not run and be heard on the recording. They ran microphones down the hall into the room where he wore rubber hip boots and marched in the dark while plunging a toilet plunger up and down in the water. The hardest part of this task was to keep from laughing long enough to get the sound they needed for the recording. It turned out great.

"Hey, Hey, Don't Throw It Away" (Miché, 1990) tells how to make money from collecting trash. It is amazing that the interest in making money begins at such a young age as four or five. Preschoolers decide that they want to work so they can make money. Teachers can put that energy to use and try a class project collecting recyclables to make money for a good cause. While you are doing that, you can sing, "Hey, Hey, don't throw it away, I can make money from your trash today. Hey, hey, don't dump that can, I'll take it to the recycle man." Then, take your class on a field trip to the local recycling center. One preschool goes every year and the teachers learn something new each visit.

Another great recycling song is "Garbage Blues" by Dennis Westphall (Tickle Tune Typhoon, 1985; Miché, 1990). This is a great rock 'n' roll recycle song to which younger children love to dance. Older kids will get out their imaginary microphones and lip sync along. This song has all the qualities of greatness. It describes gross, disgusting, yucky garbage in complete detail. "Takin' out the garbage can be such a drag, there's some crusty old gristle on an old dish rag. Sittin' on top near some moldy old beans, there's slimy green spinach that smells mighty mean. Aluminum cans full of yellowish goo, oozing over plastic caked with mildew." It also has a great beat and a catchy chorus. "Recycle, it's a better way, Uh huh. Recycle, I'm needin' a solution to this throw away pollution, what can I do? I've got the garbage blues, Uh huh." It is wonderful to make pretend microphones and get a video camera to tape the kids while they sing this song. Kids spontaneously choreograph extraordinary dancing for this song. Try it out and you might be dancing too. If you do no other recycling song, try this one.

Songs That Encourage Appreciation of Nature

Because energetic songs engage children and because teachers want to hold their attention, it is easier to find engaging energetic songs than calm, quiet ones for young children. One excellent quiet song is "Ally, Ally Oxen Free" by Rod McKuen (1994; Miché, 1990). The title does not do justice to the beauty of the lyrics and melody of the song. When doing a calm and quiet song like this, children can lay down and listen to the beauty of the music. "Time to let the rain fall all across this land. Time to let the trees grow tall, now if they only can. Time to let our children live in a land that's free. Earth and air, clear and fair, full of love and care." When the song is finished, teachers can talk in a quiet voice about the beauty of the earth and how we are here to love it, appreciate it, and care for it.

If you can, try to do an **evening activity** with children and their families once a year. This can be an evening in the park, a campfire sing-along, or camping overnight. For any of these events, the song "Go into the Night" by Steve Van Zandt (Banana Slug String Band, 1996; Miché, 1990) is a natural. In this song he teaches about different night animals and the sounds they make. "If you go into the night there's music in the night, callin' out a song that's clear." Each verse is about a different nocturnal animal and the sounds they make (Figure 5–10). "The great horned owl is a nighttime pal with a song that you can hear." The song then plays the sound of the great horned owl. During the coyote verse, "The beautiful note of a lone coyote is a song that you can hear," a few

FIGURE 5–10 Making nighttime sounds helps children overcome fears of the dark.

What science concepts can be taught with songs?

Most concepts in science can be taught through songs. You just have to find songs that fit your curriculum. The following is a list of science songs from this chapter and the concepts they teach.

A Common ??? Question

SCIENCE CONCEPT	RECORDING
Animals	
· Fear of	Bats Eat Bugs (Banana Slug String Band, 1987a; Miché 1990)
	Go into the Night (Banana Slug String Band, 1996; Miché, 1990)
	Spiders and Snakes (Axlerod, 1980; Miché, 1987)
· Habits	Bats Eat Bugs (Banana Slug String Band, 1987a; Miché, 1990)
	Newts, Salamanders & Frogs (Banana Slug String Band, 1987a; Miché, 1990)
	Romp in the Swamp (Brennan, 1984; Miché, 1990)
· Nocturnal	Go into the Night (Banana Slug String Band, 1996; Miché, 1990)
	Nocturnal Animals (Banana Slug String Band, 1987a)
· Reptiles/Amphibians	Al the Alligator (Timberlake, 1989; Miché, 1988)
	I'm a Reptile (Forest & Schimmel, 1990)
	Newts, Salamanders & Frogs (Banana Slug String Band, 1987a; Miché, 1990)
· Voices	All God's Critters (McCutcheon, 1983; Miché, 1990)
	Old Mr. Mackle Hackle (Madsen, 1999; Miché, 1988)
Nature	
· Appreciation	All God's Critters (McCutcheon, 1983; Miché, 1990)
	Ally, Ally Oxen Free (McKuen, 1994; Miché, 1990)
	Dirt! (Gailmor, 1983; Miché, 1990)
	Dirt Made My Lunch (Banana Slug String Band, 1987a; Miché, 1987)
	Garden Song (Mallet, 1997; Miché, 1987)
	Ms. Spider (Arnold, 1986; Miché, 1990)
	Mud, Mud, Mud (Miché, 1990)
	I'd Like to Teach the World to Sing (Miché, 1989)
	What Is a Tree? (Brennan, 1982; Miché, 1987)
· Ecosystems	Dirt Made My Lunch (Banana Slug String Band, 1987a; Miché, 1987)
	Niche in Nature (Miché, 1990)

continued

WHAT SCIENCE CONCEPTS CAN BE TAUGHT WITH SONGS? *continued*

SCIENCE CONCEPT	RECORDING
Nature *(continued)*	
· Respect	Banana Slug (Banana Slug String Band, 1987a; Miché, 1987)
	Old Turtle (Wood, 1992)
	Romp in the Swamp (Brennan, 1984; Miché, 1990)
	Spiders and Snakes (Axlerod, 1980; Miché, 1987)
	You Can't Make a Turtle Come Out (Reynolds, 1972; Miché, 1987)
Plants/Trees	
· Decomposers	Banana Slug (Banana Slug String Band, 1987a; Miché, 1987)
	Song of the Young Tree (Brennan, 1982; Miché, 1987)
· Gardening	Garden Song (Mallet, 1997; Miché, 1987)
	Roots, Stems, Leaves (Banana Slug String Band, 1987b; Miché, 1987)
	Workin' Together in the Sun (Miché, 1990)
· Growth Cycles	Song of the Young Tree (Brennan, 1982; Miché, 1987)
	The Sprout Song (Brennan, 1982; Miché, 1987)
	Workin' Together in the Sun (Miché, 1990)
· Parts	Bugs in Your Bark (Brennan, 1982; Miché, 1987)
	Lotta Seeds Grow (Hunter, 1985; Miché, 1987)
	Roots, Stems, Leaves (Banana Slug String Band, 1987b; Miché, 1987)
	The Sprout Song (Brennan, 1982; Miché, 1987)
Recycling/Pollution	
	All Across the USA (Brennan, 1984)
	Garbage (Hunter, 1985; Miché, 1990)
	Garbage Blues (Tickle Tune Typhoon, 1985; Miché, 1990)
	Garbage Man's Blues (Miché, 1990)
	Hey, Hey, Don't Throw It Away (Miché, 1990)
	Pollution (Lehrer, 1965; Miché, 1990)

young humanoid mammals will not be able to resist joining in. Fortunately, the song continues, or the coyotes might never stop howling. This song, in combination with "Nocturnal Animals" (Banana Slug String Band, 1987a), is great for helping young children overcome their fears of the night and appreciate the beauty of the natural world after dark. Especially with children who come from neighborhoods where nighttime can be dangerous, help them understand the difference between the threats of humans and the safety of the natural environment.

The song "I'd Like to Teach the World to Sing," by William Backer (Miché, 1989), also discussed in Chapter 7, is a wonderful song of appreciation for a world "of apple

FIGURE 5–11
Music can enhance many science curriculums.

trees and honey bees and snow white turtle doves." The chorus is very singable, and for the true '60s style, you can hold hands and sway back and forth while singing. "That's the song I sing, let the world sing today, a song of peace that echoes out and never goes away." Appreciating the world we share can be a lot of fun for all of us (Figure 5–11)!

Animals' and Plants' Responses to Music

Even young children can discover the responses of the natural world to music. It is easiest to begin with animals. If you have a classroom hamster or can have a parent bring one to visit, your class can try playing different kinds of music next to its cage. With preschoolers, have a classical selection, a salsa selection, and a jazz band selection. With early elementary grades, have children suggest different kinds of music. If students wish to bring a tape or CD from home, be sure you listen to the selection before playing it for the whole class. Ask students what they think the hamster will do. You can teach the scientific method, choosing an area of research such as animal behavior, hypothesizing the experimental outcome—for example, what you think the animal will do—and then observing the results. This exercise works even with very young children. See if the hamster moves faster or slower depending on the kind of music you play. Does it dance or jump?

Try the experiment with different animals such as a turtle, goldfish, crickets, or rabbits (Figure 5–12). Do they respond differently? If you leave the music playing next to a turtle, does he move toward it or walk away? What kind of music does he seem to like the best? If you put the speakers right next to the goldfish tank, do the fish swim toward or away from the sound? Does it matter if it is loud or quiet music? Which kind of music do they seem to like better? Of course, in all these activities, the children also learn about different kinds of animals, how to observe animal movements, the basic ideas of the scientific method, and listening and observing skills. At the same time, they focus on listening to the music.

Another **musical experiment** to consider is the effect of the music on the children, since humans are animals. With preschoolers, play different selections of music and ask how each selection makes them feel. Ask them to imitate animal movements; for example, say, "How would a kitty eat when it hears this music?" A more fanciful approach is to ask children to act like different animals in response to each musical piece. Say, "What

JEFF MORAN

a.k.a. Dr. Chordate, Collector of Science Songs for Children

Jeff Moran's early childhood experiences were pretty ordinary. He idly sang at home, in children's choir, and during the minimal music instruction provided in elementary school in the '50s. Later, he played trumpet in the junior high and high school band, which was quite demanding, because the band was always winning awards. He continued singing in school and church choirs. His real musical training began when he was a graduate student in zoology. Other graduate students in his department included people who had played guitar with Gordon Lightfoot; Peter, Paul, and Mary; the Eagles; and Exile. Several students paid their way through graduate school playing music in local bars. Moran learned a lot from them, as well as from his childhood best friend, who is now a professional musician.

Moran's son was born in 1984, and he was then compelled to learn some children's songs. He performed in some capacity most of his life, but more as an actor than as a singer. He started collecting science songs when his son was young and he has been singing original songs since 1992.

Moran learns science songs and likes a wide range of musical genres. He confesses that lyrics are more important to him than the music, but he understands that they are impossible to entirely separate. For Moran, a great song is a good story with humor and melody.

Moran does not consciously write *for children* most of the time. In fact, he thinks it is easier to get parents to take their kids to see a children's performer if the parents think there might be something at the concert for them also. He would rate some of his songs as PG, and thus inappropriate for the youngest audiences.

Says Moran, "Musical intelligence is one of Howard Gardner's eight intelligences. Some people learn better via music than any other way. Teachers need to have music as a tool to use in academic classes."

FIGURE 5–12 Children learn about animal responses by watching rabbits' behavior as different styles of music are played.

would a squirrel do when it hears this music?" In talking with children about science, use sophisticated vocabulary but follow it up immediately with a phrase or sentence that defines the word. For example, say, "How do animals respond, that is how do they act, when they hear the music?" As an early childhood educator, you'll begin speaking like this to your adult friends, defining every complex word for them. It's an occupational hazard.

The World of Sound and Music

The world around us creates music. Sometimes it is the chirping of birds, sometimes the rushing of cars, and often, the humming of machines. This world of background noise is often ignored by adults because we have learned how to hear selectively. However, young children are still learning what to tune in and out. You can help them learn how to screen out some sounds while learning to hear and identify specific sounds by teaching them how to focus on a particular sound. Help them do this by choosing a rhythmic sound that you are hearing in the environment and then moving your hands in time to the rhythm. You might hear someone sawing, or you might have one of your assistants bang softly and rhythmically in the next room. This method helps children learn not only to focus on a single soft sound but also to move in time to the rhythm.

You may be interested in taking your class on a field trip to listen in a natural setting. Let children know before the trip what sounds to expect. You can play a professionally recorded tape of nature sounds such as bird calls of your area, or you can create your own. See the next section of this chapter for hints on how to make your own recordings. With young children it is not particularly effective to describe sounds before they have heard them. That is because they are still developing their vocabulary and cannot figure out what you mean when you use words alone. Play the recorded sound and then show a picture of the animal that makes it from a natural history guide book. Do not attempt too many sounds. Three to five distinctive sounds will do. Have children try to imitate the sound after they hear it. You cannot expect them to actually reproduce the sound, but it is good for children to learn imitation at this age. Then you can add words that describe the sound and have the children also make up descriptive words. If this is the first year for your field trip and you cannot find a good set of sounds already recorded, try recording sounds for next year's group on this trip.

Listening to and Recording Nature Sounds

The process of listening to nature can be enhanced by experiencing pre-recorded nature sounds and also by letting young children record nature sounds themselves (Figure 5–13). Recorded nature sounds can be found in natural science catalogues or purchased at natural history museum stores. The birdcall recordings that have a number of bird sounds with the names and sometimes pictures of the birds are particularly helpful. These recordings are wonderful for listening to different sounds and trying to find them in nature. Another kind of nature recording is one with both music and natural sounds that are meant to be a relaxation for adults, but are also great as background music for a busy classroom. Some teachers put on a recording like this, and as the noise level in the room goes up, they walk around the room saying, "Can you hear the ocean?"

When you want to record nature sounds, focus on the sound you want. Use a sound dish with a microphone at the bottom to help cut out the background noise in an outdoor environment. Also, use a directional microphone and a tape deck with Dolby enhancement to help reduce the tape hiss noise because natural sounds are soft and difficult to distinguish from each other. You can make your own sound dish using a piece of

FIGURE 5–13 Recordings of nature sounds can be soothing to children.

cardboard, five feet long by two feet wide. Form it into a funnel with a microphone at the base. If you want even better sound, varnish the inside of the cardboard funnel. You might have to buy a good microphone for 20 to 30 dollars to get reasonable quality, but you could use it for other musical recording activities in the classroom.

The Science of Musical Sound

Musical sound has a science of its own. Though this science is not related to natural science, young children can learn about musical sound and how instruments produce it. In the movie *Fantasia* (Walt Disney Studios, 1953), children can see the oscilloscope patterns that different kinds of instruments make when producing their sounds. The patterns are given different colors to distinguish them even further. Parents can bring in instruments to show children how they are played and how each instrument makes its sound. Even beginning instrumentalists like the sixth graders can bring instruments to a kindergarten class to show children how their instruments make sound. Books like *Music* (Ardley, 1989) with beautiful pictures of ancient, classical, and modern instruments can help children see the relationship between sound and how it is produced. Books for both adults and children about musical instruments can be found at a public library. Check your local library for assistance in learning about the science of sound.

Conclusion

Science and music are often considered to be different curriculums. However, the combination of science concepts with rhyming words and catchy tunes can help children remember both concepts and their applications to nature. Not only is a child absorbing and retaining science information, the added benefit of musical development occurs simultaneously. A child is learning at many levels and in many ways. Science concepts, musical reinforcement, language learning, and nature appreciation can all be taught in the time it takes to sing one song.

KEY TERMS

decomposers	musical experiment	plant processes
environment	nature appreciation	pollution
evening activity	niche	recycling
factual songs	nocturnal animals	rodent
fanciful songs	plant parts	science concepts

DISCUSSION QUESTIONS

1. What are the elements of a successful science song?
2. What science music would be appropriate for infants, preschoolers, and elementary age children?
3. How can you incorporate a song into a science lesson?
4. What is accomplished when a song is appropriately incorporated into the curriculum?
5. How can you combine musical experiments and science learning?
6. Name six science concepts and an appropriate science song to illustrate each concept.
7. Name four musicians who specialize in science and nature music.

SUGGESTED LEARNING ACTIVITY

Design a five lesson plan unit of half hour science/music classes for your target age group. Choose an overarching unit theme and a main science concept for each half hour lesson. Include a science activity and a music activity, which can occur consecutively or concurrently, for each lesson. Provide a schedule for how to use the time in each lesson, and list the songs you will use by title, writer, recording artist, and album.

REFERENCES

Ardley, N. (1989). *Music* (Eyewitness Series). New York: Knopf.

Arnold, L. (1986). *Make believe* [cassette]. Santa Cruz, CA: Ariel Records.

Axlerod, J. (1980). *Turtles and snakes and snowstorms* [record]. Washington, DC: Smithsonian/Folkways.

Banana Slug String Band. (1987a). *Dirt made my lunch* [CD]. Santa Cruz, CA: Author.

Banana Slug String Band. (1987b). *Singing in our garden* [cassette]. Santa Cruz, CA: Author.

Banana Slug String Band. (1989). *Adventures on the air cycle* [cassette]. Redway, CA: Music for Little People.

Banana Slug String Band. (1991). *Slugs at sea* [CD]. Santa Cruz, CA: Author.

Banana Slug String Band. (1996). *Penguin parade* [cassette]. Redway, CA: Music for Little People.

Brennan, B. (1982). *Billy B. sings tree songs* [cassette]. Takoma Park, MD: D. O. Dreams Music.

Brennan, B. (1984). *Romp in the swamp* [cassette]. Takoma Park, MD: D. O. Dreams Music.

Bungie Jumping Cows. (1994). *Rockin' the foundations of science* [cassette]. Oakland, CA: C. U. D. Productions.

Cherry, L. (1992). *A river ran wild.* San Diego: Harcourt Brace Jovanovich.

Dreifus, G. (1987). *Yosemite by song* [cassette]. El Portal, CA: GLO Productions.

Dreifus, G. (1996). *National parks by song* [cassette]. El Portal, CA: GLO Productions.

The Earth Works Group. (1990). *50 simple things kids can do to save the earth.* Kansas City, MO: Andrews and McMeel.

Forest, C., & Schimmel, N. (1990). *All in this together* [cassette]. Berkeley, CA: Sister's Choice.

Gailmor, J. (1983). *Dirt!* [cassette]. Ferrisburg, VT: Philo Records.

Hunter, T. (1985). *Windows* [cassette]. Bellingham, WA: The Song Growing Company.

Lehrer, T. (1965). *The remains of Tom Lehrer* [CD]. Los Angeles: Rhino.

Madsen, G. (1999). *Old Mr. Mackle Hackle* [CD]. Berkeley, CA: G-spot.

Mallet, D. (1997). *Parallel lives* [cassette]. Cambridge, MA: Flying Fish Records.

McCutcheon, J. (1983). *Howjadoo* [cassette]. Cambridge, MA: Rounder Records.

McKuen, R. (1994). *Carnegie Hall* [CD]. Los Angeles: Delta.

Miché, M. (1987). *Earthy tunes* [cassette]. Berkeley, CA: Song Trek Music.

Miché, M. (1988). *Animal crackers* [cassette and CD]. Berkeley, CA: Song Trek Music.

Miché, M. (1989). *Peace it together* [cassette and CD]. Berkeley, CA: Song Trek Music.

Miché, M. (1990). *Nature nuts* [cassette]. Berkeley, CA: Song Trek Music.

Raffi. (1984). *More songs for young children* [cassette]. Vancouver, BC, Canada: Troubadour Records.

Reynolds, M. (1972). *Funny bugs, giggleworms, and other good friends* [cassette]. Vida, OR: Pacific Cascade.

Tickle Tune Typhoon. (1984). *Circle around* [cassette]. Redway, CA: Music for Little People.

Tickle Tune Typhoon. (1985). *Hug the earth* [cassette]. Redway, CA: Music for Little People.

Timberlake, J. (1987). *Nine green fingers and forty-seven toes* [cassette]. Oakland, CA: Author.

Walt Disney Studios. (1953). *Fantasia* [Film]. Hollywood, CA: MGM Studios.

Wood, D. (1992). *Old turtle* [cassette and book]. Duluth, MN: Pfeifer-Hamilton.

Music and Language

This chapter suggests possible ways that music can enhance language skills. Teachers already know that learning songs can help children use correct pronunciation. A lesser known fact is that music can also teach vocabulary and the synthesis of language. Children often sing songs with vocabulary they can *almost* pronounce, even though they may not understand the meaning of the words. In fact, songs can be one of the best vehicles for vocabulary development and language acquisition.

Language Acquisition and Music

Researchers have long suspected that music learning and language learning are closely connected. This connection can be seen most clearly through the development of early **language skills** with infants. In the first few months of an infant's life, adults interact with him differently than they interact with other adults. Usually, adults look directly at an infant and say things like, "coochy coochy coo," or "Hi there, sweetie." These short phrases are often repeated in high, singsong voices. The name for this kind of talk in infant research is **infant directed speech**. In addition, most adults sing lullabies to children. Lullabies are similar across all cultures; it is possible to identify a lullaby in any language, even if you do not speak the language. Lullabies are very much like infant directed speech, with simple pitch contours, repeating rhythms, and elongated vowel sounds (Trehub, Bull, & Thorpe, 1984).

Music learning and language learning have the same process until a child's third year. Most children master the basics of their native languages by age four. Many children have an adult **vocabulary** by age ten. Why do some children master language but not singing? Singing takes a longer time to develop than the basics of language. If you compare basic language to basic singing at age four, singing is less developed, while language is functional (Figure 6–1). The development of singing continues until about age nine. The growing trend in the United States is to sing in school with children only until kindergarten, age five or six. The critical point at which children learn how to sing is the point at which most classrooms stop singing with young children.

This critical point, kindergarten, is also the one at which schools should be introducing **foreign language learning**. In countries like Switzerland, children normally learn to speak three to four foreign languages. By the time they are eighteen, most Swiss teens speak French, English, German, and perhaps Italian or Rumansch (a Swiss language) as well. The Swiss have paid attention to research that shows the critical time for learning foreign languages as ages five to twelve. This is also the critical time for learning to sing and to play instruments.

FIGURE 6–1 *Singing on pitch takes years to master.*

Developing Foreign Language Skills

Although the United States has practically no public school foreign language education in preschool or elementary school you can still give your students some foreign language exposure. If children can learn to both hear and make the sounds of a foreign language when they are under twelve, they can later learn to speak the language with moderately decent **pronunciation**. For example, six-year-olds who spend time listening to Spanish songs can learn to sing those songs with a better accent. Even if children do not know what the songs mean, they still develop the ability to make the sounds. At a later age, a child may wish to learn to speak that foreign language.

If the ability to pronounce sounds has been learned before the age of twelve, a child can learn to speak the language in adulthood and to pronounce it relatively well. This is because language sounds are differentiated at an early age in the brain. In a young child who learns to speak English, the sounds of the letters *P* and *B* are placed in separate and distinct locations in the brain. For speakers of some other languages, the **discrimination** between those two letters is not crucial; therefore, those sounds are placed in one location of the brain. If a person whose language does not differentiate those sounds later learns to speak English, it is difficult to separate the sounds *P* and *B*. Similar distinctions are true for English speakers of other languages. In order to speak German or French, the brain must be able to differentiate the sounds of the vowels in "König" and "München." This difference does not occur in English. However, if a child learned to hear and replicate these sounds before age twelve, the brain placed the sounds in separate locations. This is why an adult can later draw on the foreign language pronunciation learned in childhood. Teach your students a few foreign language songs so that they will have the capability of making a variety of sounds when they want to learn to speak another language.

An excellent song that can be sung in more than one foreign language is "Tous ce que je veux." The song is by Charlotte Diamond and is available in French, Spanish, and English on her albums *Qu'il y toujours le soleil* (1988b), *Soy una pizza* (1994), and *10 Carrot Diamond* (1985). The French version can be used to incorporate all three languages. During the first verse, instead of singing in French, you can sing the chorus in English, "All I really want is peace in the world, in my heart, and in my family." During the instrumental section of the song, you can sing the chorus in Spanish, "Todo lo que quiero es paz en el mundo, en mi corazón, y en mi familia." You can include sign language with the song to add a fourth language.

Learning Foreign Languages through Songs

When you teach foreign languages and music simultaneously, choose an artist who has good recordings that appeal musically to children. A recording that has slow, poor quality music where the children cannot understand the words is difficult to use for teaching foreign languages. Then children are not motivated to sing by either the music *or* the words. When children reach six years old, they understand the words to songs. This understanding becomes part of the appeal of the song for them. If the song is in another language, the children do not understand the words, so the appeal of the song must be almost entirely musical. A catchy tune and great music make the children want to sing the song, even though they do not understand the words.

An exception is songs that are bilingual in nature. **Bilingual songs** combine two languages. A true bilingual song begins in one language and then repeats the same words in another language. If the song is mostly in one language and adds a few words from another language, it is a multicultural appreciation song, rather than a true bilingual song.

Charlotte Diamond
Trilingual Singer

Charlotte Diamond began working with music in her French classes when she was a high school teacher near Vancouver, Canada. She discovered that songs are a wonderful way to teach new vocabulary as well as the pronunciation and flow of the language. Soon, she had a group of teenagers meeting in her classroom at noon wanting to sing not only French songs but music from around the world. From this group, she formed her first chorus and within a few years, she had expanded to teaching choir and guitar. This occupation expanded even further when she became the choral director for major musicals such as *Oliver!* (Bart, 1962) and *Fiddler on the Roof* (Bock, 1964). As she says, "I had been bitten by the musical bug!"

When Diamond took time away from teaching to raise her two boys, she began writing songs for them and performing with local folk musicians. She also taught music to children and parents at the local parent participation preschool that her children attended. In 1985, Diamond took a major risk. She withdrew her teacher's pension and invested in her first recording for children, *10 Carrot Diamond* (1985). She formed the Hug Bug Band, who have stayed with her to produce ten recordings and three videos. When *10 Carrot Diamond* won three awards, it launched her career in both Canada and the United States. In her words, "I feel extremely lucky and grateful to have achieved success with my first recording. It is still my best seller."

She said, "It takes many years to prepare one's first album. All of my teaching experience and my experience as a parent aided me in the creation of songs, researching appropriate material by other writers and marketing my work." It also requires organization and dedication to detail.

The success of a song often depends on the care taken in recording and production, and Diamond loves recording! She always uses musicians rather than relying on synthesized instruments. She creates a magical world of sound with talented musicians and cooperative creativity. Once the songs are recorded, she loves performing the new material and seeing the audience react. Diamond enjoys taking children and their families into the world of imagination. The songs are the vehicle and she is the guide, but the audience is definitely involved. She is happiest when everyone is singing along, like one big choir.

Diamond enjoys touring and exploring new areas. While she is on the road, she gives workshops that encourage teachers to become involved in music and tap into their own creativity. She said, "I hope that my work inspires others to have fun with music and the arts." Diamond had the opportunity to perform with Pete Seeger in Vancouver in 1982 in a large theater. Every seat was filled, and his magic with an audience inspired her to follow her musical path.

Diamond told a great story about performing with a symphony orchestra, singing "You Never Praise Me Enough" (1986), when backstage someone accidentally bumped a lever that made the orchestra pit on which she was standing slowly descend.

Luckily, I was the only one standing on the pit. The spotlight was in my eyes so I was oblivious to the fact that I was disappearing out of sight from the audience point of view. There was a slight murmur in the audience which made me suspicious. So I turned to look behind me and the conductor was 10 feet above me with a panicked look on his face. The cello section was dangerously close to the edge. I just kept singing. What could I do? Slowly the pit rose again and by the final note I was back in place as if nothing had happened. "Well . . . beam me up, Scotty!" was all that I could think of to say. When I was signing autographs after the concert, one parent said, "I just loved the way you acknowledged the orchestra by disappearing." Quite an experience! I still chuckle when I think of it and feel a bit nervous every time I come to that song in my program.

continued

CHARLOTTE DIAMOND *continued*

Diamond enjoys singing all her songs and is constantly varying her program. She enjoys songs with a Latin American beat and has recorded several songs and one album in Spanish. For her, a great song is one that "moves people emotionally, makes people think, and becomes part of their lives." Diamond says songs also give people great little phrases that make life easier, such as "Four Hugs a Day" (1985), "Love Me For Who I Am" (1985), and "I Wanna Be a Dog" (1985). The inspiration of teachers and parents keeps her going. Her boys were also a great source of ideas as they grew. Matt helped her write "Slimy, the Slug" (1988a), and Thomas inspired "Dicky Dinosaur" (1988a).

Music is a wonderful escape for Diamond. If she were not a performer or teacher, she would still be a singer and guitarist. She sings and whistles around the house, and says, "There is always music running through my brain!" Her favorite music styles are classical and world folk and she cannot resist musical theater.

Charlotte Diamond meets the challenge of providing catchy tunes and great musical accompaniment for foreign language songs (Figure 6–2). *10 Carrot Diamond* (1985) has the double language appeal. Her recordings in French and Spanish are also excellent because of the jazzy sound of her music.

A favorite bilingual song from Diamond's album *Soy una pizza* (1994) is the song of the same name, sung in both Spanish and English. It can be used at lunch time, especially on days when the cafeteria is serving pizza. It tells the story of a pizza, with lots of special toppings, which is dropped on the ground. At the end of the song, the singer and children sign in Spanish, "Qué lástima" (What a shame).

Repetitive songs are best when you first teach songs entirely in a foreign language. You can teach a song that has only one line that repeats often in the song, such as the song mentioned previously, "Tous ce que je veux" (Diamond, 1986, 1988b, 1994) or it could be a zipper song. A song like "Vamos a cantar" by José Luis Orozco, from his first album *Lírica infantil* (Volume 1) (1986), is a good example of a zipper song in Spanish. This song,

FIGURE 6–2
Children enjoy learning foreign language songs.

FIGURE 6–3 Acting out foreign language words helps children understand their meanings.

entirely in Spanish, brings up the question of translation for teachers. Young children are happy to sing songs in Spanish without knowing what the words mean. It is the teachers who bring up the issue of translation. Certainly, a translation is helpful, but the purpose of singing the song is to experience the other language. As much as you can, act out the meaning of the words so the children can understand the song without having to translate every word (Figure 6–3).

Some teachers of elementary school children want the translation and the words written out for their students. This reading of the song in Spanish while singing is only helpful if the children are expected to be bilingual in their reading. It is difficult for first graders who are learning to read English, who have no working knowledge of Spanish, to read the Spanish while singing. It is even more difficult for children to read French while singing because the spelling of this language is not very phonetic. Chinese is nearly impossible to do with written language for non-Chinese speakers. Recognize that this is an issue of the adult learner, who relies on the printed word to give foreign language clues. It is not in the best interests of the children to teach them how to read another language unless they already speak that language. It is especially difficult for children to learn to read a foreign language during the early elementary years, the critical time for learning to read English.

One important aspect of foreign language music education is a native speaker singing in his native language. It is better for children to hear a native speaker so that they will hear the sounds of the language sung correctly and learn how to make them. For Spanish, José Luis Orozco's music is perfect. While his early volumes of songs in Spanish have a beautiful, simple, guitar accompaniment, children often prefer the later volumes with more instrumentation (Figure 6–4). His is also the most comprehensive and accessible collection of songs in Spanish available in the United States.

One of the best songs by José Luis Orozco is "Las hormiguitas," the first song on *Lírica infantil* (Volume 2) (1986). This song has the added attraction of the silly sounds, created by the speeding up of the machine, so the little ants sound a lot like chipmunks. This song is also slow enough that non-Spanish-speaking children can hear the words.

FIGURE 6–4 Instrumentation enhances participation with foreign language songs.

Another excellent choice is "Los elefantes" (Orozco, 1986) which is a wonderfully repetitive song about balancing elephants. This song includes counting in Spanish and all the advantages of repetitious words. With a clear voice and distinct pronunciation, this song is slow enough for the children to easily understand.

Though Charlotte Diamond is not a native Spanish speaker, her accent is good, and her albums have excellent instrumental accompaniment. Therefore, her songs in Spanish are a top choice for use in the classroom. One favorite of teachers is "Somos como las

Meet the Artist

José Luis Orozco
Children's Musician, Latin American and Mexican Spanish Language Songs

José Luis Orozco started singing in the Mexico City boys choir. As a child he sang in many languages: English, Spanish, Italian, and Latin. Forty-four years later, he is still performing. Orozco makes albums of Latin American songs for children in Spanish. You can hear in his voice the wonderful training he had in the boys choir. On his early albums, he sang Latin American songs in Spanish accompanied only by guitar. He added more instrumentation on subsequent albums.

Orozco enjoys his work the most when everyone is singing along. He has too many favorite songs to count. That is probably why he has recorded so many songs and albums. He likes to listen to all kinds of music, and he involves children in music through language, culture, history, and movement. Over the years, the appreciation of children, parents, and teachers has kept him going.

Orozco has been a teacher for over 28 years. He has a master's degree in multicultural education and feels that "music is magic, it brings people together." He has traveled to over 30 countries and performed for children in schools in the United States and Latin America.

Meet the Artist

Nancy Raven
Children's Musician, Multicultural Music

Nancy Raven began singing with her own kids during the folk music revival. She had wonderful mentors: Pete Seeger, Charity Bailey, Sam Hinton, Ella Jenkins, and Burl Ives. In the early 1950s, when her children were in a cooperative nursery school, she started teaching singing and musical games to all the children in the preschool. Raven began her professional career when someone saw her singing with the co-op kids and wanted to record her. She has never stopped since then.

Raven gets wonderful collections of letters and drawings from classrooms. She has about 500 favorite songs that she sings. "Great songs have singability, rhythm, and content," says Raven. "Music feeds me in ways that nothing else can."

Children were her first audience, and she loves what they give back to her. Raven gets children involved in her music by first teaching them to sing a word here or there, then gradually teaching them to sing more, until finally they are playing on the stage. Usually, an older child comes up first to play an instrument. Then a younger sibling follows, barely able to walk, grabs an instrument, and steals the show.

flores" (1994). It has a reggae beat and a great message, "Somos como las flores, en el jardín de la vida." (We are like flowers in the garden of life.) "Qué buena suerte" (1994) shares the message, "I have a happy face, shoes on my feet, what great luck, I don't need anything else." Both songs have been recorded by Diamond in English, so children can learn the songs in both languages.

Another artist whose work reflects language learning and multicultural awareness at the same time is Nancy Raven. She has recorded a wonderful rendition of "De colores" (1989). Raven's version is slow enough that children can sing along easily, with a clear vocal line that makes it easy to hear the pronunciation. Raven also features awareness of other cultures and styles in her songs.

Learning English Language Skills through Music

In the United States today, many teachers have students in their classes whose first language is not English. For these children, learning to speak English is a high priority. It is as important as learning to read, since reading also requires learning vocabulary and pronunciation. Preschool children learn to speak a foreign language through experience, not through reading, the way most adults learn a second language. Surrounding these children with English speakers is a high priority. Having printed material in English is helpful, but hearing and imitating the sound of English is the most necessary skill (Figure 6–5). Music is one of the best ways for children to hear and imitate English.

With elementary school children, adding the printed word can be very helpful in teaching English language skills. This is because children can recognize letters and are learning to read. For bilingual children, reading in both English and Spanish is a great asset to language development in both languages.

How can teachers provide language learning opportunities that give children experience in a new language? Children can learn a second language through a variety of experiential tasks, one of which is listening to and singing music.

FIGURE 6–5 Children learn best from hearing a native speaker pronounce the words.

Learning Consonant Sounds

One early language task that preschoolers must practice is the sound of the **initial consonant** of a word. Listen to a three-year-old speak, and you will notice that on larger words, he often misunderstands the initial consonant sound (Figure 6–6). For example, a child will say "uh-structive" instead of "*de*structive." He has heard and uses the word but

FIGURE 6–6 Toddlers learn initial consonants when adults add emphasis to them.

Tom Hunter
Minstrel, Consultant

Tom Hunter remembers singing with his family all the time. They sang before meals, in the car, and on backpacking trips. His father wrote funny parodies of simple songs: thank you songs, birthday songs, and general purpose songs. His family also played music. Hunter played clarinet, some piano, and occasional bassoon in high school. In college, he sang with the glee club, and taught himself guitar so he could carry one around to accompany his voice.

Hunter wrote his first children's songs in 1973 and later started writing both adult and children's songs, but the ones for children were usually better. He continued writing children's music rather than adult music " 'cause I happened to write good songs for kids." He became increasingly interested in listening to kids' ideas so that he could write songs that were interesting to them. In 1974 and 1975, he started performing in classrooms.

Hunter's favorite part of his work is listening to children's feelings as well as their words and their responses, not just to the song but to the sharing of their experiences. His favorite story is about a first grade class with which he made a list of 32 topics they wanted in songs. During recess, as he was looking at the list, a boy came in and sat down, remained quiet for a long time, and then said, "Can we really write about all those things?" Hunter replied, "Yes, if we had enough time." To which the child replied thoughtfully, "We gotta lotta work to do."

Hunter's mission is to show teachers the interactive uses of songs: allowing interruptions, having children share their experiences, and using teachable moments. He does many workshops with teachers to show them how to use songs, and he teaches families to sing more songs together. He particularly likes to hear from teachers and students about what they do with the songs he taught them.

Hunter keeps making music because "I can't help it. It's too compelling, it's too fun." He feels that singing is an entrance into sharing feelings. It touches the part of people that wants to change the world to a more loving place and to help those who feel voiceless to find a voice. Hunter believes that songs are a powerful tool for bringing peace and justice. He said,

> Peace and justice are adult notions, not necessarily the interests of the children. We need to listen more carefully to what children are saying, what their concerns are. In fact, it is an issue of peace and justice that we do listen to them. Peace and justice are accomplished by listening to the unempowered, and children are part of that group.

Reprinted with permission from Tom Hunter, Minstrel, Consultant.

---

has missed the initial consonant sound. Even on shorter words, three-year-olds often have trouble pronouncing certain sounds, so the word "star" comes out "tar." This learning of the initial sound is important for later reading skills, since many children read by using them. Therefore, preschool teachers should emphasize initial consonant sounds. You can do this easily with many simple songs the children already know. Just add emphasis on the initial consonants of important words. For example, you can emphasize the *T* in "Twinkle, Twinkle Little Star" (Collins, 1990). For *M* you can sing "Mary Wore Her Red Dress" (Seeger, 1990). You may want to try more sophisticated songs with five- and six-year-olds. "Mooey Mooey Ma" (Miché, 2001) is included on the CD that accompanies this book and is an example of a song that is excellent for consonant practice with both preschoolers and elementary school students. It uses a zipper song approach but substitutes a new consonant in the beginning of each word rather than

Bob McGrath
Children's Musician, Introducing Children to the Instruments

Bob McGrath began singing when he was six years old. His mother inherited the family upright piano, and on the day it arrived, she began playing for him. She found out that he could carry a tune when he sang a song for his father that night and he has been singing ever since.

McGrath has been a performer for 60 years and keeps going because he loves the involvement, not only with the arts, but with music and with children. He was one of the original hosts of *Sesame Street* ®, and he still sings mainly for and with children. He enjoys the creative process of producing and performing in live concerts, as well as producing and recording albums.

McGrath always includes children dancing and singing in his shows and uses live musicians onstage because he feels children in the audience should be exposed to real performers. It means extra work and extra rehearsals, but the rewards are great for the children both on and off stage. He has had the opportunity of working with choreographers and choral directors from schools all over the United States and Canada. He sends them audio and videotapes of the music and is always amazed at their ingenuity and creativity.

McGrath has some wonderful stories about children. Once, he was given a handful of pennies during a Christmas show with the Vancouver Orchestra by a little boy who came up onto the stage. After the show, the same little boy approached and said that he was the one who gave him the pennies. When McGrath asked him why, he said, "Well, Bob, I just didn't have time to buy you a Christmas present." Young children actually think that McGrath knows them and sees them on their television sets. He once received a letter from a child that said, "Dear Bob, we sold the kittens."

McGrath has many favorite songs. From his student days at the Manhattan School of Music and the University of Michigan, he enjoys singing Italian arts songs and gets ready for concerts by vocalizing with these songs. When he was young, he sang "Danny Boy" (Reeves, 1996) and "Mother Machree" (McDermott, 1999) at home. When he was a tenor on the Mitch Miller Show, he loved singing "I'll Take You Home Again, Kathleen" (Miller, 1992).

Because of his exposure on *Sesame Street* ®, McGrath was invited to perform live concerts for children. His first symphony concert was with the Minnesota Orchestra as part of their children's series. At that point, he had to make a decision to pay for the cost of having a one hour children's show arranged and scored for orchestra. It was a big challenge, creatively and financially, but having now performed with over 100 orchestras, it turned out to be a good decision. McGrath's symphony shows include his own introduction to the instruments of the orchestra. He works hard to create original concepts that make the classical repertoire accessible and fun for children. He also works with large and small bands in many other venues.

McGrath is serious about his fun and believes that children should attend arts events because of the cuts in such programs in schools. "I feel that the arts are a very strong part of what life should be. You hope it leaves some kind of impression on kids. You never know when it will light a spark." McGrath feels that music is the ideal form of communicating and the perfect way to express feelings.

Reprinted with permission from Bob McGrath, Bob McGrath Productions, Inc.

substituting whole words into the song. A number of consonants are used, but you may wish to do additional consonants not recorded in the song.

Learning the Sounds of Vowels

In kindergarten, children learn the sounds of the consonants. Most children are unaware that there are vowels in English until first grade. A wonderful song for teaching **vowel sounds** is "Apples and Bananas" (Raffi, 2000; Miché, 1985). You might already know this traditional song from other versions. The version included on the CD to accompany this textbook names the vowel sounds in order and helps children learn both the vowel names and their sounds.

Another song that focuses on vowel sounds is in Spanish and is recorded on the first album by José Luis Orozco. Its title, "Las vocales" (Orozco, 1986, Vol. 1), tells us how to sing the vowels in Spanish. This is an excellent song for either a bilingual classroom or to teach as a foreign language song.

Learning about Language Parts

Children as young as first grade begin to learn about the **parts of speech**. Nouns, verbs, pronouns, and contractions are topics that are taught in grades one to three. Children can learn information about **grammar** easily through songs. In fact, rote memory information such as the parts of speech, names of states, days of the week, months of the year, the alphabet, and multiplication tables are easily learned with music (Figure 6–7). If you have any list of items that your students should learn, they will probably learn them best if you teach them with a song. If you cannot find a song to go with a lesson, make one up (Figure 6–8).

FIGURE 6–7 Learning the alphabet is easier with music.

Katherine Dines
Children's Musician

Katherine Dines started her music career in the early '70s as an introspective, folksy singer and songwriter with horrible stage fright. She gave up music and performing altogether for five years, and after that, she began to write songs for adults in the country and pop fields. She has recorded several songs and lullabies, which have been translated into other languages. Another publisher heard the lullabies and asked Dines to write for a children's musical theater group. There she found her musical home: writing for children.

Soon, friends asked her to perform at their children's birthday parties and encouraged her to record some of her songs. With half a record under her belt, she moved from Denver to join the incredible community of songwriters in Nashville. Between 1990 and 1992, Dines worked for the Nashville Songwriter's Association International (NSAI) and became a full-time performer in 1992.

Dines once got a note from a parent who said, "Dear Katherine Dines, please stop making tapes. That's all my children want to listen to and it's driving my husband and me crazy." Another time, after she packed up at the end of a show, a woman took her by the arm and said, "I wanted to tell you that my daughter has been suffering from childhood depression and today is the first day in two-and-a-half-years that I've seen her smile." Dines explained, "It's moments like those that make everything I do truly worthwhile."

Dines involves audiences in her music by combining several techniques, including:

1. small theatrical props.
2. call and response songs.
3. sing-alongs.
4. stories and songs with lyrics that have catchy phrases and with messages that interest children.
5. homemade and unusual instruments from around the world.
6. sign language.
7. audience participation and interaction with her onstage.

Dines' joy in her work is her motivating force. Most importantly, the idea that her songs can make a difference in people's lives inspires her. She has chosen to work with children because she loves them. She feels that "Adults are too filtered. Children haven't lost the ability to play."

Reprinted with permission from Hunk-Ta-Bunk-Ta Music by Katherine Dines, http://www.hunktabunkta.com.

 ## Learning Listening Skills through Music

Listening to different languages is similar to the skill of listening to instruments and identifying their sounds (Figure 6–9). Both require complete attention. Both also promote pitch discrimination, which in turn can be correlated to the ability to sound out words for reading. Chapter 10 discusses this topic more fully. **Listening skills** are discussed here because they are part of the development of language, which, in elementary school, we refer to as language arts.

During the preschool and early elementary years, make sure your students have experience listening to and identifying different kinds of instruments. By age eight or nine, many students will choose to play musical instruments. If students connect a sound with an instrument, they are more likely to choose an instrument that sounds pleasing to them. If a child enjoys the sound of the instrument, practicing gives him an intrinsic

FIGURE 6–8 Children can be exposed to music during many activities.

reward. (*Practice Makes Perfect,* in Chapter 3, discusses intrinsic and extrinsic rewards.) Intrinsic rewards are internal to a child, so we want to foster them because they keep him practicing on his own without external praise or rewards.

Another reason to teach listening skills with instruments is to help children differentiate between timbre, or sound quality, and pitch. As you read in Chapter 2, preschool children especially need this training. The ability to hear pitch differences helps children to pronounce language as well as reproduce musical sounds.

FIGURE 6–9 Rhythm and language work together.

How do I sing with my students without ruining my voice?

You can utilize a few excellent vocal tricks that are quick and easy to learn. These tricks will save your voice during the winter months, even if you never sing.

First try to sing through your nose a bit, which gives projection to the voice and takes pressure off the vocal chords. Start with a little mouse voice. Hold your nose while singing and you will have a squeaky little voice. Then gradually sing a little louder each day. The only problem with this technique is that you will begin to have a piercing voice if you do not learn the next step.

If you do not want to sound like a buzz saw while singing through your nose, yawn a lot. This lifts the soft palate. You can locate the soft palate by putting your finger right behind your front teeth. Move your finger back along the roof of your mouth until you feel the soft roof of your mouth. That is the soft palate. The combination of lifting the soft palate and pointing the sound through the bridge of the nose makes a loud sound that is rounded off by the cave created in your mouth when you lift the soft palate.

This is the same vocal production technique that you should develop for speaking in the classroom. Try to speak more through your nose rather than using the vocal chords to produce a loud sound. Speaking in English is usually low in the vocal range, and most people do it by forcing the chords rather than passing the air through the nose.

To project sound farther, pronounce words clearly and crisply. You might have to pronounce words toward the front of your mouth. What is really hard is to hold up the soft palate and pronounce the words at the same time.

Breathing properly is another part of vocal production that provides a loud sound. Pretend you are a balloon and you are hissing out your air slowly. Put you hand on your diaphragm, right below your lungs, and feel it slowly lower. When you are out of air, quickly let go, and the air will rush in. Singing breath is nothing more than letting the air slowly out of the balloon. No hissing is necessary when singing. You need to let more air out of the balloon for higher notes.

A helpful vocal repair exercise is a yoga position called *the Lion.* For this exercise, sit down, put both hands on your knees, breathe out, open your mouth *really* wide, stick out your tongue really, *really* far and scrunch up your face. You should feel all the muscles of your face and throat tighten up. Do the scrunching for one minute and then stop and relax for one minute. You should feel a lot of blood rushing in.

If you are teaching regularly, do *the Lion* once a day. If you feel a sore throat coming on, do the position three times in a row, three times a day. To prevent a cold coming on, you can drink lots of water, take a nap, and do *the Lion* exercises. If you do get a cold, do not clear your throat. Swallow. The sound made when you clear your throat is created by the vocal chords rubbing together and is hard on them.

If you feel a gritty feeling in the back of your throat, be really careful with your voice. You can do major damage to your vocal chords if you talk loudly or sing seriously when your vocal chords are a little swollen. You can lose your voice or worse, get blisters, or nodes, on the chords.

One important habit to develop as a teacher is to try not to talk over loud noises, like a room full of loud children. Instead, clap or use a whistle.

The easiest way to learn the sounds of instruments is to use a recording made for that purpose. As mentioned in Chapter 1, an excellent example is *The Orchestra,* narrated by Peter Ustinov (1987). Other possible methods include taking students to a local concert and then visiting with the musicians afterwards so that the children can hear musicians play a few notes on each instrument. Another method is to have a group of musicians visit your school. A third option is to bring in short recordings of instruments, either playing together or alone, that you have made from your own collection of music.

Conclusion

Music and language work together. The better a child learns music, particularly a wide array of songs, the more his vocabulary and pronunciation will improve. This improved pronunciation and greater understanding of vocabulary helps him master the language. The better a child is at language, the more easily she will understand the words of the songs and sing them with enthusiasm. Educating young children this way can create a positive learning loop. Learning makes children feel more capable, and more capable children feel better about themselves and learn more easily.

KEY TERMS

bilingual songs
discrimination
foreign language learning
grammar

infant directed speech
initial consonant
language skills
listening skills

parts of speech
pronunciation
vocabulary
vowel sounds

DISCUSSION QUESTIONS

1. How are language acquisition and music learning connected?
2. Why should children sing foreign language songs?
3. At what age do most Swiss children learn foreign languages, and how many do they normally learn?
4. What is a bilingual song?
5. How is a bilingual song different from a multicultural awareness song?
6. Who is Nancy Raven and what is her contribution to music?
7. What English language skills can be taught with music?
8. How does listening to music help language development?
9. What steps can you take to preserve your voice when you teach every day?
10. What should you do if you notice you are getting a sore throat?

SUGGESTED LEARNING ACTIVITIES

Visit the Web site of one of the artists from this chapter and gather information that is not included in this book. (The Web site addresses are located in Appendix A.) Write a report on the Web sites you visit.

Do a search for songs in another language and see if you can discover any new material available for children. Write a report on the Web sites you visit and any new information that you gather.

REFERENCES

Bart, L. (1962). *Oliver!* [CD]. Toronto: Madacy.

Bock, J. (1964). *Fiddler on the roof* [CD]. Los Angeles: Capitol.

Collins, J. (1990). *Baby's bedtime* [cassette]. New York: Lightyear.

Diamond, C. (1985). *10 carrot diamond* [cassette]. Vancouver, BC, Canada: Hug Bug Records.

Diamond, C. (1986). *Diamond in the rough* [cassette]. Vancouver, BC, Canada: Hug Bug Records.

Diamond, C. (1988a). *Diamonds & dragons* [cassette]. Vancouver, BC, Canada: Hug Bug Records.

Diamond, C. (1988b). *Qu'il y ait toujours le soleil* [cassette]. Vancouver, BC, Canada: Hug Bug Records.

Diamond, C. (1994). *Soy una pizza* [cassette]. Vancouver, BC, Canada: Hug Bug Records.

McDermott, J. (1999). *Old friends* [CD]. London: EMI.

Miché, M. (1985). *Kid's stuff* [cassette]. Berkeley, CA: Song Trek Music.

Miché, M. (2001). *Easy sing alongs* [cassette]. Berkeley, CA: Song Trek Music.

Miller, M. (1992). *Favorite Irish sing-a-longs* [cassette]. New York: Columbia/Legacy.

Orozco, J. L. (1986). *Lírica infantil* (Volumes 1 & 2) [cassette]. Berkeley, CA: Arcoiris Records.

Raffi. (2000). *Raffi's box of sunshine* [CD]. Ukiah, CA: Shoreline.

Raven, N. (1989). *You Gotta Juba* [cassette]. Monterey, CA: Lizard Rock Music.

Reeves, J. (1996). *The very best of Jim Reeves* [CD]. New York: BMG/Heartland.

Seeger, P. (1990). *Song & play time* [CD]. Washington, DC: Smithsonian/Folkways.

Trehub, S. E., Bull, D., & Thorpe, L. A. (1984). Infants' perception of melodies: The role of melodic contour. *Child Development, 55,* 821–830.

Ustinov, P. (1987). *The orchestra* [cassette]. Toronto: Mark Rubin Productions.

Music and Social Learning

Music is especially well-suited to teaching children about other peoples, places, and experiences. One school program that integrates the arts into elementary social studies curriculums includes four artistic specialists in dance, drama, visual arts, and music. The regular classroom teachers suggest topic areas around which the specialists design curriculums. For example, they offer the first grade a unit on families, since that is part of their social studies curriculum. They offer fourth graders a unit on trains that the teachers requested. Each classroom teacher has three visits from each of the four arts specialists. This program is inspiring and helps both the teachers and specialists be more creative in the classroom. For example, in the unit about families, they not only talk about animal families and sing animal songs, but they also talk about instrument families and listen to the way instrument families sound. For the unit on trains, children learn some standard train songs, but they also practice train rhythms and learn about westward travel.

Teachers should think broadly about how to incorporate music creatively into their curriculums. Consider the social contexts of your students and try to touch on important issues when you choose music. Try to find songs that will bring up your target social topics. At the preschool level, consider how you can use music to open children's minds to appreciating diversity. At the elementary level, incorporate songs that will initiate discussions about conflict resolution and **self-esteem**.

Valuing Diversity

The easiest way to teach appreciation of **cultural diversity** is through music. Your class can learn songs of other cultures and words from other languages in songs. You can also listen to music of other cultures and read about the instruments of those cultures. Look at pictures of diverse musical instruments and try to find someone from another culture who plays an instrument of that culture. Perhaps she can bring that instrument to your class and play it. You can teach songs that encourage an appreciation of the differences between peoples. You can write your own songs about these differences. These ideas certainly have not exhausted the list of possibilities for teaching diversity through music, but they will give you a place to start (Figure 7–1).

FIGURE 7–1 Teaching children about other cultures helps them appreciate others.

Songs That Teach Appreciation of Our Differences

Begin by teaching your students to appreciate people who are different than themselves. This is a lesson appropriate for children as young as two. In preschool, the **differences** tend to be focused on externals: children's shoe colors, hair colors, and clothing colors. Most preschool children are so self-concerned that they tend not to notice individual differences in others. A child with Down syndrome can be fairly easily integrated into a class of three-year-olds. However, by age eight, children are keenly aware of the differences between themselves and others, and they note the behavior of a child with special needs as different. With this in mind, teachers should train children early to be kind to those whom they perceive to be different, so that by age eight they have learned to be considerate.

One favorite song for preschoolers that teaches concern for others is by Jane Timberlake called "Nine Green Fingers and Forty-Seven Toes" (1987; Miché, 1988a). The children call the song "Tiddly Tum Street." The song is about a monster who has three orange eyes, his knees on his nose, and no friends. In the song, the child is at first frightened and runs away from the monster. Then, the child notices that the monster is crying and lonely, so the child smiles and plays with the monster. They end up flying to the zoo and finding another monster for a friend. Part of the beauty of this song is that the moral is not directly stated. Instead, the song is told as a story of the wonderful fun a child can have if she is willing to play with someone different than herself.

For elementary school children, Greg Scelsa wrote a beautiful song, "The World is a Rainbow" (Greg & Steve, 1982; Miché, 1989). You can easily use sign language to illustrate the words in this song. The song compares people in the world to a rainbow of colors, "Yellow, black, and white, and brown, you see them all around" (Figure 7–2). See Chapter 9 for a description of how to do sign language with this song.

"The World is a Rainbow" is a beautifully melodic and slow song. In contrast, "Rapp Song" (1986; Miché, 1989) by Red Grammer on his album *Teaching Peace* is a jazzy and

FIGURE 7–2   The world is a rainbow.

exciting tune conveying the same kind of message. It starts with the children repeating a variety of ways to say hello in different languages. The verses are a verbal challenge to any singer.

> Now all across this big wide world,
> there are lots of boys and lots of girls,
> with different eyes and different noses,
> different hair and different clothes.
> It's a magical thing, it's a wonderful game,
> we all look different but we're all the same.

All of these wonderful words are accompanied by a reggae sound and Latin beat.

For older children is a song by Peter Alsop called "The Kids Peace Song," from his album, *Wha'd'ya Wanna Do?* (1983; Miché, 1989). This song begins with the words, "People come in different sizes, colors, shapes, and names. Though we're different on the outside, inside, I think, we're the same." It is especially considerate of feelings and ideas that we all share. It also specifically stands against wars and fighting and encourages people to "try a different way, where fighting isn't in the plan."

You can easily find more songs for teaching appreciation of differences. As you find them, make short tapes and code them, as suggested in Chapter 1. This way, you can remember which songs are a good match for different social learning units.

Singing Songs of Other Cultures

The next step in learning to appreciate differences is to help children understand that families have different holidays, celebrations, special events, and customs (Figure 7–3). Some preschools have children from Christian, Jewish, Muslim, Buddhist, and nonreligious families. In one Berkeley, California, school there were children whose families came from Turkey, Syria, Japan, China, Italy, Russia, Ireland, and countries in Africa. This may not be typical in every preschool, but teachers should still recognize the cultural differences and try to teach children as young as preschool to respect others. This can be done at the preschool level by celebrating a number of different holidays and family

FIGURE 7–3 Children learn about cultures and customs through music.

Red Grammer
Children's Musician, Teaching Teachers and Teaching Peace

Red Grammer has been writing and performing music for a long time. Before getting started in children's and family music, he performed for adults for years. Grammer and his wife, Kathy, started making up songs for their first son, David, just after he was born. Some time later his wife suggested they make a recording of them. This was in 1983, when he was performing with The Limeliters, a well-known folk group.

Two things keep Grammer going. First, the incredibly positive energy that working with children generates in his heart, and second, the knowledge that it is a profoundly good thing to uplift the hearts of children and those who work with them. Grammer does many teacher workshops, helping others to use music in their programs and showing them ideas for movement, literacy, and social and character education activities that can accompany the songs. Grammer feels he has never been particularly clever or witty, so when he gets the fan letters that say, "Red Grammer, you're the funniest man I know!", it really tickles him.

Grammer is mostly interested in songs that are both funny and touch the heart. For him, a great song is a "combination of lyrics and music that ring true." "Music is primarily about uplifting the heart and calling the human spirit to a higher place," says Grammer. He tries to reflect this calling through his work.

Reprinted with permission from Red Grammer, http://www.redgrammer.com

customs. Songs can be learned to accompany the celebrations or just played during the celebration. For example, at Chanukah, the children can learn the simple "Dreidl Song" (Various, 1994): "I have a little dreidl, I made it out of clay. And when it's dry and ready, then dreidl I will play." For the Muslim holiday Ramadan, you might ask a parent of one of your children to teach a song from her culture. For Cinco de Mayo you can play some music by José Luis Orozco, whose songs are discussed in Chapter 6.

With elementary school–age children, you can teach about other cultures by singing songs in other languages. Review Chapter 6 for the detailed discussion of songs in French and Spanish. Teachers can also add words from a variety of different languages to a single song. Tom Chapin's song "The Wonderful World of Yes" on his album *Around the World and Back Again* (1996) demonstrates how to say "yes" in a variety of different languages. It is easy to add other languages besides the ones in the song. "Rapp Song" (Grammer, 1986; Miché, 1989) is another song that lends itself to teaching various ways to say "Hello" in different languages.

Appreciating Music of Other Cultures

Music from a variety of cultures can be played for children as young as infants. Preschool teachers have a tendency to play mostly Western music. Instead, try bringing in a piece of classical music from China or India. For preschoolers and children under two years old, there are lullabies from many cultures in all different languages. In order to find titles, use the strategies presented in *A Common Question* in Chapter 1. You can post a request for suggestions of lullabies in different languages to the children's music list. The results of one such post were as follows: Try the collection of lullabies by Sara Jordan entitled *Lullabies Around the World* (2001); it includes a book of lyrics and cultural activities. The songs are in Russian, Mexican, Yiddish, Italian, Mandarin, Polish, German, Lingala (from Zaire), Japanese, French Canadian, and English. Other suggestions from the music list were: *The Planet Sleeps* from Sony Wonder Records (1997), *Global Lullabies* by Freyda Epstein (1995), and *The World Sings Goodnight* (Wasinger, 1993).

Meet the Artist

Ella Jenkins
Children's Musician, Multicultural Musician

Ella Jenkins has had music in her heart her whole life. Her early music training was informal. She listened to music at church and record shops. She and her teenage friends would make up dances and clap to the music playing in front of the record stores. The jukebox was also a great source of new music. Her Uncle Flood loved the blues, so he would play blues tunes on the jukebox. Jenkins learned to play a Marine Band harmonica at age eleven by listening to her uncle play blues. She did not have lessons, she just listened and played by ear.

In college, Jenkins started playing the drums: both conga and bongo. She had always been interested in drumming of all kinds, beginning with oatmeal boxes and coffee cans. In her early adult years, she took up the baritone ukulele. She learned a few chords from a friend but mostly taught herself, and she started playing in the minor keys. She once received a letter from Carl Orff commenting that they both played music using the pentatonic scale.

Jenkins started working with children at the YWCA as a teenager. She later sang in folk music clubs. While volunteering with some teens in the early 1950s in Chicago she was asked to do a TV commercial with them. The television producers liked her so much that they asked her to come back and do more. Pretty soon, Jenkins was doing a television program and writing call and response songs for children. Friends suggested that she record her songs. She brought a few songs to Folkways Records, which signed a contract with her for her first album in 1956. It was *Call and Response, Rhythmic Group Singing*. She has been singing with children ever since.

Jenkins said about teaching music to children:

> We who do music with children should be flexible. It's important to get the music to the children in some fashion. Use records or tapes, but don't let the tape or record determine the whole program. Use your own voice and let the children compose their own music too. However, it's also important to make music, not just noise.
>
> Start with something simple, like the many different ways to play rhythms. Have a lot of small instruments, such as cowbells, triangles, and shakers, that the child can use to make music. Have the children tap out rhythms, listen, and repeat it themselves.

Jenkins uses the traditional songs because they are basic. Sometimes she plays a tune and the children guess the tune. She said about music, "Music for me is an everyday thing. In the background I'm listening to a classical music station, but I like a variety of music: Latin music, Cuban, Puerto Rican, and jazz."

At age seventy-five, Ella Jenkins is celebrating almost fifty years in children's music.

Try to choose some music from other cultures when considering movement activities. You might use Israeli folk dance music, a Portuguese rock song, or African drums. See Chapter 9 for more movement activities to accompany music from other cultures.

Musical Instruments of Other Cultures

One hands-on way to introduce children to the appreciation of other cultures is to show them various instruments (Figure 7–4). When friends travel to other countries, ask them to bring back small musical instruments they find. When you travel, look for small musical instruments to buy in places like open markets or local general stores. Depending on where you go, you can acquire instruments like ocarinas, panpipes, guiros, wooden flutes, and pennywhistles. Bring them in one at a time to show children, and tell them about the place from which they came. Over the years, you can create your own collection.

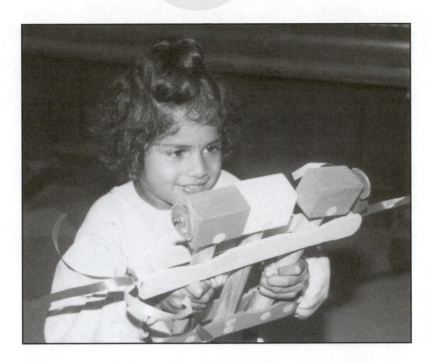

FIGURE 7–4
Children can learn culture from an Italian instrument.

A great instrument to start a collection is a gamelan. This instrument from the South Pacific has been used extensively by Orff approach teachers. It is made out of wood and hit with wooden mallets. You can easily get one from a distributor of Orff instruments on the World Wide Web. In local music stores, you can find small instruments like a kazoo or an ocarina, a clay or gourd whistle with holes in the side. You may also find a kit for an African finger piano, called mbira or kalimba. African drums are not too difficult to find in shops that specialize in African imports such as clothing or jewelry. If you visit a local Chinatown, you may find a small replica of a Chinese string instrument or wooden flute.

Finally, the Australian instrument didjeridoo is sometimes available in local retail stores. The didjeridoo even has a great song to accompany it: "What Is a Didjeridoo?" (Chapin, 1996).

Communicating Values through Song

You communicate values to students in every lesson you teach. It is easy to be unaware of the values transmitted through those lessons. What values do you want to communicate to your students? When you use songs, it is important to listen to them with an ear for their values. Sometimes you may purposely choose a song for its values (Figure 7–5). The next few songs teach the values of cooperation, peacemaking, and altruism.

The wonderful old song written by William Backer, "I'd Like to Teach the World to Sing" (Miché, 1989), was the focal point of a classic '70s Coca-Cola® commercial. Since today's children are too young to remember the advertisement, they come to the song with fresh voices. The values of cooperation and family love are beautifully expressed in its verses and chorus, "That's the song I sing, Let the world sing today, A song of peace that echoes out and never goes away."

A similar thought is expressed by Linda Arnold in her song "Find a Peaceful Thought" on her album *Make Believe* (1986; Miché, 1989). In this song, children's voices sing the chorus, "So find a peaceful thought and plant it in your heart, maybe then a

FIGURE 7–5 Music teaches children about cooperation. (Photo of Omnichord used with permission, Suzuki Corporation)

peaceful world could really start to grow." The verses give children's responses to "What is peace?" with answers like, "Peace is full of magic, peace is you and me."

Another good song for teaching values is the 1980s pop hit "We Are the World" (Jackson & Ritchie, 2001; Miché, 1989). The song was written by Michael Jackson and Lionel Ritchie and performed by a number of famous recording artists. It promotes unity: "We are the world, we are the children, we are the ones who make a brighter day, so let's start giving. There's a choice we're making, we're saving our own lives. It's true we'll make a brighter day, just you and me."

"Let There Be Peace on Earth," written by Sy Miller and Jill Jackson (Miché, 1989), is a song that touches children and adults. It encourages individual action and living together in harmony: "Let there be peace on earth and let it begin with me."

Songs and Self-Image

Some educators believe that we can teach self-image. How can you do this? A positive **self-image** is the way a person views herself when she feels competent in some areas, values those areas of competency, and is compassionate toward herself in areas of less competence. That **compassion** then extends toward others as empathy. It is possible to teach children to be compassionate toward themselves when they feel inadequate. The next two songs help children understand that all people have feelings of inadequacy and areas of less competence. It is great when children get this message.

Peter Alsop is interested in helping kids realize that "you're OK." His song "You're OK" on the album *Wha'd'ya Wanna Do?* (1983) is a great self-image builder (Figure 7–6). The chorus says, "You're OK, what do you say, no need to make a fuss, if something's wrong with you too, then you're like us." The verses feature kids who have various problems, like skinny arms, long toes, bad breath, or extra weight. Even a person who thinks she's perfect has something wrong: she thinks she's better than others.

FIGURE 7–6 Music can help build self-esteem.

Another excellent song for self-acceptance was written by Willie Welch and performed by Peter, Paul & Mary on their album *Peter, Paul & Mommy Too* (1993). The song is "Right Field," in which a child sings about how he likes to play right field in baseball because he is not a very good player and right field is an easy place to play. He sings, "Playing right field, it's easy, you know. You can be awkward. You can be slow. That's why I'm here in right field just watchin' the dandelions grow." This is a favorite song of children, who particularly like the instrumental part, where they can pretend to play baseball. It is a favorite song of teachers because it instills compassion for oneself and others.

Learning about People with Special Needs through Songs

Many teachers decide to start teaching children to be aware of people with special needs when they have a child with a disability in their class. The problem with this approach is that sometimes children can go through six years of an elementary school and never have such a classmate. In that case, children have little training in school on how to treat people with special needs. Through songs, children can at least learn a little about how to treat children with special needs.

Two versions exist of Larry Penn's song "I'm a Little Cookie." His version is on *Grandma's Patchwork Quilt* (1987), a sampler album. The second is on John McCutcheon's album *Mail Myself to You* (1988). This is an excellent song for teaching children to be sensitive to people with special needs. The inspirations for the song were a child with Down syndrome in Penn's wife's special education class and a cookie factory

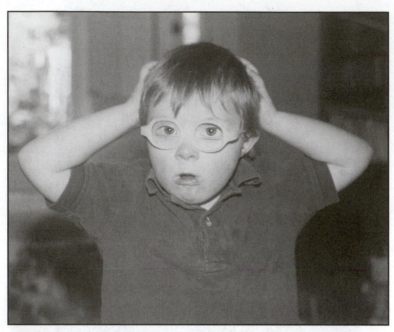

FIGURE 7–7   Songs addressing special needs help children accept their peers.

where people can buy broken cookies. He put these two ideas together and came up with the words,

> I'm a little cookie, yes I am,
> I was made by the cookie man,
> but on my way from the cookie pan,
> a little piece broke off of me.
> A little piece broke off of me, umhmm,
> a little piece broke off of me, umhmm,
> but I can taste just as good, umhmm,
> as a regular cookie can.

Another good song for this purpose is "He May Be Slow" by Tom Paxton, sung by a child on Bob Reid's album *We Are the Children* (1993). "He may be slow, but he's still in motion, he's got his own road, he's got his own hill to climb, all he needs is a little devotion, he may be slow, but he's right on time."

If you would like your children to develop a **sensitivity** toward people with visual disabilities, "Seeing with My Ears" by Tom Hunter on Bob Reid's album *Marz Barz* (1989) is a perfect song. "Seein' with my ears and seein' with my nose, seein' with my fingers and seein' with my toes, there's magic in the morning and a big surprise, all the things that I can see without my eyes."

Peter Alsop is an artist whose work is useful for addressing valuing those with differences (Figure 7–7). Peter has approached the issue of a child who has cancer in his song "Nobody Knows for Sure" (1983). In it, a child sings about a friend who may die of cancer, but nobody knows for sure. It is a sweet and poignant song, perfect for helping children understand and talk about a serious illness.

Teaching Social Information through Song

Many kinds of social information can be taught through songs (Figure 7–8). The previous sections of this chapter covered communicating values through song with emphasis on such themes as valuing cultural diversity and accepting persons with special needs. In this section we will consider ways to teach other kinds of social information through music, including:

- teaching appropriate behavior and manners in song format.
- fostering understanding of other time periods and societies through singing their songs.
- learning to say the names of other countries.
- learning the names of the 50 states and their capitals.
- teaching young children the days of the week and the months of the year.

One good song for teaching appropriate behavior is "Be Kind to Your Parents," recorded by Linda Arnold on her album *Make Believe* (1986). Children really like this song, adults think it is cute, and teachers think it gives a good message.

Another example is "Use a Word" by Red Grammer (1986; Miché, 1989), recorded on his album *Teaching Peace*. This song is best for early elementary students, but it can be used with preschoolers. "When someone makes you slip and you want to bruise their lip, Use a word!" Have the children put out their first finger and say, "Use a word" with the music. Older children will help sing the chorus, but preschoolers just yell "use a word" every time.

Songs that are good for second and third graders are "The Kindergarten Wall" by John McCutcheon on the album *Mail Myself to You* (1988) and "Pluggin' Away" by Peter Alsop (1990). The first song is about remembering the right behavior learned in kindergarten. "Of all you learned, remember this the best, Don't hurt each other and clean up your mess." The second song is about the importance of persistence. "Pluggin' away, pluggin' away, people who keep pluggin' away, they're the ones who get things done 'cause they keep pluggin' away."

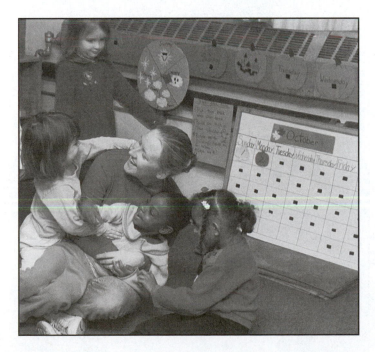

FIGURE 7–8 Children learn about social information through music.

Learning about the Events of History through Songs

Teachers and folk singers have long used music to teach information about historical events and places. Some of the events of the Bible were long remembered in song before they were written down. Some information from the medieval period only survives because it was preserved in song.

In the modern era, people still continue to write songs to remember historical events. Some are old folk songs, like "I've Been Workin' on the Railroad" (Jamboree Kids, 2000) or "Clementine" (Jamboree Kids, 2000). You can use a song like "I've Been Workin' on the Railroad" with preschoolers to talk about the kind of work people did to build trains, a topic often interesting to them. Children are not able to understand timelines until they are over seven years old, so "Clementine" is not a good song to use for teaching preschoolers about gold rush time. The tune is wonderful, but the song is better suited for teaching history to third and fourth graders. By then, they are often interested in the wild west and the gold rush, especially because third grade is the age of money awareness.

Singing the Songs of Other Eras

Teachers should try to make historical events come alive for children. For preschoolers, even the concepts of yesterday, today, and tomorrow are confusing. For them, focus on teaching relationship to the past in two basic categories: yesterday and a long time ago. You can give them experiences of a long time ago through dramatic representations, dressing up, and songs (Figure 7–9). Elementary school children need the same kind of experiences, but teachers can define the past into more specific eras because of students' more developed language skills. Second graders, for example, can understand the past in terms of yesterday, last week, last month, a few months ago, last year, when your parents

FIGURE 7–9 Drums were a primitive instrument for many cultures.

Pete Seeger
Folksinger, Song Collector, and Weaver of Music

Pete Seeger originally made music just for the fun of it. His father Charles Seeger was a musicologist and was intrigued all his life by the power of music. When the Depression came along, his father got together with a bunch of other musicians. They thought surely the proletariat would need marching songs to march to the barricades. His father decided to throw in his lot with the communists. They organized The Composers Collective, of which Aaron Copland was a member. Pete Seeger says the group's attempts to write songs for the masses was a laughable failure. Aaron Copland wrote the song "Into The Streets May 1st," but it required a piano with an expert player and had a melody that no one could quite follow.

About this time Seeger's father met with some folklorists who said, "Charlie, you know everything about European music but you don't seem to know much about American music." He had heard a little of it, but not much. There was a woman named Aunt Molly Jackson, from Kentucky, who had made up some songs during a miner's strike. Seeger's father brought her around to a meeting of The Composers Collective. They listened politely and then said, "Charlie, we're supposed to be creating the music of the future, this is the music of the past!" He took Molly back to her apartment and said, "I'm sorry. They didn't really understand you, but I know some young people that are going to be very interested in your music." His son was one of them.

As a teenager, Pete Seeger started feeling that music was more than just a lot of fun. He refused to read music, but he could strum anything they taught him in school and pop songs he heard on the radio. Aunt Molly and folklorists like his longtime mentor, Alan Lomax, made him fall in love with the five-string banjo.

Seeger and his father later put out a collection of protest songs collected by Lomax and Lomax's father, in a book called *Hard Hitting Songs For Hard-Hit People* (1999). Woody Guthrie and Pete Seeger did most of the work on it. Alan Lomax gave them several hundred songs which he'd come across. These were textile workers' songs, coal miners' songs, farmers' songs, and songs of the unemployed.

Seeger has a lot to say about music and social justice:

Makers of music have always linked up with whatever social activists were doing. Throughout history ordinary people have used music to try and survive all sorts of bad conditions.

Armies and churches and all sorts of organizations have used music for thousands of years. Plato said, "It's very dangerous for the wrong kind of music to be allowed in the Republic." There's an old Arab saying, "When the King puts the poet on his payroll, he cuts off the tongue of the poet." I think of that every time I get a job on TV.

Pete Seeger has seen a lot in his lifetime:

I've seen a bunch of strikers being given courage by union songs. We know from history that the IWW [Industrial Workers of the World] issued a little red songbook with every union card. When a bunch of Wobblies [members of the IWW] found themselves on a freight train bound for a harvest, they'd pull out a little red songbook. Everybody knew the tune. They'd shout, "To the tune of 'The Girls They Go Wild Over Me.'" That was a pop song of 1911. A Wobbly songwriter with a good sense of humor wrote a new lyric, a hilarious story of a union fellow who complains that "The cop he goes wild over me, held his club where everyone could see. The judge he goes wild over me, and the jailer goes wild over me." And then the verse, "Well the bugs they go wild over me, I'm referring to the bedbug and the flea." He has a lovely poignant verse to end, "Will the roses grow wild over me? When my soul and body part the stillness of my heart, will the roses grow wild over me?"

continued

PETE SEEGER *continued*

I've also seen how the songs have been used in the Peace Movement. During World War I, there was a song, "I don't want to march with the infantry, ride with the cavalry, shoot with the artillery. I don't want to fly over Germany, I'm in the Peace Army."

Along came the Depression and you could see that sometimes an old spiritual with slightly different changes took on great meaning. This is one of the great traditions in America. We know that church people made up hymns out of secular songs, but the reverse is even more true. "We Shall Overcome" (Seeger, 1996) was a union song before it was a civil rights song. Before that it was quite a well-known, fast gospel song. You clap your hands, "I will overcome. I will overcome. I will overcome someday." It had various versions, "If in my heart I will not yield," or, "Down in my heart I do believe." When it moved from spiritual to union song, to civil rights anthem, it slowed down. Isn't it interesting how many lives a song can have?"

Pete Seeger says:

I look upon the crises that the world faces today as one huge crisis. We will either solve or it will solve us within a few hundred years. I don't think we have another 2,000 years to learn the sermon on the mount.

It's a crisis of poverty amidst plenty. I mean there's plenty for everybody in the world, as we know, yet some people are literally starving to death. It's a crisis of ignorance amidst a glut of information. It's a crisis of various kinds of fundamentalism. My father called it the lingo-centric predicament. He said if the world fails to make it, it's because of an overdependence on words. When people around the world are firing angry words at each other, he said, use every other means of communication possible. In the arts, whether it's pictures, or dancing, or rhythms, or harmonies, or food. I used to say, "When all else fails, use strawberry shortcake!"

It's a crisis also of racism and sexism and discrimination and injustice of all sorts. We will either solve it or it will solve us. We'll put ourselves out of business. I really despair of any one organization, no matter how nobly started, doing the job that needs to be done for the world. Whether it's a church or political movement or a nation or even a United Nations. All of these have got their function, but the bigger the organization, the more it's likely to attract power hungry people, which will corrupt it in some way or another. My own suggestion is, let the little organizations proliferate till there's tens of millions of them, and there'll be such disagreements it'll be hilarious: save this, stop that. But, we will agree on a few basic things. This is it: Better to talk than shoot. Bombs always kill innocent people, whether it's in a Tokyo subway or in Oklahoma City or in Hiroshima.

I think one of the main lessons I learned from Martin Luther King was you don't expect to tackle the big problem first. Tackle a little problem first, when you succeed there, you tackle another one. I mean, who could say that riding in the front seat of a bus was the important thing? And yet it turned out to be.

After 70 years, I've been surprised. Some songs I thought would be a great success have been quite big failures, and some songs that I thought were failures surprised me by other people picking them up and showing me it's a better song than I thought. "Where Have All the Flowers Gone?" (Seeger, 1996)—I made it up in '55–'56 and sang it along with a batch of very short songs. I only sang three verses. Then I forgot about it, I had guessed it was one more unsuccessful attempt. Joe Hickman added rhythm to it and put two more verses, he now gets 20 percent of the royalties. Then Peter, Paul & Mary (1998) got hold of it, and the Kingston Trio (1995), then Marlene

continued

PETE SEEGER *continued*

Dietrich (2000) took it around the world. The German translation sings better than the English.

I've met some of the most wonderful people that anybody could want to meet. All around the world. People that are trying to stop a war here, or organize people there. A wide range of people. Of course, I've made a lot of big mistakes. One of them was I left my wife to raise three kids while I was gallivanting around the world. I have a cartoon on the wall of my office showing a harried woman with a kid pulling at her skirt, and she's on the phone, "No, he's not here. He's out trying to save oppressed people."

A high point would be singing one of the world's shorter songs, "Give Peace A Chance" (Lennon, 1998). Just nine words, "All we are saying is give peace a chance," over and over and over, for half a million people in front of Washington's Monument, November 13, 1969.

So what would I say to the young musician who is thinking about trying to save the world? Oh, you'll have a hell of a lot of fun. You won't get rich, probably, but you'll meet an awful lot of good people. The funny thing is that if you stick with it long enough, you actually do make a living. After 20 years I was able to take a vacation, and after 50 or 60 years royalties were coming in for songs that I never thought would earn a penny. I pay my taxes with royalties, so now I can afford to sing for union minimum.

Thanks to Tom Chapin, president, Sundance Music, Inc., for permission to reprint this interview with Pete Seeger.

were children, when your grandparents were young, before your grandparents, a long time ago, a long long time ago, and a very long time ago. They still have trouble differentiating 100 years ago, 2,000 years ago, or 20,000 years ago. Thus, they may think dinosaurs lived at the time of the invention of the train.

In order to give children an experience of another era, you can design a unit around an event in that period, including drama and songs. An example is to study the life and times of Dr. Martin Luther King, Jr. First you could begin by reading a picture book about Martin Luther King, Jr., to your students. One favorite is *Happy Birthday, Martin Luther King* (Marzollo, 1993). You could then teach a few songs like "We Shall Overcome," "If I Had a Hammer," "Down by the Riverside," and "A Tribute to Martin Luther King, Jr." Excellent recordings of the first three songs are available on a composite album called *Around the Campfire,* released by Peter, Paul & Mary in 1998. "A Tribute to Martin Luther King, Jr." is recorded on *Holly Daze* (Miché, 1988b). These four songs form an excellent basis for a unit on understanding the freedom movement. The first three songs were sung by the freedom groups. The last song explains what Martin Luther King, Jr., did and why his work is so important. Put these songs together with a short dramatization of Rosa Parks riding the bus that children can perform themselves, and you have an experience that children will remember into their adult years.

Songs That Teach about Geography

As mentioned earlier, children can learn rote information through songs. One great example is the song "Fifty Nifty United States" (Miché, 1985). Children as young as kindergarten are able to name off *all* 50 states in alphabetical order because of this song.

FIGURE 7–10 *Songs about geography help children learn about the world.*

In one school, fifth graders who had to learn the information for an upcoming test begged younger children to teach them the song.

Other songs also help teach about geography (Figure 7–10). On his album *Mother Earth* (1986), Tom Chapin included a song called "The Picnic of the World" in which he names 79 different countries. Even though it is too hard to sing all the names, children can sing the chorus to this song. They love listening to the verses and singing, "All the nations sitting on a blanket, having a picnic, the picnic of the world." Have elementary school–age children listen carefully to the verses and remember the names of two countries. After the song is finished, each child can say the name of a country she remembers. You can even get a globe and look for one or two of the countries in the song. After listening to the song a few times, children can remember as many as five names of countries. This song has a super message: "Knowing at the deep down heart of it, we're all a part of it, the picnic of the world." This song has an additional, hidden benefit. It is sung to a tune from a famous operetta, "Orpheus in the Underworld," by Offenbach, which is a tune you may already know as "The Can-Can."

Tom Chapin has recorded two other excellent songs about geography. One is "State Laughs" (1986), in which he sings about the different styles of laughter in each state. "In Ohio, they go ho, ho, ho. In Tennessee, they go hee, hee, hee." Once you have learned this song, you can use a large map of the United States to point out where the various states are.

The other great geography song is on Chapin's album *Around the World and Back Again* (1996) and is called "Going to Borneo." The song is about a kid and his friend who ride bicycles across the United States, take a parachute across the Pacific Ocean, and arrive in Borneo on the same day. An occasional third grader notices that they passed over the International Date Line, but the rest of the children just think it is a really fun trip. The best part of this song is tracing their journey on a globe or map from Buffalo, New York, to Borneo. Even if *children* forget, *you* will always remember the location of Borneo because of this song.

What should I do when a parent complains about a component of my music curriculum?

Sooner or later someone will complain about a song or something you have discussed with children. When this happens, keep in mind that you will work with hundreds of children over the years and only a few parents will complain. You should pay attention to the parents who give you feedback because it can be helpful. However, remember that parents are not usually aware of what is typical for a child's age group and are unfamiliar with the range of behaviors they should expect. Since you will probably work with the same age group over many years, you will have a much broader knowledge than will individual parents about children in that age range.

Here are some of the factors to keep in mind when dealing with criticism. First, consider the source. Is this a parent who has done a lot of complaining in other programs? Is the parent new to your program or school? Does the parent have one of the younger children in your program? Does the parent have a girl or boy? Does the parent have more than one child? Could she be reacting to some element of her own educational past that may have nothing to do with you?

Often, parents of the younger children in a moderately wide age range, say a four to six year span, are not yet used to the expectations for those children. Parents seem to be always catching up to the age of their children. In one outdoor school, some parents of eight-year-olds were shocked that teachers expected children to make their own sandwiches at lunchtime. This is just an example of how parents have not caught up to the changing abilities of their children. Parents of younger children are sometimes overprotective and react with a need to protect their kids from a perceived threat. Parents of girls, especially preschool girls, seem to have more concerns than parents of boys. Parents of only children usually have more complaints because they may not be familiar with the range of normal behaviors. Some parents try to be perfect, so when you present a song about a sensitive topic, such as death, illness, or vomiting, they may perceive the song as inappropriate for their children's developmental age.

No matter what the cause, parents who complain are providing you with honest feedback. If a parent complains about the violence in a song and the children are between three and five years old, you may not want to do that song with that age group. Songs like "The Cat Came Back" (Penner, 1992), in which a man tries to get rid of a cat, are better for older children and are inappropriate for preschoolers. This song is wonderful for ten-year-olds who understand satire and metaphor and know that the song is really a protest against violence to animals. Other songs, like "Throw It Out the Window" (Beall & Nipp, 1996), in which things are thrown out a second-story window, may only be perceived by parents as violent. Just as parents have a hard time keeping up with their children's social abilities, they also may not be familiar with their children's cognitive development, and they may be vigilant against any violence, no matter how innocuous. Throwing things like snakes, King Cole's pipe, Jack's crown, silver bells, and cockle shells out the window is hilariously funny to children. The song is probably not teaching them to be violent.

Sometimes all you need to resolve a complaint is to calmly listen to the concern. If you need to make a response to the parent, respond at a later time, after you have had a chance to consider your reasons for teaching a particular song. If you need to continue singing the song with children, address the parent's concern in some way. Either change the song to meet their concern, or call them back to explain why you cannot change the song. Sometimes it may be easier to drop the song from the repertoire this year and sing it when the child is no longer in your class.

continued

WHAT SHOULD I DO WHEN A PARENT COMPLAINS ABOUT A COMPONENT OF MY MUSIC CURRICULUM? *continued*

In one first-grade class, a parent's complaint was about the song "Tomorrow" by Barry Polisar (1993), who writes songs for older children. In the song, a child keeps putting off the jobs he is supposed to do until tomorrow. At the end, his grandmother promises to give him chocolate cake, but all the adults say, "Tomorrow, tomorrow, you'll get it then." The complaint about this song is an example of underestimating children's cognitive abilities. When asked, first graders all clearly understood the meaning of the message: children should not put off jobs until tomorrow. This was a case of a parent who did not know that first graders are sophisticated enough to understand the message.

In dealing with complaints, you need to decide if the complaint or the parent making the complaint needs to be taken seriously. If you are not sure, you can always consult with other teachers in your program to help you get a perspective about the appropriateness of your songs and the validity of the complaint.

Sometimes the song is not the issue; rather, the problem is a discussion you had with children about the song. For example, one song taught in the first grade mentioned throwing up, and one child said that her babysitter made herself throw up. This, of course, raised concerns about bulimia, and there was a short discussion about teenage girls who sometimes make themselves throw up and how dangerous that is. The children were interested in a problem that they or their friends could possibly face as teenagers. A parent later said that she was upset to hear that bulimia had been discussed with children so young. In this case, listening objectively is important, while recognizing that it is not possible to change the discussion you had in the past.

Should teachers talk with early elementary–age children about problems they could possibly encounter in the teenage years, such as smoking, drugs, bulimia, suicide, and gun violence? This is a serious issue. Adults disagree about how much we should discuss with young children. When you talk about serious subjects with young children, modify the vocabulary used to their developmental level, and limit discussions to what the least mature children in the group can handle.

Learning about Music History

Teaching music history can be called teaching "**music appreciation**." This is an area of music education that is often taught to college students. In a college music appreciation class, students listen to a variety of classical music and some nonclassical music from all different periods and styles. Usually, students learn about various composers and different kinds of musical styles, from symphonies to operas. Children do not need to wait until college to appreciate music (Figure 7–11). So how can you teach music appreciation to young children?

First, you need to appreciate music yourself. Even if you are a complete novice, you have probably absorbed many musical phrases and bits of history from our culture. However, even the most musically educated people have some blanks in their musical education. For example, most classically trained musicians do not have much experience with jazz or blues or how to play them. We can all learn to appreciate and develop our sensitivity to types of music that are new to us.

One way to learn is to simply listen to music. Begin with your interests and expand from there. If you like voices, try choral music. If you like violins, try symphonies. If you

FIGURE 7–11
Older children can inspire music appreciation in young children.

Tom Chapin
President, Sundance Music, Inc.; Children's Musician, Music of the World

Music was a constant in Tom Chapin's life from his earliest memory. His father was a jazz drummer; music was his job and he loved it. Chapin's mother played piano, and she really loved opera. Every Saturday afternoon the Metropolitan Opera radio broadcast could be heard wafting through the house.

When Chapin was a teenager, his oldest brother James, who sometimes called himself "the nonmusical Chapin," was a faithful listener to pop radio. Because of him, all four Chapin boys knew every song on Top 40 radio in the late '50s and early '60s.

In 1953, Chapin and his brother Steve joined the Grace Episcopal Church Choir of Boys and Men in New York City. There, they learned to sing harmony, sight-read music, and experience the discipline and delight of making music with other people.

In the summer of 1958, the Chapin boys—Tom, James, Steve, and Harry—found a Pete Seeger record, *The Weavers at Carnegie Hall* (The Weavers, 1956) that inspired the rest of their musical lives. They listened to it all summer, and the end of the summer, Harry said, "We could do that!" And so they did. Harry got a five-string banjo and the Pete Seeger book, and he began to play. Tom scraped together $25 for his first guitar, and, with Steve on bass, they became "The Chapin Brothers." Harry later went solo and became the famous Harry Chapin.

Flash forward 35 years. Tom is now a professional musician who makes a living doing what he loves. He is a writer and singer of songs for old and young people. He still travels the road that the Weavers record introduced him to so long ago.

Chapin was an adult performer until 1988, when his daughters were eight and six years old. Then he started writing songs for kids. His girls had outgrown the Raffi songs, and he could not find music for older kids. He teamed up with John Forster and Michael Mark to create some new songs for elementary school–age children. This group of trained musicians–turned–fathers played around with ideas for kids' songs, and they had a great time together.

Chapin likes folk music. He said that it is not a "watch me do this" kind of style; rather, it gathers people together to become a community event. Children occasionally approach him, amazed that he knows all the Tom Chapin songs. One child said to his mom, "I thought he lived in our tape recorder."

like a particular instrument, find pieces that feature that instrument. You can also listen to the radio and then note the name of pieces you really like. You can buy music at a local record store or online, you can check out tapes or CDs from the library, or you can buy albums at a used music store.

Another way to learn to appreciate music is to read an adult book about music. *Classical Music for Dummies* (Pogue & Speck, 1997) is readable and informative, even if you already have a musical background. You can read biographies about composers or check out books about music history from the library. You can read about music online. No matter what age you are, you can become a music enthusiast.

Once you have a personal appreciation and feel somewhat informed, you can pass that attitude on to your students. If you attended a great concert, tell children about it. If you listened to a piece of music that you really liked, play a little of it for children. If you are enthusiastic about music, your enthusiasm will inspire your children.

The next challenge is to add purposeful music appreciation to children's environment. Do not sit them down for a listening lesson in classical music. Preschoolers and early elementary children won't sit for it. Music appreciation for young children has to be done with movement, art, or other participation. Plan another activity, like putting together puzzles, and then place the classical music at the puzzle table, so children get a dose of music in the background while doing another activity in the foreground.

Conclusion

Music is part of our society. Most of us do not notice that it weaves its way through the fabric of our lives. Music is in the background of children's lives as well. Teachers should choose a few of the threads and make sure they are woven into children's lives. These threads may help them remember the lessons of compassion and care that they need to survive in this diverse world.

KEY TERMS

compassion	music appreciation	self-image
cultural diversity	self-esteem	sensitivity
differences		

DISCUSSION QUESTIONS

1. Name five ways to help children value cultural diversity through songs.
2. List the titles of three culturally diverse lullaby albums to use with children.
3. Name five musical instruments from countries other than the United States.
4. List the titles of four songs that teach cooperation or peacemaking.
5. Outline your response to a parent who complains about a component of your music educational program.
6. List the titles of five pieces of music you will use to teach your children music appreciation.
7. Name four children's musicians who write songs about appreciating diversity.

SUGGESTED LEARNING ACTIVITY

Design a unit to teach children about another historical era. Define the time period, outline the kinds of activities you will use, and provide the titles of five songs you will use. Besides the song titles, include the composers, recording artists, and album titles.

REFERENCES

Alsop, P. (1983). *Wha'd'ya wanna do?* [cassette]. Santa Cruz, CA: Flying Fish Records.

Alsop, P. (1990). *Pluggin' away* [cassette]. Topanga, CA: Moose School Music.

Arnold, L. (1986). *Make believe* [cassette]. Santa Cruz, CA: Ariel Records.

Beall, P. C., & Nipp, S. H. (1996). *Wee sing silly songs* [cassette and book]. Los Angeles: Price Stern & Sloan.

Chapin, T. (1986). *Mother Earth* [cassette]. New York: Sony Wonder Records.

Chapin, T. (1996). *Around the world and back again* [cassette]. New York: Sony Wonder Records.

Dietrich, M. (2000). *Legends of the 20th century* [CD]. London: EMI.

Epstein, F. (1995). *Global lullabies* [cassette]. Redway, CA: Music for Little People.

Grammer, R. (1986). *Teaching peace* [cassette]. Toronto, ON, Canada: BMG Music.

Greg & Steve. (1982). *We all live together,* Volume II [cassette]. Acton, CA: Young Heart Records.

Jackson, M., & Ritchie, L. (2001). *Salute to the 80's* [CD]. New York: Legacy.

Jamboree Kids. (2000). *Hickory dickory dock* [cassette]. New York: Jamboree Records.

Jenkins, E. (1956). *Call and response, rhythmic group singing* [record]. New York: Folkways Records.

Jordan, S. (2001). *Lullabies around the world* [cassette and book]. Niagara Falls, NY: Author.

The Kingston Trio. (1995). *The Capitol years* [CD]. New York: Capitol.

Lennon, J. (1998). *Anthology* [CD]. New York: Capitol.

Lomax, A. (1999). *Hard hitting songs for hard-hit people.* Lincoln: University of Nebraska Press.

Marzollo, J. (1993). *Happy birthday, Martin Luther King.* New York: Scholastic.

McCutcheon, J. (1988). *Mail myself to you* [cassette]. Cambridge, MA: Rounder Records.

Miché, M. (1985). *Kid's stuff* [cassette]. Berkeley, CA: Song Trek Music.

Miché, M. (1988a). *Animal crackers* [cassette and CD]. Berkeley, CA: Song Trek Music.

Miché, M. (1988b). *Holly daze* [cassette and CD]. Berkeley, CA: Song Trek Music.

Miché, M. (1989). *Peace it together* [cassette and CD]. Berkeley, CA: Song Trek Music.

Penn, L. (1987). *Grandma's patchwork quilt* [cassette]. Guilford, CT: American Melody Records.

Penner, F. (1992). *The cat came back* [cassette]. Ukiah, CA: Shoreline.

Peter, Paul & Mary. (1998). *Around the campfire* [cassette]. Burbank, CA: Warner Brothers.

Peter, Paul & Mary. (1993). *Peter, Paul & Mommy, too* [record]. Burbank, CA: Warner Brothers.

Pogue, D., & Speck, S. (1997). *Classical music for dummies.* Foster City, CA: IDG Books.

Polisar, B. L. (1993). *Teacher's favorites* [CD]. New York: Orchard.

Reid, B. (1989). *Marz barz* [cassette]. Aptos, CA: Blue Bear Records.

Reid, B. (1993). *We are the children* [cassette]. Aptos, CA: Blue Bear Records.

Seeger, P. (1996). *Link in the chain* [CD]. New York: Columbia.

Sony Wonder Records. (1997). *The planet sleeps* [CD]. New York: Author.

Timberlake, J. (1987). *Nine green fingers and forty-seven toes* [cassette]. Oakland, CA: Author.

Various artists. (1994). *Happy Chanukah songs* [CD]. Toronto, ON, Canada: Madacy.

Wasinger, T. (1993). *The world sings goodnight* [cassette]. Boulder, CO: Silver Wave Records.

The Weavers. (1956). *The Weavers at Carnegie Hall* [CD]. New York: Vanguard.

CHAPTER **8**

Music and the Arts

How do you integrate music into the other arts? Of course, music is itself an art, but in this chapter the term *the arts* refers to visual and dramatic arts.

One of the best ways to get children to listen to music is to combine it with a visual art project. Both adults and children find it difficult to just sit and pay attention to music. We tend to be much more visual than auditory, so we often combine music with theater, as in opera, or music with film, as in movies and music videos. The same combination interests children.

Music and Emotions

A 1995 experiment by Lewis, Dember, Schefft, and Radenhausen studied the effects of musical sound and video images using an optimism-pessimism questionnaire. The pieces of music and video clips were first assigned to a positive or negative mood category by experts. The researchers found that music, but not videos, affected the **mood** of the people in the study. Positive music produced increased positive moods, and negative music produced negative moods. The effect was greater for women. Therefore, it was concluded that somehow music imparts its mood to listeners, especially women.

In 1995, Chastain, Seibert, and Ferraro did a similar study in which they played music of a particular mood and had college students study various words during the music. The students paid more attention to the words that matched the musical mood than words that did not match. The mood of the music that matched a word affected students' ability to remember that word.

In a 1989 study of art and music, Stratton and Zalanowski first studied paintings and music alone to see if either induced moods. They then showed paintings while playing music of different moods. The study subjects paid more attention to the music than to the painting when deciding the mood of music-painting combinations. So, if sad music was played, they felt the painting was sad-looking, and if happy music was played, they judged the painting to be happy. This effect is also true of movies. Researchers found that people's expectations of a film's outcome is set by the mood of the music in the film. Also, their recall of the film's events is better when the music matches the film's outcome (Boltz, Schulkind, & Kantra, 1991).

In 1995, Bouhuys, Bloem, and Groothuis did an interesting experiment in which they matched faces with music. First, students looked at a variety of faces and determined which ones were happy, sad, neutral, or ambiguous. Another group of students listened to happy or sad music. They then looked at faces that had positive, negative, or neutral expressions. They rated the mood of the facial expressions. The people who listened to depressing music judged the neutral faces to be sad. Is it a wonder that teenagers who listen to depressing music have their moods intensified by it?

What we call **background music** also has an effect on our moods and even on how we shop. In a study of background music in a supermarket chain, the use of *slow* music increased sales effectively. Shoppers stayed in the store longer and bought much more. The average gain was from about $12,000 per store to $16,700 (Milliman, 1982), which is almost a 40 percent increase! For this reason, everywhere we go shopping, we hear background music. Next time you shop, listen to the background music and see if stores are playing slow music as this research indicated they should.

What are the implications of these studies for your classrooms? Background music does have an effect on our children. If you want them to "shop" longer in the book area, you can play slow classical music in your room, and if you want them to be energetic, play fast, exciting music. If you want babies to be peaceful and happy, play lots of quiet, joyful music.

Does this kind of response to music require training? In a 1994 study done in Italy by Robazza, Macaluso, and D'Urso, some children and adults who were musically trained and some who were not matched pieces of music with the emotions happiness, sadness, anger, and fear. All the groups matched the emotions equally well. This research clearly suggests that children and adults respond to music similarly, even without specialized musical training. However, children perceived more feelings of happiness and less feelings of anger than adults. Music has a natural way of communicating emotions.

Music and the Development of Creativity

Why is creativity a quality that we encourage in children? **Creativity** is the ability to take two or more known ideas, put them together, and produce a new viewpoint or product. For example, Thomas Edison took the concepts of a vacuum tube, a filament, and electricity running through the filament to invent the lightbulb. All the components existed before he put them together, but he invented a new product by combining existing ideas. We want children to have knowledge, but they also need to know how to put different pieces of information together to solve problems. In order to be creative, a person must be knowledgeable but must also have flexible thinking in order to be able to form new ideas (Figure 8–1).

How do we measure creativity? How do we help children develop it? Several ways of measuring creativity have been developed by psychologists. You may have heard of the Unusual Uses test developed by Guilford (1967), in which someone is asked to suggest as many uses for a common object as possible. Very creative people can think of 10 ways to use a key, while others only think about using it to open a lock. He also developed the Unusual Situations test, in which questions such as "What would happen if no one had to sleep anymore?" are asked. Creative people come up with all kinds of new activities and new consequences of the questions. Others just think about watching TV. The Torrance Test of Creative Thinking (Torrance, 1962) is another test that is widely used to measure creativity in children.

Creativity is widely thought to be enhanced in children by giving them many new and different experiences and opportunities. Children can be given opportunities to make up stories, to write, to produce art, and to create projects. However, creative projects in elementary school are often limited to certain areas, mostly art and writing. Children can also be given projects in other subjects, such as science or mathematics.

FIGURE 8–1 Children should learn to be creative.

Accumulated findings show that music training enhances creativity, not only within music, as we would expect, but in other areas of intellectual achievement. According to Norman Weinberger (1998), one of the earliest studies was performed by Simpson in 1969.

Simpson gave 173 high school music and 45 non-music students tests of creativity devised by Guilford. He reported that music students scored more highly than did non-music students on several measures of creativity. The findings are correlative, that is they show a significant relationship between music and creativity. Whether or not music education caused creativity scores to be enhanced cannot be determined from this report.

Weinberger also reviewed an unpublished dissertation by Wolff (1979), which studied the effects of 30 minutes of daily music instruction for an entire year on first graders.

All students were tested at the beginning and end of the year on the Torrance Test of Creative Thinking and also with the Purdue Perceptual Motor Survey. A control class received no music education. Wolff found that the music students exhibited significant increases in creativity. As it happens, they also developed a significant increase in perceptual motor skills. This study indicates that the creativity of children as young as first graders can be enhanced by music education, if it is a sustained part of the curriculum rather than a periodic addition to the school day for a few months.

Music can also increase creative thinking for children younger than first grade. Again, according to Weinberger (1998):

Magda Kalmar (1982) studied the effects of music instruction on preschool children of three and four years of age. Working in Budapest, Hungary, Kalmar obtained test scores both for the Torrance Creativity Test and the Binet Intelligence Test and also for the Oseretzky Scales of motor development. The experimental group received singing music lessons and musical group play twice weekly; the relatively modest amount of music education was offset by the fact that this treatment was continued for three years. The author found that the music students scored higher than a non treatment control class in creativity.

In addition to the previous studies, Weinberger (1998) reviewed two controlled studies, both performed by the same group at Kent State University, who studied high school and university students.

In the first of these studies, Hamann, Bourassa, and Aderman (1990) obtained scores on the Guilford Unusual Consequences Test for university students who either were or were not music majors. They found significantly higher creativity scores in music majors. Of course, this is a purely correlative finding; no causal relationship can be inferred from these data. However, the authors also determined the relationship between creativity and the total amount of music education. They discovered that students with more than 10 years of music education exhibited significantly greater creativity than those with less than 10 years of experience. . . . these findings are quite consistent with the idea that creativity increases as a function of the amount of music education.

In another study, Hamann, Bourassa, and Aderman (1991) tested high school students whose experiences included theatrical and visual arts. Once again, the authors found that music students exhibited greater creativity than non-music students. Theater students also scored significantly higher, but, unexpectedly, no effects were found for visual arts students in this particular study. Again, the issue of possible causality was approached by determining the relationship between length of music education and the creativity scores, based on the number of academic units of music classes. A statistically significant relationship was observed: the greater the number of music class units, the greater the creativity scores.

In 1992, Mohanty and Hejmadi studied preschoolers, ages four and five. They used a variety of methods to teach the names of body parts. Four matched groups received:

1. verbal instruction.
2. verbal instruction plus acting out movements.
3. music and movement, in which instruction was given by song accompanied by dance movements.
4. no specialized instruction (control group).

After only 20 days of training, all the groups showed improvement over the control group. The music/dance group showed the greatest improvement both in learning the body parts and on the Torrance Test of Creative Thinking. From this study, we can infer a few important conclusions. First, teaching and training children made a difference in their learning. Second, music was the most effective training method for this kind of task. Third, music/dance treatment not only taught children the body parts, but it also affected their ability on the creativity test (Figure 8–2).

Because they include control groups, these studies show that music is not just something that creative people happen to study more often than others; rather, studying music actually enhances creativity. The study by Mohanty and Hejmadi (1992) has a significant implication for educators. Educators often think certain knowledge is important for children to learn. They can choose from a variety of teaching methods to deliver that information. For example, the alphabet can be taught through the "Alphabet Song" (Bartels, 1980), through reciting the alphabet, and through pointing to the alphabet cards. Most methods are effective, but some are more effective than others. In addition, some methods, such as using music, have side effects that are beneficial to the neurological development of the brain.

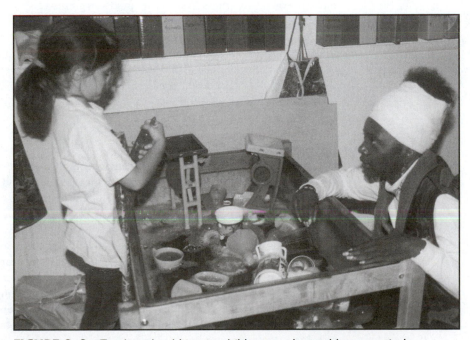

FIGURE 8–2 Teachers should inspire children to solve problems creatively.

HAP PALMER'S VIEWPOINT ON CREATIVITY

Q: *What does creativity mean to you?*

A: Flexibility, curiosity, open-mindedness. The ability to see different options and solutions to problems, and to see a variety of ways tasks can be accomplished. It's a way of thinking that includes not only the arts and literature, but also science, mathematics, and everyday life situations.

Q: *Did you exhibit qualities of creativity as a child?*

A: I was fond of asking questions that began with "What if." Things like, "What if we attached wings to the car and drove real fast, would we fly?" or "What if I wrapped myself up in mattresses and jumped from the top of the house?" I would string these ideas together ad nauseam until one or both my parents would say, "What if you stopped talking and finished your dinner?"

I started lessons on the clarinet and saxophone when I was nine years old. By seventh and eighth grade, I was playing in bands and small combos. I really enjoyed improvising, responding to chord progressions, and creating melodies. I was playing by ear and only later in college began to learn the theory of harmony. I realized there is a balance between knowledge and intuition; they are equally important in the creative act.

Q: *What did your parents do to encourage your creative abilities?*

A: I don't remember my parents specifically encouraging creativity. They didn't meddle or fuss over me much. I had great amounts of unstructured time and a garage full of things that I could fiddle with; things like tools, wood, wire, parts of old pin ball machines, electrical gadgets, old motors, record players, amplifiers, speakers, screws, bolts, and nails of every size. My father had all these things organized, sorted, and labeled in boxes. Much to his understandable annoyance, I never learned to put things away. We also had boxes of old clothes and a large collection of records: jazz, swing, classical, and musicals which I was free to play.

There were times when my parents would discourage creativity. I liked to invent and make my own gifts, things like a flower inside an empty toilet paper spool attached to a wood base, until my mother told me these were not real gifts, they were just junk. Another time my sister and I were making up a play with some neighborhood friends. We were laughing and jabbering away, wearing old clothes we'd found in the garage, when Mom suddenly came in and got very upset because we were ruining the things she'd saved for the Goodwill. Looking back on these memories, the main thing I would tell parents is, "Relax, you don't have as much power as you think." If a child has a drive to create, nothing you can do will stop it.

Q: *What did your teachers do?*

A: Creativity and imagination were not encouraged in my early school years. I struggled to focus my mind and learn basic skills, which I realize as an adult are also necessary for creative pursuits. My kindergarten teacher sent a note home to my parents saying that I was one of her problems. She wrote, "Hap is interested in everything and can apply himself to nothing."

When I was in third or fourth grade we had a school talent show. I had nothing prepared, but I had a sudden spontaneous urge to get up on stage. Claiming I had a comedy act, I got up and started improvising. I ran over to a speaker and said "this needs fixing." I got inside the enclosure and pantomimed wiggling wires. Then I pretended to get an electric shock. I leapt back and rolled around the stage. As all the children laughed, the teacher came up and pulled me off the stage, saying something like, "You don't know what you're doing." Which of course was true, but it could

continued

HAP PALMER'S VIEWPOINT ON CREATIVITIY *continued*

have been an opportunity to show how one moves from the brainstorming phase of creativity to forming and setting a piece.

Q: *Was there anyone else who was a major influence on you in this area? How so?*

A: I met the people who had the biggest influence through books. In junior high school, I enjoyed reading biographies, and many of them were about creative people. I was especially fascinated with Will Rodgers and Thomas Edison. I took hope from the fact that Edison, like myself, was a poor student. Books gave me insight into how creative people worked.

Q: *Are there any special activities you would recommend to parents to foster creative thought and action in their children?*

A: Provide opportunities for exploring and experimenting (Figure 8–3). Have lots of materials available for children to choose from. Some examples: arts and crafts—paper, felt tip pens, clay; drama—kitchen utensils, old pans, plastic dishes, and old clothes in a costume box for playing make-believe; music—rhythm sticks, tambourine, drum, woodblock, triangle, bells, and a cassette player with recordings of a variety of musical styles; dance—provide young children with opportunities for movement exploration rather than emphasizing competitive sports and formalized dance training. As children mature, let them choose the disciplines that catch their interest. Take children to classes and lessons when they are interested and ask for them.

Q: *Any other helpful hints for parents?*

A: Recognize that creativity often occurs in stages. At first, preparation: becoming familiar with materials, exploring, discovering; followed by generation of ideas or brainstorming. For a free flow of ideas, don't pass judgments during these processes. Following these stages, let evaluations come primarily from the child. Creativity is a peculiar paradox of both freedom and discipline. There are techniques and principles inherent in any pursuit, which enhance and guide the creative impulse and creative bursts often follow periods of patient, persistent effort. Ideally, the discipline should come from within the child. As children mature, let them delve into what excites and interests them. Children are more likely to excel in those pursuits that are chosen by them rather than imposed by adults.

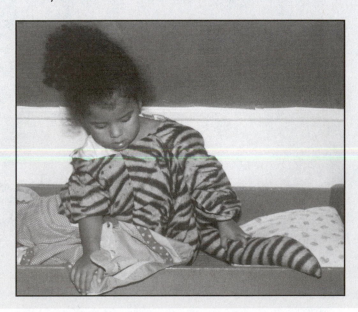

FIGURE 8–3 Creativity is enhanced through dramatic play.

To summarize, Norman Weinberger (1998) makes this point:

In summary, the findings to date provide solid support for the claim that music increases creativity. Moreover, it appears that active music making is more effective than passive music experience. But it must be realized that there is not nearly enough research on this issue. We need detailed and systematic studies of the types and amount of music education for groups of all ages. In addition, a broader range of measures of creativity should be used to fully explore this critical dimension of the intellect. It is very important that creative potential can be increased. It should be glad tidings for everyone that music appears to be an effective means of accomplishing this goal. After all, what is the greatest source of potential benefit to our planet if not the potential of our imagination linked to rational and unselfish action?

Representing Music through Visual Art

The easiest way for children to listen to music is to listen while they do something with their hands. At every age level, you can play music for children and provide them with some kind of artistic medium. You can then ask them to represent the music in art. For example, if you choose paint, ask children to pick colors that they hear in the music. If you choose clay, ask them to put the feeling of the music into the feel of the clay (Figure 8–4). By choosing a piece of music and an **artistic medium**, you set the parameters of the production but allow the children to be creative in their art.

Virtually all art teachers encourage teachers to provide the medium but not to predetermine the product. You probably already know that art teachers deplore coloring

FIGURE 8–4 Children can express music through clay creations.

Sally Rogers
Children's Musician and Educator

Sally Rogers began her musical studies sitting under her mother's grand piano. As a child, her family listened to the Limelighters, Harry Belafonte, and Rodgers and Hammerstein musicals. Besides playing the piano, Rogers' mother played the organ in church, where she sang with the choir.

When Rogers was in the eighth grade, her family moved to Brazil for a year. There, she fell in love with samba and bossa nova music. In high school, Rogers was in a theater program that performed musicals and plays. She also sang in the choir and played in folk groups. It is no surprise that Rogers went on to be a music major in music education at Michigan State. After college, she played in coffeehouses; taught dulcimer, guitar, and voice lessons; and was the director of a school of folk music. Rogers started in the children's music business in 1979 when she auditioned for the Winnepeg Festival in Canada. There, she performed for adults and began doing children's concerts.

Currently, Rogers leads teacher workshops focused on integrating the arts into school curriculums. She is a teaching artist in HOT (higher order thinking) schools and works with EastCon, a resource center for interdistrict grants. She particularly loves to do projects based on local oral history and songwriting. She assigns students to go into the community and do oral interviews with local people. They then write songs based on the local history they learned.

Rogers works with music for children because "that's where the future lies." She feels that music is becoming rare in the schools and that children are treated as consumers and not as musicians—passive takers, not active participators. Her job is to reactivate them. Rogers loves watching kids get excited, and she gets excited by their excitement. She involves children by having them sing along, write songs, and play instruments. She feels she has learned something valuable and worth passing on.

books where the lines are predetermined. Instead of predetermined cut and paste art, try to pick a medium such as watercolors, pastels, papier-mâché, collage, rubber stamps (with different colored inks), or modeling clay, and then allow children freedom in exploring the medium (Figure 8–5). Do not forget to provide different genres of music—jazz, classical, folk, reggae, etc.—with this variety of media.

FIGURE 8–5 A three-dimensional collage is an expressive music/art activity.

Illustrating a Song Book

To illustrate a song book, choose a song that you plan to sing fairly often with your class. If your children are between four and six years old, write one line of the song in large print at the bottom of each page. For preschoolers, pick an easy song with few words and few pages. You should have about five to ten pages when you are finished. Make copies of each page for your students. Put the pages together so that each student has a booklet, and have the children illustrate the booklet (Figure 8–6). Remember, children do not have to illustrate the book in crayon or colored pens, two commonly used media by teachers. They could use other media. You can consider having them do collages or use rubber stamps. You can also give them a variety of media and allow each child to select which one he wants to use. While you sing the song, have the children follow along with the words in their booklets. Preschoolers are likely to get lost in the turning of pages, so keep in mind that following along is really an activity in tracking the print and turning pages.

With second graders, you can either make the preprinted pages or have them copy words to the song into a blank song book as a writing exercise. If you plan to do copying, the text needs to be short. Again, children can illustrate their books with a medium that you or they select.

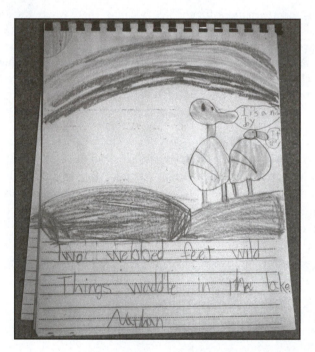

FIGURE 8–6 Children enjoy making illustrated song books.

Making Musical Instruments

You can acquire a book or a video with directions for how to make instruments. A great book is *Kids Make Music, Clapping and Tapping from Bach to Rock!* by Avery Hart (1993). It has good ideas for how to use the instruments once you have made them. Most of the ideas are for elementary school–age children, but some can be adapted for preschoolers. In addition to this book, Cathy Fink and Marcy Marxer have a video, *Making and Playing Homemade Instruments* (1992). It teaches you how to make an oatmeal box banjo, a washtub bass, bottle cap castanets, and other musical instruments from recycled materials. Fink and Marxer are featured in Chapter 9. You may prefer using a video because you and the children can watch it together. Students may notice information that escapes your attention. Watching the video piques the children's interest in making instruments. It is easier to make instruments after you have watched someone else do it. Reading directions in a book can be confusing. However, in Hart's book, there are many other ideas for music making other than just making instruments.

Integrating Music with the Dramatic Arts

Music has been integrated with dramatic performances since the time of the Egyptians (Figure 8–7). In ancient Greece, no play was complete without a musical interlude. Though we do not know much about ancient music and what it sounded like, we do know that it has been a part of the dramatic arts for a long time.

Musicals

Bob Blue has written many **musicals** for children. Blue takes popular children's books like *Charlotte's Web* (White, 1987) and turns them into scripts. He looks through the book and then takes the text in quotation marks and makes it into the script. After he has a script, he adds songs. Significant moments in the script become the points where there are songs. For example, in his musical *Charlotte's Web* (Blue, 1987), Blue included a protest song called "The Runt of the Litter," which Fern sings when her father is about to kill Wilbur, the runt of the litter.

You can also do musicals with preschoolers. Use Blue's idea of picking a popular book, but this time the entire text becomes the script, which an adult reads as a narrator.

FIGURE 8–7 A mirror can enhance dramatic play to music.

Children can act out the story while the adult reads. Pick two significant moments in the book and write new words to an old tune for the songs of the musical. You can also just pick two songs written for children and insert them in an appropriate moment. You can pick a book like *The Salamander Room* (Mazer, 1991) and insert the songs "Newts, Salamanders & Frogs" and "Bats Eat Bugs," both by Steve Van Zandt (Banana Slug String Band, 1987; Miché, 1990), mentioned in Chapter 5. If you really get into the production, you can create scenes, involving the visual arts (Figure 8–8). What better songs to play while making sets than the ones you will sing in the performance?

You're a Good Man, Charlie Brown (Gesner, 1967) can be done with elementary school–age children. The songs are fun and the drama is done in small skits. Teach all the songs to the children, rather than choosing children for solos. This avoids creating a competitive atmosphere encouraged by solo singing. The children not chosen for a solo may tell themselves they are not talented enough and remember it for the rest of their lives. There is time enough for those kinds of disappointments later in life.

Choosing Background Music for a Video

As discussed earlier in this chapter, the type of music played during a movie or film affects the mood of viewers even more than visual cues (Figure 8–9). One hilarious activity to do with children is to view different videos with the children's choices for music. This can be done by playing a video on a television with the sound turned off. Children can suggest different recordings that they already sing in class. You can play the recordings next to the video and watch the kids' reactions. If there is a mismatch between the video and song, you will have a hilarious time viewing the combination. Another fun activity is to have a parent videotape your class. Play back the video with the sound off.

FIGURE 8–8 Music complements plays and puppet shows.

Bob Blue
Educator, Teacher Trainer, and Writer of Children's Musicals

Bob Blue started teaching in 1969. Due to multiple sclerosis, he retired from full-time teaching in 1974, but he still volunteers at a local elementary school. He assists children with reading and writing and talks with children about their problems. He has been writing songs since 1969 and writing articles about parenting and teaching since 1974.

Blue was inspired by wanting to teach and write, wanting to have an impact on what happened in the world, and believing that this was how he could help others.

Blue started writing musical plays for children in 1976. He has written 12 musicals for elementary school children, ages six to twelve. He has written about 150 children's songs, but he considers only 80 of them to be good. Peter, Paul & Mary have performed his songs, and 25 other children's musicians have recorded his songs. The most popular of his songs is a parody of Paul Anka's song "My Way" (1997), named "Their Way" (1984). Another of Blue's best-loved songs is "Courage" (1990), which has been performed in the United States and abroad. For 30 years, loving children has kept him going. He most enjoys talking with and listening to children.

Currently, Blue helps student teachers through his articles, and he really appreciates feedback from teachers. One teacher wrote him, "Your articles are kind of like good maps. They remind the reader of the territory of children and parents and teachers, and will help us pay attention to the unique realities of the people we encounter." His favorite quote from a child is, "Uh-uh! Real magic is make-believe! Only make-believe magic is real!"

FIGURE 8–9 Music can change the mood of a video, film, and even the viewers!

Have the children choose different songs to try with the video and see which one fits. Another video activity is to videotape the class with the sound off while they are dancing to one kind of music, and then put on a different kind of music when you play back the video.

203

As a child, Linda Arnold listened to opera and Broadway musicals, and sang a lot of folk songs around campfires. When she was ten, she chose the flute for her first instrument because it looked pretty. At eleven, she went to summer camp, where the counselors played guitar. She really wanted to play, so she took guitar lessons and learned from her friends. Arnold was influenced by Joni Mitchell, Joan Baez, and Gordon Lightfoot. She started writing songs in high school and also taught guitar. In college, she did musical comedy and completed a theater arts degree at UC Santa Cruz.

When Arnold was pregnant, she began writing songs about pregnancy and put out an album of those songs two years after her daughter was born. When her children were small, she began looking for music for them. Arnold sang with her children, wrote songs for them, and put on musicals with them. In the early '80s, she began volunteering in her daughter's classroom and started writing songs for the class. By the mid-1980s, she had put out her first album of original children's songs. Her own children still perform with her "like a family vaudeville act." In her circus show, her son wears a dinosaur costume, her daughter is Miss Kitty the poodle trainer, and Arnold is the ringmaster, an apt analogy for a mom.

Arnold was once performing in Syracuse, New York, when suddenly it was as if a wind swept the audience away. All the preschoolers ran out of the room. Her competition was a guy in a rented Barney® suit singing with a tape recorder. "Every good children's performer has to be upstaged by Barney® at least once," said Arnold. During another concert, her four-year-old son stuck his singing teddy bear out of the side curtain. "Every children's performer has to be upstaged by [her] own children at least once." At a holiday concert, Arnold was doing a costume change while her daughter sang a song. Unfortunately, the costume change took longer than either had expected. Her daughter finished the song and stood on stage yelling, "Mom, Mom, where are you?"

Arnold involves children in her performances by having them participate in choruses with lots of movement. Her imaginative storytelling also draws them in. Sometimes, she brings children up on stage to help her sing. Arnold prefers children; they are her favorite people. They are creative, spontaneous, and loving. They are also a lot of fun!

In speaking about music, Arnold said, "Music reaches into the soul and connects us to our emotions. Music has a very healing quality. And it's fun." She cannot imagine her life without performing music.

Creating Audio for Drama Productions

Children love doing plays and dramatic productions, even at very young ages. Because children have difficulties speaking loudly enough and remembering their lines, teachers can make an audio tape of the children to accompany their play. If the children help create the tape, that is even better (Figure 8–10). This way, you can turn the tape player up so the children can be heard, they do not have to remember lines, and the flow of the play is controlled by the audio playback. If the children forget part of the play, they can just listen to the tape and continue acting. For this kind of a recording, try to use a good microphone. Microphones that comes with portable tape recorders are usually low quality, and the sound is accompanied by a loud hum when played back. Occasionally, you can find a tape recorder with an acceptable microphone. Try it out before buying a separate microphone.

Joanie Bartels
Musician, the Magic Series

Joanie Bartels recorded her first album for children, *Lullaby Magic* (1985), as a singer working for Discovery Music. Bartels loves what she does, and the joy of sharing music with children and their families motivates her. She loves meeting kids after her shows. What she enjoys most is watching how children respond to music—how it carries them to their own special world where they can sing along and dance with total abandon. She also loves fan letters and has many pen pals all over the country. She gets wonderful letters and drawings; some of the letters are very funny. Bartels's favorite quote is from a young friend, who drew a beautiful picture of them both and wrote, "I love you, I am ctr [meaning *cuter*]!"

Funny things always happen when you work with children, but one of the most endearing of Bartels's stories happened years ago, when she was performing in concert. During one of the songs, a two-year-old boy got onstage and started hugging her around the knees. The next thing she knew, all the children came up and made a huge "hug sandwich." Hug sandwiches are now a frequent occurrence during shows, but the first one was the best!

Many different components contribute to the making of a great song, but for Bartels the key is *relate-ability*, be it tickling a funny bone, making her cry, making her smile, or just making her want to dance. She feels it is crucial to involve children in music, and during her shows there is plenty of opportunity to sing along, get up and dance, do sign language, come onstage to play percussion, or even to act like a dinosaur! She performs a variety of music for many ages and different musical styles to keep it interesting.

Bartels feels that music is one of the great healing arts. For her, music ranks behind only breathing, eating, and sleeping. Music is the second greatest universal language after smiling.

FIGURE 8–10 Creating audio recordings for dramatic productions helps children remember their lines.

How to Record Music with Children

You can record the voices and songs of young children in a number of ways. You can create a **semi-professional recording**, which gives children the experience of visiting a real studio, or you can create a studio situation in your school environment (Figure 8–11). You can also create a **nonprofessional recording**, using a basic tape recorder and microphone to capture the joy of young children's voices for their parents to remember.

Creating Nonprofessional Audio Productions

Children enjoy hearing the sound of their own voices, so creating a homemade **audio production** is a great motivator. Children can tell a story or sing a song into a tape recorder. They can read books into a tape recorder, creating a book on tape for other children. This is an especially good idea for a child who is sick at home or away on a trip.

In one family, whenever someone is far away from home—for instance, in college or the Peace Corps—the family will set up the tape recorder during special celebrations such as Thanksgiving or Christmas and record the comments, conversation, jokes, and songs of the celebration. The distant family members often find it the most popular tape in their circle of friends.

Young children can easily be involved in making a tape of their songs and stories as a gift for parents or grandparents. All it takes is practicing a few songs, recording their voices, and then taking the master cassette to a local tape duplicator. The quality of the tape does not have to be high. Parents and grandparents enjoy having a memory of their children's young voices.

Class recordings are fun projects for older children, but these children are also ready for a bigger project, such as making a radio show or visiting a radio station. First, teachers should explain what a radio show is and that children's grandparents or great grandparents had only radio and no television. Then, a class has to decide what kind of radio show they will create. They choose songs to play or sing on the show. They choose an announcer and maybe even decide on commercials. This project is guaranteed to teach a lot about cooperation and music listening.

FIGURE 8–11

A field trip to a recording studio can be informative and fun.

Sharon, Lois & Bram
Children's Musicians

Sharon Hampson has been surrounded by music all her life. She comes from a close-knit, socially conscious, and compassionate family. She grew up with the songs of Paul Robeson, Pete Seeger, and other politically and socially active artists. Much of her commitment to music and her sense of community reflects those early influences. She took piano lessons as a child and played cello in her high school orchestra. Her music teachers had a strong influence on her enthusiasm for music. As an adult, she toured the folk clubs and festivals of North America and did television performances. Through her warm and gentle manner, her joy of singing, and her love of children, Hampson immediately establishes a bond with all her audiences.

Hampson lives in Toronto with her husband Joe, a singer–songwriter and member of The Travelers. Their home is filled with music. Joe plays bass and a bit of everything else, their son and daughter play piano, and Hampson occasionally finds time to play her guitar. When she, her family, and her friends gather for a party, they invariably end up singing.

Lois Lilienstein made a less than spectacular debut in show business at the age of five. At an amateur talent show, she nervously stepped onstage, looked over the audience and announced, "I be back when I be six." She has since overcome her stage fright and now she is a dynamic performer whose natural exuberance and sense of fun put audiences immediately at ease. Lilienstein was introduced to music, mostly pop, jazz, big band, and American musical theater, by her father, who sold insurance by day and played piano at weddings and bar mitzvahs by night.

Her mother enrolled her at a school for tap dancing, where Lilienstein learned and her mother watched and picked up steps. They became the Goldberg Sisters, and together they provided a total entertainment package at family gatherings and special events. Lilienstein is an accomplished classical and jazz pianist. She graduated with a Bachelor of Music degree from the University of Michigan. When her son David was three years old and they had recently arrived in Toronto, Lilienstein enrolled him in a cooperative school. The head teacher asked her to play the piano for the children. Lilienstein said to her, "But I play Bach and Beethoven." The teacher said, "Whatever you play will be better than what we can do!"

Lilienstein began working with children and music, delving into folk music and introducing children to singing, creative movement, and musical games. She was highly respected for her work in the classroom and gave seminars and workshops on children and music for educators. Due to her long-standing fascination with children's street play, she has become a collector of playground rhymes and games, many of which appear on Sharon, Lois & Bram albums.

Bram Morrison, ex-school teacher, professional folksinger, and modern-day pied piper, toured with the noted folklorist and singer Alan Mills for four years. They traveled across the United States and Canada, while Morrison built his own extensive repertoire in English and French Canadian folk songs. Between tours he was active in the Toronto folk music scene, singing frequently on television and at the Mariposa Folk Festival.

Morrison's first performing experience was as an actor during his high school and university days. Many of the qualities that give special distinction to his musical performance today are part of the actor in him: his comic timing, sense of the burlesque, narrative skill, and masterful gift for mimicry.

Through his association with Alan Mills, Morrison became interested in working with and performing for children. He entered Teacher's College and taught in the Toronto school system for seven years, five of them as an itinerant music teacher. His work with children, teachers in the field, and teachers in training was known and respected all over Ontario.

Morrison's easy rapport with children and tongue-in-cheek sense of humor reveal the mischievous child in him. Morrison's family, like Hampson's, is thoroughly musical. He credits his wife with inspiring and increasing his knowledge of popular music, Broadway show tunes,

continued

and classical music. His six grandchildren keep him singing at home as well as in concert. The young ones call the trio "Sharon, Lois & Papa."

Making music, improving their musicianship, and seeing the delight of young children when they make music keep this trio going. All of them, early in their solo careers, combined teaching and music, and as a trio they have always enjoyed working with teachers to pass on the message that "music as pure entertainment is a wonderful thing."

Creating Semi-professional Audio Productions

Many resources are available for recording children. You should first ask the parents of your class if any of them work in a recording studio. You may find a parent, aunt, uncle, or friend of your students who owns a small recording machine or who works in a professional studio. They will be invaluable for helping to record your students.

The first step is to decide whether you will record your students at the school using a four-track recording machine or go to a recording studio. If you decide to record at school, you will need to find a four-track recording machine with two or three microphones. A parent or one of their friends may have access to a recorder. A four-track recording machine may be somewhere in the school district. You may be able to rent one from an audio rental company. There also may be a band in your area that has a four-track recorder.

Once you have located a machine, you have to obtain the proper kind of tape and find someone who can set up the microphones and operate the machine for you. It is best if the person can set up the recording equipment in another room, like a library or an auditorium, rather than your classroom because it takes time to set up microphones and test the equipment. This kind of setup is difficult to do with children milling around, asking questions, and trying to touch things.

Once the equipment is set up, record the instrumental tracks first, such as guitar or piano. Remember, with four tracks, you only have enough room for three instrumental tracks and one voice track. You can record piano on one track, guitar on another, and then two tracks of children singing. Children find it difficult to come in and sing live on a blank tape. So, begin with piano and record the accompaniment to two or three songs. This will take about two hours because the machines need to be calibrated to the level of sound and the pianist usually does not play perfectly the first time through.

Once the piano tracks are recorded, you can record a lead vocal, which you can keep or discard later. The reason for the lead vocal is so the children have a clear, well-pitched voice to follow when they are recording. Next, the children are recorded, usually as a group with two or three microphones hung overhead and in front of the children. This eliminates the problem of a few children being too near the microphones.

Try to find a rug for the children to sit on while they are recorded. This not only eliminates excess sounds from their feet on the floor, but it also defines the area where the children are to sit for the recording session. Prepare children ahead for the quiet and patient behavior that they need to have for the recording session. Generally, it takes at least three takes of a song to get it right. Each time you do a take, you have to listen to it afterwards, which adds to the time. Plan for about an hour of recording time for each song.

Once the children have finished, add the other instruments. You can record another instrument like a guitar over the lead vocal track that you used to help the children record. Since it takes time to set up and take down the equipment, you can understand why it may take as long as three school days to record only three songs. This recording time at school can be shortened if you have the pianist and the recording engineer do the piano tracks at home or in a studio before you add the children's singing. The other instruments could also be added in the studio or at home after the children finish their part. Do not have the guitar and other instruments playing while the children are singing. This is because you will later have no control over the loudness or softness of these instruments in comparison to the children's voices. Also, children are distracted by instruments playing right next to them while they are trying to sing and control their behavior.

When you have finished recording all four tracks, usually the process of mixing the sound down to two tracks occurs so that it can be duplicated onto a cassette or CD. Hopefully, your sound recording person will be able to help you. Once you have a master cassette or CD, the cheapest way to make copies is to have someone make enough copies on a home system that everyone can keep one. If you plan to sell a few more at school and do not want to spend the time duplicating the tapes one by one, you can take them to a small duplication company where they make high-speed copies, usually three at a time, from a master copy. If you really want to sell copies, then you can have 500 made at a regular cassette duplication company. They have a setup fee, but it usually includes the cost of cassette cases and the plastic wrap on the outside. You have to provide your own paper card inserts, called J-cards.

If, instead of recording at school, you want your students to have the experience of going to a real recording studio, it will save you the trouble of finding a four-track tape recorder and someone to run it (Figure 8–12). The hourly fee of the studio usually includes the cost of a sound engineer. Currently, recording studio time costs about $60–80 per hour. However, if you find a parent who has a studio connection, you may get some time during the week when the studio is not booked. For example, most recording studios are not booked from 10 AM to 1 PM on a Wednesday. A small local college may have a recording studio. You may find what you need in a small television studio. Perhaps a local cable channel will provide you access. By law, cable channels are required to provide some local access. Hopefully, you will find one that can provide you with

FIGURE 8–12 Children learn about recording music at a studio.

When do I need to get copyright permission?

Generally speaking, you must get copyright permission when you intend to sell written music. When you intend to sell recorded music written by someone else, you are required to find, notify, and pay the songwriter according to a rate specified by law, unless you and the songwriter make some other legal agreement about payment. This is called a mechanical license. You can only record the song if it has been previously distributed to the public. The songwriter has the right to record it first. If you are an educator and you want to make a copy of a single song from a CD *that you bought,* you are permitted to do this for educational use. It is illegal to borrow a tape, CD, or record from a friend and copy the whole thing onto a cassette tape. If you do this because it is for educational use, you, the school, and the district can be sued for copyright infringement.

In one school, kids sang a great song for Chanukah. They said they had learned it from their teacher's tape. That teacher had a copy from another teacher in the school who had a copy from a friend's CD. Such practices are common in schools, but they do serious financial damage to small record companies, such as the ones that produce music for children. Many of these companies cannot sell enough copies to pay for the initial recording expenses (about $10,000 per album), so they regularly go out of business. You can find great children's songs on albums that never survived past the first thousand copies.

At a conference, a teacher approached one artist and told her how much she liked her tape and that she had all of her students bring in blank tapes so that she could make copies for each child. The artist was not thrilled. Teachers often feel justified in copying children's music tapes because it is for the children. They do not realize the financial hardship it can cause.

If you ever consider making a recording of children's music, a great resource is a book called *How to Make and Sell Your Own Record* by Diane Rapaport (1984). Unfortunately, this book is out of print, but many libraries have a copy. One local library has a copy that is used so frequently that they keep it in the reference section.

In general, if you have great songs you have written and want to record them, it is best to make a simple demo tape using a four-track recorder then send the songs to recording artists who may choose a song or two for an album. The artist would then record your songs in a studio with instruments and vocals, and would pay you royalties, about eight cents per recording sold.

If you wish to make your own recording of children's music, you need enough money to make an initial recording and at least 100 copies. If you are careful with your studio time and record your songs with simple, tuneful accompaniment, you can produce an album for the cost of a small mortgage on a home. Before you do this, get advice from some of the artists in this book. You might as well know where the rocks on the path are before you hit them.

about 12 to 15 studio hours, in blocks of about two to three hours. This would be enough time for your group to record about three songs with piano and one other instrumental accompaniment.

The recording schedule at a studio is similar to the four-track recording scenario. You will need to buy appropriate tape for the machine you will use. You will need two to three hours to record the piano tracks without the children. The next two hours will be needed for the lead vocalist to put down tracks that the children will use for their reference vocal. The next three hours will be used for the children recording in the studio. The next two to three hours will be used for adding the other instruments to the tracks. The final three hours will be utilized for mixing the songs down to two tracks. Be sure to tell the studio that you want a cassette backup, because in most studios they now mix down to a digital audio tape (DAT) or CD. You can use the cassette backup to make home copies. A recording made in a studio is probably going to be better quality than one made on the four-track machine; however, the choices will depend on what you find available. In either case, the experience for children will be one that they remember for a lifetime.

The scenarios outlined will produce a relatively high quality sounding product. Perhaps you do not want to spend this much time and energy. If that is the case, then you can record the piano, the children, and the instruments all at once on just two of the four tracks of the four-track machine. If you are in a studio, you can record everyone at once on just two tracks. The biggest problem of this method is that the mistakes are permanent. The children usually do not sing in tune as well, and there are often piano and instrumental mistakes that cannot be fixed. The benefit is that children still get an experience of recording that may inspire them to develop an interest in sound engineering, radio, or television.

Conclusion

Although curriculums are full and teachers have little time for teaching the arts, if you arrange your time wisely, children can learn many subjects at the same time. There is time for drama if you combine it with teaching health. There is time for the visual arts if you combine them with social studies. There is time for music if you use it to reinforce reading and mathematics. This is an important consideration for regular classroom teachers who are required to teach a great amount of information in a short amount of time.

KEY TERMS

artistic medium
audio production
background music

creativity
mood
musicals

nonprofessional recording
semi-professional recording

DISCUSSION QUESTIONS

1. Name five kinds of artistic media you can use with children. Specify the age group.
2. Describe how to make a song book for preschoolers, age four.
3. Describe how to do a musical with preschoolers.
4. Who is Linda Arnold and what is her contribution to music?
5. How can children be involved in choosing sound for a familiar video?
6. What is the difference between a nonprofessional and a semi-professional recording? List both kinds of semi-professional recordings.
7. Name three types of nonprofessional productions.
8. What is legal and what is illegal in copying recordings?
9. When do you need to get copyright permission and how do you get it?
10. Why is it important to develop creativity in children and adults?

SUGGESTED LEARNING ACTIVITY

Choose five kinds of artistic media and five pieces of music. Outline how you would combine the music and art. List the titles of the songs, along with the composer, recording artist, and title of the album.

REFERENCES

Anka, P. (1997). *The very best of Paul Anka* [CD]. New York: RCA Camden.

Banana Slug String Band. (1987). *Dirt made my lunch* [CD]. Santa Cruz, CA: Banana Slug String Band.

Bartels, J. (1980). *Sillytime magic* [CD]. Sherman Oaks, CA: Discovery.

Bartels, J. (1985). *Lullaby magic* [CD]. Sherman Oaks, CA: Discovery.

Blue, B. (1984). *Their way* [cassette]. Newton, MA: Baker Street Studios.

Blue, B. (1987). *Charlotte's web (a musical).* Unpublished manuscript.

Blue, B. (1990). *Starting small* [cassette]. Newton, MA: Wellspring Sound.

Boltz, M., Schulkind, M., & Kantra, S. (1991). Effects of background music on the remembering of filmed events. *Memory and Cognition, 19,* 593–606.

Bouhuys, A. L., Bloem, G. M., & Groothuis, T. G. G. (1995). Induction of depressed and elated mood by music influences the perception of facial emotional expressions in healthy subjects. *Journal of Affective Disorders, 33,* 215–226.

Chastain, G., Seibert, P. S., & Ferraro, F. R. (1995). Mood and lexical access of positive, negative, and neutral words. *Journal of General Psychology, 122,* 137–157.

Fink, C., & Marxer, M. (1992). *Making and playing homemade instruments* [video]. Washington, DC: Community Music.

Gesner, C. (1967). *You're a good man, Charlie Brown.* New York: Jeremy Music.

Guilford, J. P. (1967). *The nature of human intelligence.* New York: McGraw-Hill.

Hamann, D., Bourassa, R., & Aderman, M. (1990). Creativity and the arts. *Dialogue in Instrumental Music Education, 14,* 59–68.

Hamann, D., Bourassa, R., & Aderman, M. (1991). Arts experiences and creativity scores of high school students. *Contributions to Music Education, 14,* 36–47.

Hart, A. (1993). *Kids make music, clapping and tapping from Bach to rock!* Cincinnati, OH: Williamson.

Kalmar, M. (1982). The effects of music education based on Kodály's directives in nursery school children—

from a psychologist's point of view. *Psychology of Music, special issue,* 63–68.

Lewis, L. M., Dember, W. N., Schefft, B. K., & Radenhausen, R. A. (1995). Can experimentally induced mood affect optimism and pessimism scores? *Current Psychological Development, Learning, Personal, Social, 14,* 29–41.

Mazer, A. (1991). *The salamander room.* New York: Knopf.

Miché, M. (1990). *Nature nuts* [cassette and CD]. Berkeley, CA: Song Trek Music.

Milliman, R. E. (1982). Using background music to affect the behavior of supermarket shoppers. *Journal of Marketing, 46,* 86–91.

Mohanty, B., & Hejmadi, A. (1992). Effects of intervention training on some cognitive abilities of preschool children. *Psychological Studies, 37,* 31–37.

Rapaport, D. (1984). *How to make and sell your own record.* Tiburon, CA: The Headlands Press.

Robazza, C., Macaluso, C., & D'Urso, V. (1994). Emotional reactions to music by gender, age, and expertise. *Perceptual and Motor Skills, 79,* 939–944.

Simpson, D. J. (1969). The effect of selected musical studies on growth in general creative potential (Doctoral dissertation, University of Southern California, 1969). *Dissertation Abstracts International, 30,* 502a–503a.

Stratton, V. N., & Zalanowski, A. H. (1989). The effects of music and paintings on mood. *Journal of Music Therapy, 26,* 30–41.

Torrance, E. P. (1962). *Guiding creative talent.* Englewood Cliffs, NJ: Prentice-Hall.

Weinberger, N. M. (1998, Spring). *Music Research Newsletter.* [Retrieved from http://www.musica.uci.edu, October, 2001.]

White, E. B. (1987). *Charlotte's web.* New York: HarperCollins Children's Books.

Wolff, K. L. (1979). *The effects of general music education on the academic achievement, perceptual-motor development, creative thinking, and school attendance of first-grade children* (Doctoral dissertation, University of Michigan, Dissertation, 1979). *Dissertation Abstracts International, 40,* 5359A.

ADDITIONAL RESOURCES

Schmidt, D. T. (1958). Living creatively with children and music. *Education, 79,* 109–114.

Vaughan, M., & Myers, R. E. (1971). An examination of musical processes as related to creative thinking. *Journal of Resources in Music Education, 19,* 337–341.

Webster, P. R. (1990). Creativity as creative thinking. *Music Educators Journal, 6,* 22–28.

Music and Movement

Music and movement are a natural combination for children. Bouncing begins in infancy, and much of a preschool teacher's time is spent controlling the moving energies of young children. Training children in movement techniques helps them learn to move with a rhythm and to control their muscles and body parts. Music is an excellent tool to guide and direct a child's movement.

Using Movement to Teach Musical Concepts

Chapter 2 presents musical information and musical expressions that a regular classroom teacher can teach to students. This chapter discusses how some of those ideas and terms can be taught, not only through music, but also through **movement**.

Rhythm and Movement

The rhythm of a piece of music can be tapped by a foot, clapped by a hand, slapped on a knee, drummed on a tummy, banged on an elbow, or whacked on a thigh (Figure 9–1). Rhythm lends itself to movement expression. With preschoolers, you can choose a simple rhythm, like *ta ta titi ta,* and then practice it in the different ways just mentioned. This same activity can be done with early elementary students, using a longer *rhythmic pattern.* You can start with the same pattern and then double it or use a slightly more complex pattern. Try not to get too fancy, or you may lose your students.

Try using an electric piano or a QChord, discussed in Chapter 1, with one of the preprogrammed rhythm patterns to add excitement to a rhythm exercise. You can begin by having children listen to the pattern, then clap to it, then switch to tapping on their knees. Select a child to be the group leader who calls out different movements to the rhythm. Of course, be sure to rotate the privilege. The child can say, "change to elbows" to get the class to slap their elbows with the opposite hands, or "change to stomping," and the class will stomp their feet to the rhythm. One caution for this activity: if the rhythm is too fast, the children may have difficulty following the beat or listening to directions. Also, make sure the music is loud enough to be heard over the movements.

If a class is learning a song, you can take its rhythm and translate it into motions. Something as simple as the song "Jingle Bells" (Bartels, 1990) can be used with preschoolers. Clap the rhythm and say, *"titi ta, titi ta, titi titi ta."* Then stamp the rhythm with your feet or tap the rhythm on your shoulders. Of course, with this song you can pretend you are riding horses.

FIGURE 9–1
Knee-tapping helps children learn rhythm.

Hap Palmer
Children's Musician, Teacher, and Trainer in Early Childhood Music

Hap Palmer's records are a fixture in most teachers' classrooms. Palmer has specialized in doing music for preschoolers and early elementary students for over 30 years. Perhaps he is the standard by which teachers measure music for the classroom.

When Palmer was nine years old, he told his mother that he wanted to play the drums. She said the drums were too noisy and bought him a clarinet. This was in the early '50s, when rock 'n' roll was becoming popular, so he also took up the saxophone, which is played similarly to clarinet. He later acquired a guitar and became really excited about it because he could sing a melody and provide rhythmic accompaniment at the same time. During the '60s, he started singing folk songs and leading sing-alongs as part of his job with the Hollywood YMCA.

After he graduated from college, Palmer went into teaching. He would often play the guitar and sing folk songs with the children. It was a struggle to get the students to stay in their chairs and sing because they kept wanting to get up and move. So after a few exhausting sessions, he said to himself, "Why not work with this energy rather than against it?" This motivated him to write songs which tapped the natural desire of young children to move and be actively involved. Palmer found that active participation was an effective way to reinforce the school curriculum, so he wrote many songs that would involve children in activities such as moving and naming body parts, identifying directions, and learning colors, numbers, and letters of the alphabet. After 20 years of writing songs for use in classrooms and day care centers, he expanded into creating music for audio and video cassettes that children and parents could enjoy in the home setting.

While teaching, he discovered he got more satisfaction writing songs for children than writing commercial songs for adults. He's written songs about everything from a hippopotamus to a roller coaster and is still fascinated with the breadth of topics about which he can sing with children.

Palmer is not fond of airports, flying in planes, the feeling of nervousness before a performance, and having to be concerned with his personal appearance. Fortunately, he overcomes his dislikes and does workshops at conventions and conferences for educational organizations.

Palmer says:

It is difficult to put in words what is important about music. Why does the artist paint? the dancer dance? the poet write? the musician play? An indescribable passion propels one onward. Music and movement are my passions. Music is an important part of the human experience and children should be exposed to music at a young age along with other creative activities such as art and dance. Children should be exposed to a variety of artistic forms, then allowed to choose and pursue what catches their fancy. Also, the arts are not isolated subjects; they relate to other areas of a child's growth and development. Music can involve the whole child: mentally, physically, and emotionally and aid in the child's development of motor skills, language, and imagination.

Hap Palmer, the educator, goes on to point out:

Gardner's theory of Multiple Intelligences suggests that music is an independent intelligence that may be helped by influences at home and school. If music is overlooked, essential learning stages may be missed in early childhood and the potential intelligence may diminish.

You can also play a **musical game** with this rhythm where students guess the song from the rhythm only. With early elementary students, start with three simple tunes: "Jingle Bells" (Bartels, 1990), "Twinkle, Twinkle Little Star" (Collins, 1990), and "Mary Had a Little Lamb" (Jenkins, 1993). Have children practice only the rhythm for various songs. Use a variety of movements to reinforce learning the rhythms. To practice, play the guessing game with the teacher giving the clue by tapping out the rhythm of one song. The children have to guess the song. After you have played this game with your class for a while, you can begin letting the children give the clues.

Later, you can expand the repertoire to include a few other songs. While you should limit the number of songs for preschoolers, with elementary school–age children, you can graduate to using rhythms from songs they sing in class. Second and third graders love to include more difficult rhythms, like the original *Star Wars Theme* by John Williams (Monardo, 1977), when they play this game. They also love to try to stump the teacher, so start practicing your rhythm patterns!

Tempo and Movement

Tempo is the speed of the music or movement. Once you begin exploring this dimension with movement, you will hit a funny bone. Faster motions are universally funny to children (Figure 9–2). With fast-forward movement, the children go wildly out of control and fall on the floor laughing. They also find slow motion amusing.

With this information in mind, start playing music at a reasonable speed. You can use a percussion or electronic instrument for this purpose. Get the beat going at a steady pace, so the children move in time with it. Start with a simple movement, like foot stomping. Then gradually speed up the beat. While you are doing the steady beat, say, "Moderato, moderato." As you speed up, say, "Accelerando, accelerando." When you get to a fast, steady pace, say, "Presto, presto." You can do the same activity with another movement, such as slapping your hands on your thighs. Again, use the words moderato and accelerando, but to give students more exposure to a variety of musical terms, for the fast beat say, "Vivace."

FIGURE 9–2 Fast motions are universally funny to children.

For the slowing down activity, start with a walking pace, and use the word andante instead of moderato. If you teach preschoolers, stick with the word moderato. After the children are moving at a moderate pace, slow down the beat and say, "Ritardando, ritardando." When you get to a slow beat, say, "Lento, lento." Another choice for a slow beat is "Largo, largo." Consult Chapter 2 for a discussion of more tempo words that you can use for this activity. Remember, keep the students focused on staying with the beat for all these rhythm activities.

Dynamic Levels and Movement

Dynamic levels refer to the loudness or softness of the music. In classical music there are six dynamic levels. Chapter 2 covers these levels in detail. Dynamic levels can be represented with movement. For the softest level, pianissimo, have students crouch down to the floor and whisper, "Pianissimo, pianissimo, it's the softest sound." For the next dynamic level, piano, children can paw the ground like a cat and say, "Piano, piano, soft as kitty paws." The next level is mezzo piano, or medium soft. Say, "Mezzo piano, mezzo piano, we can say it medium soft." Have children kneel on the floor and pretend they are petting a dog. Mezzo forte is next. Tell them to put their hands up to their mouths like a megaphone and say, "Mezzo forte, can you hear me now? I'm talking to you, medium loud." Forte is a loud voice. The forte movement is like a cheerleader with pompoms, saying, "Forte, forte, rah rah rah." For fortissimo, stand up, put your hands up in the air, and jump, while saying, "Fortissimo, fortissimo, it's the loudest loudalissimo" (Figure 9–3). If you survive movement with the six dynamic levels, you can progress to musical expressions.

Musical Expressions and Movement

You can teach many **musical expressions** to young children through movement. Movements that accompany words help reinforce the words. Children can use long arm swaying for legato, short finger flicks for staccato, and a fist pounding on an open hand

FIGURE 9–3 Raising arms over your head symbolizes fortissimo.

for marcato. Children can also say the word and its meaning while doing the motion. For legato, say, "smooth and connected"; for staccato, say, "short and choppy"; for marcato, say, "mark each one." Switch between saying the meaning and saying the word while continuing to do the motions.

In addition to staccato, marcato, and legato, you can do a hand movement for *sforzando.* This word means to accent a note that has *sfz* written over it. For sforzando, choose the note to accent, and as you sing the scale, sing the note loudly and punch your fists into the air.

Use the list of musical expressions in Chapter 2 to develop other movement activities to match words. For example, *maestoso* means majestically, so you can play a piece of majestic music, such as Handel's "Coronation March" (Johnson, 1987) and have students do a variety of movements in a majestic manner. Classical music is great for this activity, but you may also want to use music students already know. Try listening to your music and see what vocabulary words it inspires. Use those words with the music and add your own motions to invent your own music movement and vocabulary building activity.

Another favorite movement activity used to teach musical expressions is using the whole body for pitch recognition. This is a sneaky way to get children to exercise, as well as to teach a lot about music. The toes are number one, knees are number two, waist is three, shoulders are four, head is five, six and seven are above the head, and high number one is as far up as students can reach. Then you can sing numbers and have students do the corresponding movement. Many tunes can be used for this movement exercise. Try "Twinkle, Twinkle Little Star" (Collins, 1990) with the numbers using this movement activity. If you do not remember the numbers for the song, refer to Chapter 2.

Some other simple songs work with the number system and the movements just described. Instead of singing the words to "Mary Had a Little Lamb" (Jenkins, 1993), sing the tune with these numbers:

three two one two three three three, two two two, three five five,
three two one two three three three, two two three two one.

"My Bonnie Lies Over the Ocean" (Peter Pan Kids, 2000) is:

> one six five four, five four two one low six,
> one six five four, four three four five,
> one six five four, five four two one low six,
> one two five four three, two three four.

"Here Comes the Bride" (Various, 1999) is:

> one four four four, one five three four,
> one four six one, six four two, five three four.

"Michael, Row the Boat Ashore" (Peter, Paul & Mary, 1998) is:

> one three five three five six five, three five six five,
> three five five three four three two, one two three two one.

Notice how each of the last three songs begins with a jump from one to three, four or six. Each song teaches a different interval jump, for instance, a third, fourth, or sixth. "Twinkle, Twinkle Little Star" starts with the jump of a fifth.

You can do the same movement exercise with the letters of the musical alphabet. Since only the first seven letters of the alphabet are used in the musical alphabet, use the same body locations as the numbers. The toes are A, knees are B, waist is C, shoulders are D, head is E, and above the head are F and G. To go all the way to the top of the scale, reach for high A. This order is the preschool version; it keeps children from being confused about the order of the alphabet. For elementary children, try using C at the toes, D at the knees, E at the waist, F at the shoulders, G at the head, and A and B above the head. The top of the scale is high C. Older children who already know the alphabet can learn that the musical alphabet is different.

The duration of a musical note can also be taught with movement. One way is to assign a motion to sixteenth notes, eighth notes, quarter notes, half notes, and whole notes. (Refer to Chapter 2 to review how these notes look.)

- ♪ Begin with quarter notes, with children moving their heads forward and back for each note, saying, "Ta" with each head motion.
- ♪ For eighth notes, children move their heads from side to side and sway their shoulders. They say, "Titi" with each movement.
- ♪ For sixteenth notes, kids slap their hands on their thighs and say, "Ticka ticka."
- ♪ For half notes, they sway from side to side and, using long arm movements, say, "Too-oo."
- ♪ For whole notes, they turn in an entire circle and say, "Whole two, three, four" (Figure 9–4).

Using Movement with Songs

Most teachers agree that using movements with songs helps children understand and remember the words. With children under the age of eight, some kind of movement should be done with every song that you teach. If you do not know any movements to go with a song, make them up. If you do not want to invent motions, have children do their own creative movements while listening to the song. Then, observe the children and choose motions that they create. After you have observed the motions that seem to fit best, put them together into a coordinated whole. This way, students will participate in

FIGURE 9–4 To symbolize whole notes, children can turn in an entire circle.

creating motions and then will be able to perform motions together. This is also a wonderful way to discover the choreographic talent of your students.

You can do different kinds of motions with a group of children.

- ♪ *Full body motion* is when children stand up and use their whole bodies to move to the music.
- ♪ *Hand motions* are done only with the hands and arms.
- ♪ A third kind of motion uses standard signs from *American Sign Language.*
- ♪ There are many different types of *dance,* which could be considered full body motion, but dance is usually stylized and not free form.

Full Body Motion

Preschool children are not yet adept at finer movements, so **full body motion** is good training for them. With two-year-olds, motions often consist of just standing up and jumping to music. Certainly, full body motions are great for acting out songs. Two favorite songs for this kind of activity are "Romp in the Swamp" by Bill Brennan (1984; Miché, 1990) and "Workin' Together in the Sun," written by Al Einhorn (Miché, 1990). With "Romp in the Swamp," children pretend they are wading into a swamp, looking around, holding a bird's nest, putting on insect repellent, and slapping at mosquitoes. For "Workin' Together in the Sun," children pretend that they are digging up the ground, planting seeds, pulling up weeds, and working together in the sun. During the chorus, they play hand jive, which is a pattern of slaps to the knees and claps of the hands. For preschoolers, hand jive can be as simple as tapping the hands of another child. First graders clap and tap their partners' hands. Second graders clap, tap, and slap their knees.

Third graders can do an entire hand jive routine, usually one that they make up themselves, complete with knee slaps and hand shakes (Figure 9–5).

Hand Motions

In elementary school, children transition from standing up and jumping with music to being able to sit and represent the words of the song in **hand motions**. Most songs sung with early elementary students are accompanied by hand motions. Students enjoy doing hand motions until about the end of third grade. By fourth grade, children consider hand motions too babyish and will only do them to perform for a younger group like kindergartners.

Preschoolers require the gross motor training that full body motion provides. However, hand motions are also excellent practice for them to learn how to train smaller muscles by using only their hands and arms for movement. So, preschool teachers should sing some songs with hand motions and some songs with full body motions.

You can sing and do motions to the same song with preschoolers and early elementary students. A good example is "Jim Along Josie," a traditional song performed by Pete Seeger on his album *American Folk Songs for Children* (1953). For preschoolers, get up and jump each time the singer sings, "Jump, Jim along." For elementary school students, sit and raise your hands and arms on the words "Jump, Jim along." In each verse, Jim walks, crawls, or hops. Have preschoolers do these movements with the song. With elementary children, have them use their fingers to walk across the top of a desk, use their hands and arms to pretend to crawl, and use their hands to pretend to hop.

Another example of a song that uses hand motions is "The Haunted House" by Gerry Tenney (1985; Miché, 1988). The words to the song begin, "As I walked into the haunted house." Children can pretend to walk with their hands into the haunted house. They put their fingers to their lips, "trying to be quiet as a mouse." Then they pretend "to climb the stairs" with their hands. "The room was cold, the walls were bare." They hold their shoulders and then reach out to the bare walls. "And who do you think was standing there, standing there at the top of the stairs?" Point up to the top of the stairs. "Standing there with a whole lot of hair?" Have them hold out their hair, full length. "It was King Kong, the gorilla." Have them pound their chests with their fists, two times, one for King and the other for Kong. "Playing ping pong with Godzilla." Hold up

FIGURE 9–5   *Children of all ages enjoy doing hand jive rhythms.*

imaginary paddles and pretend to play ping pong, then put up three fingers on each hand for Godzilla.

This is a very popular song with children from three to eight. You will have to limit the period during which you sing it with children. A good time is from the beginning of school until Halloween. Otherwise, you may end up singing it every week for the entire year.

American Sign Language

You can teach **American Sign Language** to preschoolers. Many children with hearing disabilities begin signing younger than age two. However, in elementary school children really become interested in learning sign language, and by then most children are able to learn the correct way to make signs. Most songs can be signed as well as sung, but some songs lend themselves particularly well to signing. One favorite is a song by Greg Scelsa, "The World is a Rainbow." This song is recorded on the Greg & Steve album *We All Live Together,* Volume II (1984; Miché, 1989). Do not do a sign for every word in the song; instead, do signs for the important words. Sign *world, rainbow, colors,* and *see them all around. World* is the letter *W* on both hands, with the hands revolving around each other (Figure 9–6). *Rainbow* is holding out four fingers on each hand, with the right hand making the shape of a rainbow. *Colors* is tapping the fingers of your right hand on your chin. *See them all around* is two fingers from the right hand touching the right side of your eye and then stretching your arm out as if it were looking all around.

Another song that adapts easily to sign language is "Spiders and Snakes" (Axlerod, 1980), mentioned in Chapter 5. Use only four signs, one for *spider, snake, love,* and *no matter.* The *spider* sign is two hands with the hands overlapping. The *snake* sign is two fingers on your right hand, shaking the whole hand downward. The sign for *love* is two closed fists, with arms crossed over your chest. The sign for *no matter* is two hands slapping the fingers of each other, kind of like a swinging door banging on itself. If you would like to learn how to do all these signs correctly, find someone who signs to show you the correct way to speak sign language.

FIGURE 9–6 The *world* in sign language.

Dance and Music

Dance is a stylized form of movement. A pattern is usually followed to ensure that the dancers do the same kind of movement. The dance may be creative, like modern dance. It may be prescribed, like square dancing and folk dancing. It can be very formal, like ballet, or informal like dancing to rock 'n' roll music.

Creative Dance. In **creative dance**, a few kinds of patterns are determined, and the dancers are free to do the patterns in their own ways (Figure 9–7). One of the best examples of creative dance for children was shown on Sesame Street®. Children created their own movements to short clips of different kinds of music. About 30 seconds of each of six different kinds of music were used. The music selections included reggae, ballet, march, lullaby, tap dance, and rock 'n' roll. This is a great project to ask a parent to create for you. You can select a few pieces of music that you already have and ask a parent to put together a creative dance tape. Emphasize the need for *short* clips. Once you have the tape, you can play it for years to come.

Square Dance. Many ways are available for teachers to do **square dance** activities with students. Even preschoolers love to learn the rudiments of square dancing. They can learn to swing their partners, do an elbow swing, do a two-hand swing (Figure 9–8), circle around, and with practice, do-si-do. Older children can learn those movements and a slide, right-hand star, left-hand star, and right and left around. These right- and left-hand activities are particularly good for first through third graders. Of course, you need the right kind of music for square dance activities. Fink and Marxer have a bluegrass sound that is great for square dancing, but it does not have the square dancing calls integrated into the music. "Hands" is a particularly good song to use for square dance routines. It is a song about the work done by everyone's hands, and it lends itself to simple square dance calls, like right- and left-hand stars. The song is recorded on the album *Air Guitar* (Fink & Marxer, 1987; Miché, 1989).

Another children's musician who has a country folk music sound is John McCutcheon. His song "The Pumpkin Man" (Miché, 1988) is well-suited to creative square dancing for children.

FIGURE 9–7
Creative dance comes in all forms.

Where can I get square dance and line dance music?

Supreme Audio is a large distributor of square dance music. They have a book with a CD called *Square Dance Now* (Rusf, 1998). The book gives an overview of how to square dance with children and includes a graduated level of dances. Another set, called *Step Lively* (Rose, 1998), is especially good for younger children and has 14 dances. An entire line of 45 rpm square dance records for callers and for line dances, hoe-downs, contra dancing, and quadrilles is also available. You can also order individual records with one dance on each record. Visit http://www.supremeaudio.com.

FIGURE 9–8 A two-hand swing is appropriate for preschool square dancers.

Line Dances. **Line dances** are actually part of a larger group of dances called **contra dances**. "The Virginia Reel" is a good example of a line dance. These dances are done with lines of couples. Two lines, traditionally one of men and one of women, move opposite, or contra, each other. Children of elementary school age usually enjoy everything about contra dances except holding hands with the opposite sex. This problem is easily solved by having children choose a partner of any sex rather than forcing boys and girls to dance with each other.

Cross-Cultural Dance. **Cross-cultural dances** include Chinese Lion dances, Mexican folk dances, Balkan step dances, Jewish circle dances, and African tribal dances, among others. Dances exist for any culture you are studying. Every nation has dances. Some may be too difficult for preschoolers, but you can always use the music to these dances as a creative dance activity. Put on the music to a Jewish folk dance and see how

Cathy Fink and Marcy Marxer
Bluegrass for Children

Cathy Fink always loved singing. Her first real memory of singing was at age three or four, when her mother played piano and she belted out her favorite songs, "Beautiful Dreamer" (Dreamsisters, 1997), "Little Brown Jug" (Miller, 2000), and "Bicycle Built for Two" (Cedarmont Kids, 1995). Fink learned to play piano by ear and took lessons for a few years in elementary school. Her family did not sing much, but she sang in every school and community chorus she could.

Fink had fun with children and music at day care centers in Montreal while attending McGill College. Then, while student teaching at Rough Rock Demonstration School on the Navajo Indian reservation, she got involved in children's music. There was no music teacher, and she had a guitar, so she became the *de facto* music teacher. Everyone had a great time, and from then on, she looked for opportunities to sing with children. Fink has continued performing folk and country music for 25 years.

Marcy Marxer's family was musical. Her mother and sisters sang jazz and swing songs in three-part harmony. Marxer's grandmother, who spent a lot of time with her, played barrelhouse blues and honky-tonk piano. Marxer's grandmother showed her guitar chords and played songs with her. When Marxer was twelve she took classes in voice, piano, and guitar at Capital University. She grew up singing in a church where the members were mostly African-American. Marxer remembers, "The community was very involved in the civil rights movement and many social issues. Music was an amazing tool for spreading messages and it was a real boost to our spirits when the going got tough. Music was the glue that helped us all unite towards our common goals. It was also some of the best music I've ever heard!" Marxer later taught special education at the High Point Center in Ann Arbor, Michigan. She used music and drama to aid in teaching the curriculum. In the early 1980s, Marxer worked with the Wolf Trap Institute for Early Learning through the Performing Arts to bring music to Head Start classrooms. Since 1983, she has toured and performed as a duo with Fink, continuing to perform for both children and adults.

Fink and Marxer feel that many important qualities are needed for effective children's music.

> It's important for the music to be fun and it's important for it to be meaningful and it's important for it to be accessible. It's also a wonderful opportunity for children and parents to enjoy music together.
>
> There's so much out there these days, we don't feel we need to add to the quantity of children's music. We feel that each project, each song, needs to make a contribution that is different from what's already available.
>
> Different songs are great for different reasons. Perhaps it's the catchy chorus, perhaps it's the message of the song, a great melody, a great arrangement. Certainly, the content of the song must be meaningful to the listener and participator to get them interested.

All of Fink and Marxer's concerts are participatory. Families sing along from the first song. They teach new songs, teach sign language to songs, and show hand motions to songs. They also involve children when recording their albums. All of their children's recordings feature groups of children singing on the chorus.

Reprinted with permission from Cathy Fink and Marcy Marxer.

FIGURE 9–9 Learning dances from other cultures teaches appreciation of other societies.

preschoolers respond. Teach them only one simple step, and they can "do the hora." With first graders, you can put on the same music and do a simplified routine of holding hands, walking sideways in a circle, walking toward the middle, backing up, and clapping on the correct beat. If you integrate this dance into your appreciation of different cultures and include ideas from Chapter 7, you can teach movement, dance, music, valuing cultural differences, and appreciation of other social styles all at once (Figure 9–9).

Parades

A movement activity with young children that is usually not considered a musical activity is a **parade**. Two occasions that are great for children's parades are Halloween and the Fourth of July. Children like Halloween because they can show off their costumes. The Fourth of July is great for waving flags and can be tied in with teaching history. Parades can also be done for other occasions: birthdays, holidays, and the end of the school year. A favorite musical parade is one with instruments. For preschoolers, this is the perfect opportunity to use homemade musical instruments. See Chapter 8 for a discussion of how to make some homemade instruments. If you do not have time to make instruments, pretend instruments are just as much fun. The slide trombone is a popular pretend instrument, outranked only by pretend drums. Pretend instruments come in all shapes and sizes. Best of all, they are lightweight for children to carry.

If you are going to have a parade, you need marching music. John Philip Sousa marches are best known for this purpose. You can look in a used record store or even a thrift store for an inexpensive Sousa march album. You may wish to march to a more modern song. "Chickens for Peace" by Peter Alsop (1986; Miché, 1989) is a good choice. Put on your chicken wings for this march and "bawk" to the music.

FIGURE 9–10 Exercising to music is healthy and fun!

Exercising to Music

Doing physical exercises to music, such as running in place or doing push-ups, has traditionally been done by exercise physiologists, and new research encourages this practice. In a 1998 study by Szmedra and Bacharach, researchers studied the effects of music during treadmill running in 10 well-trained adult males in their 20s. Many physical measurements were done before and after running either with or without music. Running with music resulted in a significant decrease in heart rate, blood pressure, and lactic acid buildup in the muscles. The results, especially the reduced lactic acid, indicated that music seems to reduce muscle tension and probably also reduces stress, even in well-conditioned individuals.

Teachers should include music as an essential element in physical exercises with students. Exercise can reduce stress levels for students and you too, right there in the classroom (Figure 9–10).

Musical Games

Two high quality books about musical games are *The Big Book of Music Games* (Pressnall, Malecha, & De Paulis, 1988) and *101 Musical Games for Children* by Jerry Storms (Storms, Griffiths, Storms, & Hurd, 1995).

The first is a book of music-oriented materials to help elementary school-age children read musical notes, signs, and expressions. This book is full of ideas about how to play music reading games.

The second book is inexpensive and contains lots of great games for early elementary students. Some of the games are good for preschool. In one game from the book, children sit on the floor in a circle. One child is asked to think of a song and to tap out the beginning of the song on the back of the next child. The neighbor passes it on to the next child, and so on around the circle until the last child claps the rhythm out loud for the whole group. The group then hears the first child's rhythm to see if they match. If they

FIGURE 9–11 Musical games capture children's attention.

do, then the children try to guess the song. If they do not match, the children have to do the whole back tapping routine again. Many other games in the book also employ movement of some kind (Figure 9–11).

The Dalcroze Method

The **Dalcroze method** of music education was developed in the 1890s by Émile Jaques-Dalcroze, a Swiss educator. It uses movement to teach the basic elements of music: rhythm, dynamics, tone, and form. The purpose of the Dalcroze method is to use all of the senses. It has three branches.

1. **Eurhythmics**, which trains the body in rhythm and dynamics.
2. *Solfège,* which trains the ear, eye, and voice in pitch, melody, and harmony.
3. **Improvisation**, which puts it all together according to students' own inventions: in movements, with voice, or with instruments.

Using this method, children move, sing, and play as they engage in a variety of activities involving listening, responding, and inventing.

Where can I find space to do movement with my students? My classroom is full of stuff.

If you teach at a preschool, you may have an outdoor play area. Outdoor space can be transformed into movement space with the purchase of a camping canopy. They are usually 10 x 10 feet in size, and that is large enough to provide some movement space. Even in winter, if the canopy is located near the classroom door, the children can bundle up and move around in the outdoor space for 10 to 15 minutes. Of course, you should not do this during a rainstorm or blizzard.

If your school does not provide enough of the right kind of outdoor space, you can look for a space within walking distance of the school. If there is a church, senior center, or recreation center nearby, it may have a large room you can use. Many centers have large spaces that may be available for 45 minutes once a week (Figure 9–12). You could take your students on a field trip to the large movement space. You could even take them regularly for a movement class.

Children love to go on field trips to another school. Perhaps there is a movement space available at a local high school or junior high school. Maybe another preschool has a good space for movement, and the cost of a music/movement specialist could be split between the two schools. A popular field trip in one preschool was a visit to a local gymnastics center. It was a nominal fee to rent the gym with equipment and pay a gymnastics teacher for an hour. Another preschool arranged for a series of 10 visits to the same gymnastics center. They had a reduced hourly fee because they booked multiple visits.

Preschools may be able to arrange visits to a local elementary school to use a multipurpose room, either once or in conjunction with a kindergarten movement class. Elementary schools often have a large space that can be reserved by teachers. If the space is being used by a small group, you may be able to trade the use of your classroom for the use of the larger room. If you need equipment for a movement activity but you do not have the finances for it, an after school recreation program may provide the equipment in exchange for use of the school space. The equipment could then be stored at the school and used by both groups.

FIGURE 9–12 Schools and community centers will often rent space for movement programs.

JOY YELIN, DALCROZE SPECIALIST

Joy Yelin is a Dalcroze specialist. She gives workshops and presentations about the Dalcroze method. Yelin studied piano from age eight to age 16. She was so accomplished on the piano that she accompanied the orchestra and choir in junior high and high school. Yelin became a piano teacher 30 years ago when a friend asked her to teach her daughter. Yelin loves the challenge of working with students, each with different needs and goals. She also enjoys teaching graduate workshops as a Dalcroze trainer.

Yelin involves children in music through diversified improvisation, imagery, theatrical presentation, and movement. She likes to listen to classical music when she is alone. About music, Yelin said, "It lifts my heart, it challenges my brain and body."

Conclusion

A variety of opportunities are available for combining music and movement, but not all the possibilities have been covered. An excellent book to consult for more in-depth training in movement is *Experiences in Movement with Music, Activities and Theory*, Second Edition, by Rae Pica (2000). The book has an excellent chapter on combining music and movement with some additional ideas for teaching music and movement.

KEY TERMS

American Sign Language
contra dances
creative dance
cross-cultural dances
Dalcroze method
dance

eurhythmics
full body motion
hand motions
improvisation
line dances

movement
musical expressions
musical game
parade
square dance

DISCUSSION QUESTIONS

1. Name three ways to teach rhythm and movement.
2. What should you be aware of when teaching preschoolers about tempo with movement?
3. What is the difference between full body motion and hand motion? When should each be used?
4. For what age group should sign language be used?
5. At what age is it appropriate to stop using hand motions?
6. What is the Dalcroze method?
7. Name five ways to find space for movement activities.
8. Name six kinds of dance you can do with preschoolers.

9. What square dance movements can you do with first graders?

10. Describe a musical game and name one source for finding musical games.

SUGGESTED LEARNING ACTIVITIES

Create hand motions to two children's songs. Teach the motions to two adults or to the class. Use a recording of the song for teaching it to the class.

Learn a dance from another culture and teach a simplified version to two students or local children. Or, you can teach this dance to your class.

Outline a plan for teaching a simple square dance to first-grade students. Include at least four square dance steps. Be sure to list the name of the piece of music you will use with this square dance. Also list the song's author, recording artist, and album title. Make a short tape of the music for later classroom use.

REFERENCES

Alsop, P. (1986). *Take me with you!* [cassette]. Topanga, CA: Moose School Records.

Axlerod, J. (1980). *Turtles and snakes and snowstorms* [record]. Washington, DC: Smithsonian/Folkways.

Bartels, J. (1990). *Christmas magic* [cassette]. Sherman Oaks, CA: Discovery.

Brennan, B. (1984). *Romp in the swamp* [cassette]. Takoma Park, MD: D. D. Dreams Music.

Cedarmont Kids. (1995). *School days* [cassette]. New York: Author.

Collins, J. (1990). *Baby's bedtime* [cassette]. New York: Lightyear.

Dreamsisters. (1997). *Beautiful dreamer* [cassette]. Windermere, FL: Family Planet.

Fink, C., & Marxer, M. (1987). *Air guitar* [cassette]. Washington, DC: High Windy Audio.

Greg & Steve. (1984). *We all live together* (Volume II) [cassette]. Acton, CA: Youngheart Records.

Jenkins, E. (1993). *Early childhood songs* [cassette]. Washington, DC: Smithsonian/Folkways.

Johnson, A. R. (1987). *Handel: Coronation anthems* [CD]. New York: Uni/Philips.

Miché, M. (1988). *Holly daze* [cassette and CD]. Berkeley, CA: Song Trek Music.

Miché, M. (1989). *Peace it together* [cassette and CD]. Berkeley, CA: Song Trek Music.

Miché, M. (1990). *Nature nuts* [cassette and CD]. Berkeley, CA: Song Trek Music.

Miller, G. (2000). *Swinging mood* [CD]. New York: Columbia River.

Monardo, M. (1977). *Star wars and other galactic funk*. New York: Millennium Record Company, Inc.

Peter Pan Kids. (2000). *Nursery songs sing-along* [CD]. New York: Peter Pan.

Peter, Paul & Mary. (1998). *Around the campfire* [cassette]. New York: Warner Brothers.

Pica, R. (2000). *Experiences in movement with music, activities and theory* (2nd ed.). Albany, NY: Delmar.

Pressnall, D. O., Malecha, L., & De Paulis, M. (1988). *The big book of music games*. Grand Rapids, MI: Instructional Fair.

Rose, M. (1998). *Step lively* [book and CD]. Vancouver, BC, Canada: Community Dance Project.

Rusf, B. (1998). *Square dance now* [book and CD]. Whittier, CA: Wagon Wheel Records.

Scruggs, J. (1984). *Late last night* [cassette]. Austin, TX: Shadow Play Records.

Seeger, P. (1953). *American folk songs for children* [record]. Washington, DC: Smithsonian/Folkways.

Storms, G., Griffiths, A., Storms, J., & Hurd, C. (1995). *101 music games for children: Fun and learning with rhythm and song*. Alameda, CA: Hunter House.

Szmedra, L., & Bacharach, D. W. (1998). Effect of music on perceived exertion, plasma lactate, norepinephrine and cardiovascular hemodynamics during treadmill running. *International Journal of Sports Medicine, 19,* 32–37.

Tenney, G. (1985). *Heart will carry on* [cassette]. Oakland, CA: Lost Tribe Productions.

Various artists. (1999). *Songs for your wedding* [CD]. Maple Plain, MN: K-Tel International.

CHAPTER 10

Music with Reading and Writing

In a 1975 study by Hurwitz, Wolff, Bortnick, and Kokas, the researchers asked, "Does music training improve reading performance in first-grade children?" The experimental group received Kodály training, which included hand signals for higher and lower pitches. The control group consisted of children who were matched with the test group in age, IQ, and socioeconomic status at the beginning of the study and who received no special treatment.

The music instruction lasted five days a week, 40 minutes per day, for seven months. Students were tested on reading ability at the start and end of the school year. After training, the music group had significantly higher reading scores than the control group. Trained students scored in the 88th percentile, while the control group scored in the 72nd percentile. The experiment continued, and after an additional year of Kodály training, the experimental group was still superior to the control group. These findings clearly showed that music training helped children to read.

In a 1994 study, Sheila Douglas and Peter Willatts tested 78 second-grade children on vocabulary, reading, and spelling. They also tested the same group on their musical skills, especially the ability to detect slight differences between rhythms. The authors found a significant correlation between reading ability, spelling ability, and rhythmic ability. They then ran a study with two groups, one that had a music program for six months and the other that had specialized instruction in verbal skills. After six months, the music students showed significant improvement in reading, but the verbal instruction group did not.

Music Instruction and Reading Readiness

What is it about music training that helps children read better? To answer this question, consider how children learn to read. Typically, they learn to recognize letters and environmental print, words like *Stop* on a stop sign or *Bank* on a bank building, beginning around age three. By age five, most children can recognize the letters of the alphabet and write their own names. In kindergarten, most children learn to associate the shape of a letter with the sound it makes. Some children also learn to read simple sight words such as *cat* and *dog* as whole words, without sounding out the individual letters. In first grade, age six, approaches to teaching reading diverge. Three systems of teaching are used: phonetic/graphic, syntax and vocabulary semantics, and the **phonemic awareness** method, which concentrates only on sounding out words. All three methods have a phonemic component. Music training is helpful to children in developing **phonemic ability**.

Music learning assists phonemic awareness because children learn to distinguish closely related sounds. In music, this is called **pitch discrimination**. Children learn to hear slight differences between musical notes. A 1993 study by Lamb and Gregory showed that the ability to distinguish pitches and the ability to sound out words are closely related skills. The researchers began by testing children of kindergarten age on their ability to read. The children were given four tests: concepts about print, word matching, letter sounding, and word reading. They were given a phonic reading test, which tested the ability to read blends and nonsense syllables. The children then listened to pairs of musical notes and chords and reported whether they thought the notes or the chords were the same or different. In an additional test, the children were assessed on pitches that had different timbres; that is, the pitch remained the same but the note was played with a different sound quality. Finally, the children's phonemic awareness was tested by having them listen to spoken, single-syllable words and then tell if the words began or ended with the same sounds. The experimenters then did a statistical analysis of the children's scores on various tests and found a correlation between pitch discrimination and simple reading, pitch discrimination and phonic reading, and pitch discrimination and phonemic awareness (Figure 10–1). The ability to differentiate timbre did not show a relationship to reading ability.

The ability to hear pitch differences is associated with children who have better reading ability. Children who have good pitch discrimination may be good readers *because* of

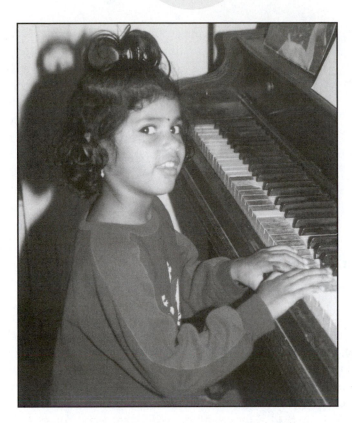

FIGURE 10–1 Increasing pitch awareness helps a child's reading ability.

the pitch discrimination. This study suggests that possibility, but further research needs to be done to find out whether teaching children to hear different pitches helps them learn to read.

Development of musical skills promotes reading achievement, as the research clearly suggested. Yet the question remains: How does music promote reading achievement? Music education helps to support reading development in a number of different ways.

♪ First, children who have poor auditory discrimination have difficulty using **phonemic clues** when in learning to read. For instance, they cannot hear small differences in sounds, so they do not hear the difference between *P* and *B*. Because they cannot rely on sounding out words, these children have to learn to read every word by sight. This is not too difficult for some words, but other words like *insight* and *inside* look similar. The research by Lamb and Gregory (1993) showed a direct correlation between children with good pitch discrimination and those with good reading ability. Therefore, the training of the hearing and pitch discrimination learned through music is probably one of the mechanisms that supports reading achievement, particularly affecting the phonemic ability of a child.

♪ Next, when children learn to read, they need to learn vocabulary. Reading specialists cite knowledge of vocabulary as one of the most important factors in children's **reading ability**. If a child can sound out the word *captain* but does not know what the word means, he will not be able to comprehend what he has read. If that same child sings a song about the sea that has the word *captain* in it, he is more likely to understand the meaning of the word. If the teacher discusses the vocabulary in the song with the class, the student is even more likely to understand the word when he reads it.

♪ A third reason why music promotes reading achievement is because musical information is stored in different locations all over the brain. There is a different brain wave pattern for singing than for dancing or reading. If children sing a text rather than reciting it, a new pattern is created in the brain, and it stores the information in new locations. The same is true for dancing or writing a text rather than reading it. When teaching reading, experienced teachers have students write, sing, and dance a text in addition to reading it.

♪ Teachers who present many songs to their classes often accompany these songs with printed text of some kind. If students look at song lyrics while they are singing, they not only spend time on music, they also spend time looking at the printed words; that is, they spend more of their time reading. The beauty is that they think they are practicing music, and do not notice that they are reading.

Reading Stories to Musical Accompaniment

As discussed in Chapter 4, research shows that music helps adults recall words they learned while listening to the same background music (Figure 10–2). If children read or hear a story with **musical accompaniment**, especially the same music repeatedly, they will able to recall the words to the story. They are cued by the music. This kind of learning is sight/word based and not phonemic, so students with phonemic difficulty may do better in this activity.

You can read a story to music in different ways. You can play a recording and read a story to children while the music plays. Then, a few days later you can put on the same music and children can read the story aloud with you. After a few more days, you can put on the music and have one student read the story to the class. Finally, you can have small

FIGURE 10–2 Reading with background music increases memory skills.

How can I find songs to go along with books that I already use in my classroom?

To find songs that go with the books you already use, make a list of the concepts in your curriculum that are presented in the books you use. When you have a clear concept of what subject areas you want to emphasize, it will be easier for you to find songs to support your ideas. Now you can begin the search. First, ask other teachers if they know of a song, say, about the ocean. Once in a while, someone has the perfect song on a record, tape, or CD in his classroom. At other times a teacher will say, for example, "No, but I have a great song about amphibians." Keep that knowledge tucked away. You may decide to do a unit on amphibians next year.

The next group to ask is parents and students. You may find that a family has an incredible collection of children's songs. You also may find that a child has a great song on a CD-ROM that accompanies a computer game.

The next option is the Internet. Start with http://www.childrensmusic.org. This Web site has a list of various musicians. Post your question to the list of children's musicians. You can ask if anyone knows of songs that teach a particular concept or that go with a particular book. Many people on the list are experienced music teachers and children's musicians. You can also consult P. J. Swift of *Pickleberry Pie Radio* by e-mail (see Appendix A). With 5,000 albums on hand, she probably has a good suggestion.

groups of children read the story to you with the music playing in the background. Use music without words for this kind of activity.

In choosing the background music for a story, you can pick something that you enjoy, or you can choose a style of music that goes with the story. For example, if you read *Happy Birthday, Martin Luther King* (Marzollo, 1993), you can play gospel-style music in the background. Music without words is better for remembering spoken text, because words in the song can distract from hearing the text.

Music and Story Combinations

A **music story combination** is not quite the same as reading a story to background music. Rather, a song that is related to the theme of a story accompanies it. You can, for example, combine the song "The Wheels on the Bus" (Raffi, 2000) with a book about a bus or about wheels. You usually begin with a song that students enjoy and then look for a book to go with it. This is fairly easy because you first pick the song and then you can consult a librarian for a book that goes with the topic or concepts in it. You can also do it the other way around: you can take a favorite book and look for a song or two to go with it. However, finding the right song is harder than finding a book that goes with a song.

Read-Along Sing-Along Books

A **read-along sing-along book** usually begins with the writing of a song. The song is later published in book form. The words of the song are accompanied by illustrations, and sometimes a tape also accompanies the book so that readers can hear the original song (Figure 10–3). At other times, the song is printed in music form at the end of the book. A surprising number of these books are available. Many Raffi books have been

Raffi
Children's Musician

Raffi Cavoukian was born in 1948 in Cairo, Egypt, to Armenian parents. When Raffi was ten, his family immigrated to Canada and settled in Toronto. Raffi's father was a renowned portrait photographer who also played the accordion and sang in the Armenian church choir. Raffi learned to play the guitar as a teenager. He started composing on his own, and in 1970 he began his career as a singer/songwriter.

Raffi began performing for children in 1974. He visited the Toronto nursery school where his stepmother was the director. Raffi's sincerity and playfulness appealed to the young children, and they loved singing silly songs with him. After talking with parents and teachers, Raffi realized the need for good recorded children's music. He felt that children should have as much of a selection of recorded music as adults. In 1976 Raffi released his first album, *Singable Songs for the Very Young*. Since then, he has recorded many albums, videos, song books, and picture books based on his music. Raffi has played a major role in generating interest in children's entertainment. He paved the way for other children's artists.

Raffi feels that the system of licensed animated characters that are advertised to the public is geared to make money, not to serve children. He makes a point of not participating in mass marketing. He will not push his albums in commercials aimed at kids, whether on radio or on TV. Raffi has kept himself separate from the commercialization of the music industry in other ways as well. He was the first artist who refused to let his album be packaged in the environmentally taxing cardboard long boxes.

Raffi feels that society offers children entertainment, mostly in the form of TV, that is at odds with what educators and child development specialists say children need during their formative years. He feels that current kids' culture is so trivialized that it does not provide for children's exposure to positive role models. He stresses reading and music rather than computers and CD-ROMS as the keys to helping children develop what he calls the "most powerful software," their minds and hearts.

FIGURE 10–3 Song books can increase language skills.

published in this format. Many *Big Books* for kindergarten and first grade are based on songs. Some of the more popular books based on songs are:

♪ *All God's Critters* (Staines, 1993).
♪ *Follow the Drinking Gourd* (Winter, 1992).
♪ *Inch by Inch: The Garden Song* (Mallett, 1995).
♪ *The Wheels on the Bus* (Zelinsky, 1992).

Children can make their own read-along sing-along books. See the directions for making and illustrating a story song book in Chapter 8.

Exploring the Vocabulary Used in Songs

Children can develop their vocabularies by singing songs. Sometimes they can figure out the meaning of a new word from the context of the song. Other times, they do not even notice that they are singing words that they do not understand. A perfect example of this is "Fifty Nifty United States" by Ray Charles (Miché, 1985). The words to the chorus are, "Fifty Nifty United States from the thirteen original colonies, fifty nifty stars in the flag, that billow so beautifully in the breeze. Each individual state contributes a quality that is great, oh each individual state, deserves a bow, we'll salute them now." Most young children have no idea what the words *billow, contributes,* and *quality* mean. Be sure to go over the pronunciation and meaning of larger words in a song.

Any time you sing with children, no matter what the age group, stop and discuss the vocabulary. It also helps to say the hard words to isolate them from the blur of the other words as they go by. Do not discuss all the new words at one time. This is too difficult for preschoolers and too boring for older children. Instead, choose a word or two each time you sing the song, and discuss the meaning of that word.

Reading Song Words while Singing

Children love to sing lots of different songs. In order to help them learn to read while singing, kindergarten and first-grade teachers often make sentence strips that have the words of a song on them. It is particularly helpful to use some kind of pointer to track the words as the children sing (Figure 10–4). To do this, you need a pocket chart, a pointer, and sentence strip paper. A pocket chart is a hanging plastic poster that has long pockets so you can put individual words or sentence strips in the pockets for the children to read. Pocket charts can be used with children as young as three. For preschoolers, just put a few words in large print on the chart instead of entire sentences. For kindergarten, put only the chorus of the song or a short and simple zipper song on the pocket chart. If you record a song on a five-minute tape as suggested in Chapter 1, and then you write the words to the song on sentence strips, you will have a great educational aid to use for many years to come.

If you do not have a pocket chart available, you can also write out song words in large print on a big piece of paper to make a chart that the whole class can read. If you have second or third graders, you can photocopy the words to a song and have children make song books of all the songs that they have sung during the year.

Sarah Pirtle
Children's Musician, Peace Educator, and Songwriter for Children

Sarah Pirtle taught herself to play the guitar in eighth grade. Even when she was young, she was passionately interested in songs about peace and respecting nature. She subscribed to *Sing Out!* magazine and rehearsed songs from Woody Guthrie, Joan Baez, and Pete Seeger after school each day.

Pirtle taught elementary school and included music daily with her students. She called her music time *discovery,* and she found that music and movement helped her students to learn to cooperate. During that period she wrote her own songs. When she started to work full-time as a music educator, the Young Audiences Program in Cleveland brought only classical musicians into the elementary schools. She persuaded them to let her audition, and they hired her to perform elementary school concerts about ecology in the Cleveland schools.

For the last 30 years, Pirtle has been researching and developing ways to teach alternatives to violence. She finds that music and communication activities introduced by music are among the most effective avenues. Once, a school asked Pirtle to do a four-day residency on the theme of nonviolence in a city where many children were exposed to domestic abuse. She called her program "The Hammer and the Candle." She talked with the students about the options to either pick up the hammer, metaphorically speaking, and address a problem with force and aggression, or to light the candle and reach for peacemaking abilities.

Pirtle works with music each summer in a peace camp she directs. Young people ages seven to twelve learn songs about nature and help write songs for the annual pageant in the woods. During the school year, Pirtle leads residencies in elementary schools and early childhood centers. She also trains teachers how to use music to teach positive social skills and teaches a course in music for Lesley College, where she helps teachers find ways of infusing music throughout their curriculums.

On her tours, Pirtle thinks of each show as an opportunity for a new conversation. She discovered that even if she did the same songs, each concert or classroom workshop could be different because of the group's participation and contributions. Now, she loves to invite jokes and incite creativity. Not only is it more fun, but it ties each group together.

Pirtle loves creating new songs to respond to the children she meets, especially when the songs help them connect with their feelings. One such experience occurred when Pirtle met with the mother of a three-year-old Tibetan girl to learn words and phrases in Tibetan. The child had been overwhelmed at a new family childcare setting, so together Pirtle and the mother made up a bilingual friendship song. She taught it to the children in the day care so that everyone could work on both languages. A second songwriting experience happened during an elementary school residency. Pirtle usually lights a candle with the children before working on songs related to conflict resolution. As she lit the candle, she saw kids flinching. The children told her that there had been a devastating forest fire in their town and the fire chief had died of a heart attack. So Pirtle and the children made up a song about how the fire started, about their sadness that the fire chief had died, and about how the fire affected them and their families. They gave it a chorus that showed how hard everyone had worked:

Help comes when you need it. Help comes when you call.
Help comes when you're hurt and help comes when you fall.
There are people who are kind. There are people who care.
Yes, people will be there.

continued

SARAH PIRTLE *continued*

They made up verses about their experiences:

> The fire came in close. Can you imagine how I felt?
> I heard a firefighter say, he thought our house might melt.
> I saw the fire burn in lines, like waves along a track.
> The grass around our yard is still burned black.

According to the principal, the song provided healing for the community. When they sang it in the classrooms, the children had a chance to cry together. The students performed it at an assembly for parents and gave copies to all the firefighters. The wife of the man who died came to the assembly. The song helped the community grieve in a very special way.

Pirtle loves working with other teachers to help them feel that music belongs to everyone. She encourages them all to bring music into their classrooms. She also likes to show how new songs can begin wtih interesting questions. Teachers can ask students something related to the curriculum, like, "What would it feel like to be walking in the rain forest at night?" or "What do you do if someone leaves you out of their group?" and create a song from students' answers. Pirtle wrote a book about cooperative songwriting to give teachers song patterns they can use with their science, ecology, and language arts curriculums.

Pirtle particularly likes two kinds of songs: songs that help children feel they are a direct part of nature and songs that help children deal with interpersonal issues. Both kinds contribute to building self-esteem, and she feels that esteem comes from feeling connected, especially to nature.

Pirtle recorded her first album, *Two Hands Hold the Earth,* in 1984, and it included a song in Spanish. Later, she began writing new bilingual Spanish songs, such as "Good Morning to the Sky/Buenos Días al Cielo." She said, "I want to help connect children by helping them learn each other's languages."

FIGURE 10–4 Pointing to words on a song chart as they are sung helps with identification.

Writing Development and Music

Children need to have a reason to write; it should be something they want to save on paper. It can be a list of their friends, a letter to someone, a story of some activity they did, or the words to a song that they want to remember.

Writing Practice

One excellent way for children to explore reading and writing is by writing the words to songs. In preschool, the writing will be done by adults. As children get older, they will graduate to writing single words in kindergarten and by second grade, whole sentences (Figure 10–5).

One excellent writing idea is a personal photo album that first graders create. Teachers can take many pictures of the class, have them developed, and let the children choose photos for their own albums. In addition to the photos and the children's creative writing, the photo album can include the words to a few favorite songs they have sung during the year.

Writing Feelings while Listening to Music. When listening to music, children identify with the feelings they hear. You can put on a piece of music for children and have great success if you ask them to listen for the feelings. This is an excellent open-ended activity because any feelings they suggest are correct.

If you teach preschoolers, play the music for one minute or less, and then ask children what feelings they had while listening. Write down the words they suggest. Play the music again and list the feelings suggested. Try to pick out one word for that piece of music that describes a feeling, then write it in large print on a card. After you do this activity on five different days with five different pieces of music, you will have five cards with words on them. After a few weeks, pick out one of the cards, show it to the children, and see if they can match the word to one or two of the pieces of music. Some of the children will even be able read the word on the card. By the next month, they should be able

FIGURE 10–5
Children learn new words by writing the lyrics to songs.

Greg & Steve
Children's Performers

At five years of age, Steve learned to play piano by ear by listening to his mother play. His mother and father loved to dance, so he grew up listening to big band and swing music. At seventeen, he played drums in his school marching band and taught himself to play guitar. He joined a rock band and played for school dances, clubs, and music events. In 1967, Steve and Greg began to perform together.

Greg's parents had music playing constantly. His father played piano and was an audio buff. Greg sang in the school choir and heard lots of religious and secular music. He took piano lessons at age ten. He performed in the trio "Lock, Stock & Barrel" with his brothers: John on the drums, Bud on the guitar, and Greg on piano. Greg picked up the guitar at age fifteen and soon after wrote his first song. He formed a rock band at age seventeen. After high school graduation, he went to Berklee School of Music in Boston for one semester. He returned to Los Angeles and started teaching.

Steve became interested in children's music while working in Los Angeles city schools in special education classrooms. As a teacher's assistant, he performed all his classroom duties and played guitar and sang with the kids. Eventually the playing and singing took over. He was sent from classroom to classroom to sing and to teach children to sing and perform.

Greg was doing the same thing at another school. Greg and Steve would often visit each other and share ideas. Steve loved his job and continued for seven years as a singing teacher's assistant. Both Steve and Greg started as volunteers in special education classrooms and later were offered jobs. They worked in separate schools, but both started experimenting using music to teach skills and enhance curriculum. Both started writing original songs and adapting traditional tunes to classroom use. In 1975, they recorded their first album together and developed the magic of Greg & Steve.

What keeps Steve going is children's enthusiasm for fun music. Greg loves children and loves performing. He enjoys feedback from the fans and appreciation for what he and Steve have created. They love involving children in the show by having them participate, and they enjoy hearing ideas come to life in a recording studio.

Greg and Steve teach others by giving workshops and music presentations to teachers, childcare providers, and parents. They also support and encourage other children's artists.

Once in concert, Greg and Steve took suggestions from the audience for verses to "She'll Be Coming Round The Mountain" (Various, 2001). One little boy piped up with, "Oh we'll all flush the toilet when she comes." Teachers, parents, and children all joined in, happily, making the sound of the flushing toilet. As Steve says, "Sometimes you just can't anticipate what a child will say." Another time, while in the middle of a workshop, Steve bent over and ripped his pants. They were playing a game called "What If." So he stood up and said to the group, "What if you were in front of a group of people and you ripped your pants and had to leave and change your clothes?" Then he backed off the stage with a gaping hole in his pants.

Once, during a performance a fire alarm went off in the theater. Everyone filed outside into the night rain. Even though Steve, Greg, and the audience were all dripping wet, they wanted to finish the show, so all happily went back in, slipping and sliding all the way.

Steve loves any kind of music that makes him feel something. He is, however, partial to the blues. For Steve, a great song has the ability to involve children in the music. He loves good rhythm and simple lyrics. Greg enjoys all kinds of music, from classical to pop to rhythm and blues. For Greg, a great song has four elements: good melody; good beat; simple, to-the-point lyrics; and the ability to touch your emotions.

Greg's and Steve's advice to teachers is, "The best way to involve children in music is to show them how much fun you can have with it. Be the example. Sing songs that almost do it by themselves. Don't sing down to kids, but draw them in."

continued

GREG & STEVE *continued*

Steve says, "I love all music. I am happy that children have chosen to like Greg & Steve in the role of children's performers because it is a role we truly love playing." Greg says, "We simply fell in love with doing music for children. However, we still involve ourselves with music for 'grown-ups' in various ways because adults and teachers are some of our biggest supporters."

For Steve, music is a great social equalizer. Everyone can clap or stomp their feet to the beat all together at the same time. It's fun! Greg feels that one can really get to know who Greg and Steve are simply by listening to their music. He says, "It's truly the soundtrack to our lives. Tucked away in many tunes is a philosophy and purpose to what we do. Music gives voice to what is in our hearts and minds. To quote one of our songs, 'Music is the sound of life, reaching out for love. Everybody has music inside.'"

to pick out the correct music from five choices to match the word. You can use these same words about feelings in your rhythm band activities, as described in Chapter 2.

For kindergartners and first graders, you can do the same activity, but write down two feeling words and have the class choose a name for each piece of music. You will then generate a pile of cards to go with your music. It is okay if some are duplicates. When you play one of the pieces of music, have a child pick out the three word cards that the group used for that piece of music. You and your students will probably always remember Beethoven's Moonlight Sonata (The Sentimental Strings Orchestra, 1999) as "Walking in the Forest at Night," or whatever creative name the children choose. With second and third graders, you can make the game interesting if you match up a creative name, three feeling words, and the real title of the piece of music.

Handwriting Practice with Songs

As children progress into second and third grade, practicing handwriting becomes important. Years ago there was just handwriting practice, no background music, no copying of words to a song, nothing useful, just thousands of letters in a row, perhaps for the sheer boredom of it. If your students are ready to do handwriting practice, include some interesting background music. Vary the music with the letter that your class is practicing. If you can, have students copy the words to a song or a poem rather than just writing random letters. If you want to make some real progress in handwriting, call it calligraphy, and have them try to create an art piece of their favorite song lyrics to hang on the wall. They will be practicing letters like mad so that they can get them right on the final product.

Songwriting

An aspect of writing that is often neglected in schools is music composition and songwriting. A new program of studies in Great Britain includes music composition at all grade levels. This is an area of study that has long been advocated by composers and writers and should be taken seriously by educators.

How to Write a Song. When composing music with children, you can either write the words or the music first. If you write the words first, you can ask for feedback from your friends and colleagues. They may suggest some tunes. People who have an easy

FIGURE 10–6 Some songwriters hear the words to music in their heads.

time putting tunes to words tend not to pay much attention to the difficulties of melody writing. They hear the words to music in their heads, right from the beginning (Figure 10–6). But not all songwriters use the same process, and not all songs are equally easy to write.

If you begin with the words, you need an idea of a song topic. Children are usually really good at suggesting topics, especially ones that they find interesting. Preschoolers will often ask you to make up a song about such topics as dinosaurs, candy, or balloons. If you do not let adult standards of rhyming perfection get in your way, you and your class can make up a perfectly good song about almost any subject. One first-grade class made up a wonderful song, with no rhyming words, about a stuffed monkey who was their class mascot.

Writing New Verses to Old Tunes. The easiest way to begin songwriting is to add new words to old tunes. Even preschoolers can easily add in new words to zipper songs. By replacing only one or two words, they can easily suggest new ideas for the lyrics. Preschoolers can also give you suggestions for topics they want in a song. Preschoolers are easily satisfied with whatever new words you create for old songs on the topic that they request. In fact, the creation of new words to familiar tunes is an excellent way of practicing the same tunes with preschoolers so that they can learn the pitch relationships of that song. With older children, you can begin your songwriting activity by using an existing tune. After you have some experience writing songs with your class, try to see if a tune emerges from the group before rewriting an existing tune.

Poetry and Music

Poetry and music are closely related. If you have a good children's poem, you are halfway to a song (Figure 10–7). The poems of Jack Prelutsky (1984) and Shel Silverstein (1975) are particularly good for songwriting activities. After you have taught a class to speak a poem, try asking, "Can anybody sing this poem?" Once you have a tune, you no longer have just a poem, you have a whole song.

FIGURE 10–7 Music helps establish a poem's mood and rhythm.

Reading Poems while Music Is Playing. You can combine music and poetry in all kinds of ways. If you want children to get some classical music listening, play a classical piece in the background and read a few poems aloud. Ask them to pick the poem that best fits the music. They will usually pick the poem that they like the best, not necessarily one that best fits the music. If you have some rhythm instruments available, you can let the children play them while either you or they recite a poem. If they want to recite the

Meet the Artist

Lisa Atkinson
Children's Songwriter

Lisa Atkinson was an active folk singer in New York when she found out she was pregnant. It was then, in 1982, she started writing songs for kids. All these years later, kids' smiles still keep her going. Songwriting and performance are creative outlets for her. The support and inspiration from colleagues in children's music helps her to continue. But she really enjoys performances the most.

Atkinson conducts songwriting workshops with elementary school students and provides inservice programs for preschool teachers and librarians. Occasionally, she performs at a few birthday parties. At one party, she played for a little boy, age four, who loved her cassette *I Wanna Tickle the Fish* (1988). In fact, he had memorized the order of the songs and insisted that she play them in that order. After each song he'd raise his arm over his head, bow his head and shout "Oh, yes!" Then, he would faithfully announce the next song to be performed. After Atkinson performed every song from both sides of her album, he stood up, looked at his fellow party goers, and said, "Wow, that was awesome, let's go get cake." She felt like Bruce Springsteen.

Atkinson works with children to help them create their own songs and makes her concerts interactive. She enjoys working with children rather than adults because she feels that children are more open-minded and less disillusioned than adults. Also, working with kids gives her time for her own children. When Atkinson is alone she listens to other folksinger-songwriters.

LISA ATKINSON, CHILDREN'S SONGWRITER

Something to Sing About: Lisa Atkinson's Advice on Facilitating a Songwriting Session with Children

Some children feel overwhelmed at the thought of writing a song, so Lisa Atkinson always begins by saying, "We are going to *make up* a song." She then asks, "How many of you have ever called up somebody on the telephone, written a letter, or told someone how you feel? A song is just another way to tell somebody what's on your mind, how you feel or what you are thinking about." Then the group starts to put together the words. Sometimes, picking a topic can take a whole hour, so when Atkinson visits a class of children to write a song, the children and their teacher have usually already picked the topic before she gets there. It needs to be a topic that the children already know about, not something that they are going to study later. They need information to start brainstorming.

At that point, Atkinson says, "Pretend I don't know anything about your topic. Tell me everything you know about this topic." She advises that at this phase, the song leader or teacher should be open to what the kids want in their song.

After brainstorming, they talk about rhythm and rhyme. Atkinson brings up her favorite comparisons: bumper stickers and your brother's shoe. Bumper stickers have to be clever and succinct, getting their point across in a few clever words. Your little brother's shoe is too small for your foot. These two ideas combine to help the children realize that you have to make the words to a song fit. The group then tries to find the words for a chorus or a first verse that has a rhythm. Atkinson explains that the words create a rhythm of their own. She takes the words suggested by the kids and says them with a rhythmic beat.

Once the group determines the words to a chorus or a first verse, Atkinson asks, "Can anybody sing it?" Ninety-nine percent of the time, a child will speak, not sing, it back to her. Then, she speaks the words to "Twinkle, Twinkle Little Star" (Collins, 1990) and asks, "What's wrong with this picture?" The children know right away that she is speaking and not singing. She again asks if anyone can sing it. About half of the time, one child in the class will come up with a tune. At other times, they resort to using a familiar tune and then re-craft the words to fit to that tune. Occasionally, Atkinson comes up with a tune for the group.

After they have a tune, the children sing it with the words to get the tune in their heads. Then they look back at the brainstorming they did previously. Sometimes the second verse just falls into place. When they get stuck, they just sing what they have over again. The energy in the room is wild by now. Teachers cannot understand how Atkinson can still function in the chaos. She loves it. Of the process, she said,

> You are thinking on your feet and you are trying to hear all the ideas at once. This is one of the areas where children definitely have more talent than adults. They are open-minded, they are expressive. They are not judgmental and offended in the way that adults are sometimes possessive of their own ideas.

Not every song is destined for the Top 40, but the teacher has a great new addition to next year's curriculum. The children feel a real sense of ownership and they experience the creative process firsthand.

poem, they can read it from a pocket chart. If you have an electric piano, select a rhythm on it that fits the mood of the poem and adjust the speed to go with it. If you have a guitar, try strumming along while you or a child reads the poem aloud. If you have a QChord, you can choose a rhythm and a speed, then strum along while reading a poem. If you play music while reading the poem, your children are much more likely to come up with a melody of their own.

Performing Choral Readings. **Choral readings** are group recitations of poems or song lyrics. They are almost like singing, but the words are said in rhythm, without a tune. In adult choruses, the conductor sometimes asks the singers to speak the words to a piece of music. In one professional chorus, when a group practiced Dona Nobis Pacem (Rumbel, 1995) from Mozart's Requiem, the conductor had them say the words and do soft-shoe tap dancing at the same time. He was trying to give them a sense of the strong rhythm under a passage that was long and flowing. With children, saying the words to a song helps ensure that they can hear individual words (Figure 10–8).

FIGURE 10–8 Reciting a song to music helps children hear individual words.

Conclusion

This chapter presents some ways to integrate music into an existing reading curriculum. Many more ways exist to teach both music and reading simultaneously. One additional source is a book by Ruby Chroninger, *Teach Your Kids About Music* (1994). It is inexpensive and full of excellent suggestions for combining music and children's literature. Hopefully, you can create some new combinations of music and reading as you develop your own curriculums.

KEY TERMS

choral readings	phonemic ability	pitch discrimination
music story combination	phonemic awareness	read-along sing-along book
musical accompaniment	phonemic clues	reading ability

DISCUSSION QUESTIONS

1. How can music learning help children develop reading ability?
2. What is phonemic awareness?
3. Describe the process for finding songs to go with books you use in your classroom.
4. Describe the process for writing a song with a group of children.
5. What is a music story combination?
6. What is a read-along sing-along book?
7. What kind of music should be used for musical accompaniment to reading a story?
8. Choose a familiar tune, then write new words for it. Be sure to state the name of the tune.
9. Choose a song for students that has challenging vocabulary for the target age group. Write the words and underline those that you will discuss and define for students.

SUGGESTED LEARNING ACTIVITIES

Choose a children's song appropriate for the age group with which you plan to work. Make sentence strips to fit into a pocket chart for that song. Make a short tape of the song. Be sure to list the title, author, recording artist, and album for the version on the tape.

Then, choose a children's book appropriate for reading aloud to the age group with which you plan to work, select appropriate background music for the book, and make a short tape of the music. Play the recording and read the book to a small group of adults or children. List the title, author, recording artist, and album of the recording. List the title, writer, publisher, and date of the book.

Finally, get a book of children's poetry. Choose a poem and make up a tune to match the words. Practice the poem with the tune and teach it to an adult friend or classmate. Perform the poem with your new tune for a group of children or adults. If you play an instrument, you can perform the song with accompaniment.

REFERENCES

Atkinson, L. (1988). *I wanna tickle the fish* [cassette]. Albany, NY: A Gentle Wind.

Chroninger, R. (1994). *Teach your kids about music: An activity handbook for parents and teachers using children's literature.* New York: Walker.

Collins, J. (1990). *Baby's bedtime* [cassette]. New York: Lightyear.

Douglas, S., & Willatts, P. (1994, Sept.). The relationship between musical ability and literacy skills. *Journal of Reading Research,* 99–107.

Hurwitz, I., Wolff, P. H., Bortnick, B. D., & Kokas, K. (1975). Nonmusical effects of the Kodály music curriculum in primary grade children. *Journal of Learning Disabilities, 8,* 45–51.

Lamb, S. J., & Gregory, A. H. (1993). The relationship between music and reading in beginning readers. *Educational Psychology, 13,* 19–26.

Mallett, D. (1995). *Inch by inch: The garden song.* New York: HarperTrophy.

Marzollo, J. (1993). *Happy birthday, Martin Luther King.* Dayton, OH: Scholastic.

Miché, M. (1985). *Kid's stuff* [cassette]. Berkeley, CA: Song Trek Music.

Pirtle, S. (1984), *Two hands hold the Earth*. Albany, NY: A Gentle Wind.

Prelutsky, J. (1984). *A pizza the size of the sun*. New York: Macmillan.

Raffi. (1976). *Singable songs for the very young* [cassette]. Cambridge, MA: Rounder Records.

Raffi. (2000). *Raffi's box of sunshine* [CD]. Ukiah, CA: Shoreline.

Rumbel, N. (1995). *Notes from the tree of life* [cassette]. Milwaukee, WI: Narada Productions.

The Sentimental Strings Orchestra. (1999). *Classically romantic* [CD]. New York: BMG.

Silverstein, S. (1975). *Where the sidewalk ends*. New York: Doubleday.

Staines, B. (1993). *All God's critters*. New York: Puffin.

Various artists. (2001). *Kids klassics* [CD]. Maple Plain, MN: K-Tel International.

Winter, J. (1992). *Follow the drinking gourd*. New York: Knopf.

Zelinsky, P. O. (1992). *The wheels on the bus*. New York: Dutton.

ADDITIONAL RESOURCES

Frith, U. (1985). Beneath the surface of developmental dyslexia, In K. E. Patterson, J. C. Marshall, & M. Coltheart (Eds.), *Surface dyslexia* (pp. 301–330). London: Lawrence Erlbaum Associates.

Nichols, B. L., & Honig, A. S. (1995). The influence of an inservice music education program on young children's responses to music. *Early Child Development, 113,* 19–29.

Pirtle, S. (1988). *The wind is telling secrets*. Albany, NY: A Gentle Wind.

Pirtle, S. (1988). *Magical Earth*. Albany, NY: A Gentle Wind.

Sing Out! The Folk Song Magazine. For additional information, visit their Web site at: http://www.singout.org.

Upitis, R. (1992, Jan.). Synthesizing music into activity based classroom. *Output,* 14–19.

Upitis, R. (1995, Spring). Fostering children's compositions: Activities for the classroom. *General Music Today,* 16–19.

APPENDIX A

How to Reach the Artists

At the time of publication, this is the most current contact information for the artists in the book. If you find that any information is inaccurate, please check our Web site at http://www.weavingmusic.com.

Peter Alsop	E-MAIL:	peteralsop@earthlink.net
	WEB SITE:	http://www.peteralsop.com
	PHONE:	(800) 676-5480
	FAX:	(310) 455-4192
	ADDRESS:	Peter Alsop
		P.O. Box 960
		Topanga, CA 90290

RECORDINGS:
Chris Moose Holidays; Pluggin' Away; In the Hospital; Stayin' Over; Take Me with You; Wha'd'ya Wanna Do?; and *Silly Songs and Modern Lullabies*

VIDEOS:
When Kids Say Goodbye; Get Real!; Wake Up!; When Jesus Was a Kid; Costume Party; and *Opening Doors*

BOOKS:
Stayin' Over Songbook; Take Me with You Songbook; In the Hospital: A Guide for Parents and Nurses (with Bill Harley); and *Wha'd'ya Wanna Do Songbook*

Linda Arnold

E-MAIL: lindaarnoldmusic@aol.com
WEB SITE: http://www.youngheartmusic.com
ADDRESS: Linda Arnold
P.O. Box 2999
Santa Cruz, CA 95062

RECORDINGS:
Circus Magic: Under the Big Top; Happiness Cake; Lullaby Land; Make Believe; Peppermint Wings; Sing Along Stew; Splash Zone; and *The Rainbow Palace: Broadway Classics and More*

VIDEOS:
Linda Arnold's World of Make Believe

Lisa Atkinson

E-MAIL: scooptunes@earthlink.net
PHONE: (650) 574-2709
ADDRESS: 317 West 41st Ave.
San Mateo, CA 94403-4305

RECORDINGS:
I Wanna Tickle the Fish; The One and Only Me; The Elephant in Aisle Four; and *Something to Sing About*

Banana Slug String Band (*see* Steve Van Zandt)

Joanie Bartels

E-MAIL: joanietones@aol.com
WEB SITE: http://www.joaniebartels.com
ADDRESS: Joanie Bartels
419 N. Larchmont Blvd., PMB 13
Los Angeles, CA 90004

RECORDINGS:
Lullaby Magic; Morning Magic; Lullaby Magic 2; Travelin' Magic; Sillytime Magic; Bath-time Magic; Dancin' Magic; Christmas Magic; Jump for Joy; The Rainy Day Adventure; The Extra-Special Substitute Teacher; Adventures with Family and Friends; and *Put on Your Dancing Shoes*

Peter Blood and Annie Patterson

E-MAIL: bloodpat@erols.com
PHONE: (610) 399-0684
ADDRESS: The Blood-Pattersons
22 Tanguy Rd.
Glen Mills, PA 19342

RECORDINGS:
Deep Roots; Planet Swing; Hep Cat Holiday; and *Rise Up Singing*

BOOKS:
Rise Up Singing

Bob Blue

E-MAIL: bblue@k12.oit.umass.edu
PHONE: (413) 256-8784
Blue prefers e-mails to phone calls. Please e-mail him if at all possible.

MUSICALS:
The Real Thief; Charlotte's Web; The Hobbit; The Wizard of Oz; Alice in Wonderland; and *The House at Pooh Corner*

VIDEOS:
What Matters

BOOKS:
A songbook and upcoming book of children's musical plays are available from:
    PHONE: (215) 625-8892
    ADDRESS: Julie Gordon
             810 Kater St.
             Arlington, MA 02474

Bram (*see Sharon, Lois & Bram*)

Tom Chapin

E-MAIL: ChapinTom@aol.com
ADDRESS: Sundance Music
         100 Cedar St., Ste. B-19
         Dobbs Ferry, NY 10522-1022

RECORDINGS:
Family Tree; Moonboat; Mother Earth; Billy The Squid; Zag Zig; In My Hometown; Around The World and Back Again; and *This Pretty Planet*

Charlotte Diamond

ORDERS:
    E-MAIL: orders@charlottediamond.com
    WEB SITE: http://www.charlottediamond.com
    PHONE: (604) 931-7375
    FAX: (604) 931-2727

CONCERT BOOKINGS AND GENERAL INFORMATION:
    E-MAIL: bookings@charlottediamond.com
    PHONE: (604) 274-8216
    FAX: (604) 274-8210

Children and adults are welcome to join the Hug Bug Club:
E-MAIL: fanmail@charlottediamond.com
ADDRESS: Box 58067
         Vancouver, BC, Canada V6P 6C5

Diamond responds to fans all over the world in English, French, and Spanish. She reads each letter that arrives, which keeps her in touch with her audience. She is pleased to hear from teachers and conference and concert organizers.

RECORDINGS IN ENGLISH:
10 Carrot Diamond; Diamond in the Rough; Diamonds and Dragons; My Bear Gruff; The Christmas Gift; Diamonds and Daydreams; and *Charlotte Diamond's World*

RECORDINGS IN FRENCH:
Qu'il y ait toujours le soleil and *Bonjour l'hiver*

RECORDINGS IN SPANISH:
Soy una pizza

VIDEOS:
10 Crunchy Carrots and *Diamonds and Dragons*

BOOKS:
Diamond's latest book is called *Charlotte Diamond's Musical Treasures* and features 22 of her best-known songs from all of the recordings. It contains activities, sign language, and lyrics in English, French, and Spanish for most of the songs. The music is arranged for piano with guitar chords. There are also Song Cards or Big Books available for many of the songs.

Katherine Dines

E-MAIL: kdines@mindspring.com
WEB SITE: http://www.hunktabunkta.com
PHONE: (303) 298-7122
ADDRESS: 2000 Little Raven Street, No. 1-C
Denver, CO 80202

RECORDINGS:
Hunk-Ta-Bunk-Ta BOO; Hunk-Ta-Bunk-Ta BOO-2; Hunk-Ta-Bunk-Ta BED; Hunk-Ta-Bunk-Ta GNU; Hunk-Ta-Bunk-Ta SPOOKY; Hunk-Ta-Bunk-Ta CHANTS; and *Hunk-Ta-Bunk-Ta FUN*

Feel free to contact Dines for assemblies and teacher inservice programs. She would love to hear from you.

Gail Dreifus

E-MAIL: gdreifus@inreach.com
PHONE: (209) 379-2764
ADDRESS: P.O. Box 66
El Portal, CA 95318

RECORDINGS:
Yosemite by Song; Red Sneakers; Animal Tracks; National Parks by Song; Grand Canyon by Song; Grand Teton Tunes; Carlsbad Cavern by Song; and *Homeplanet Harmony*

VIDEOS:
Nature Notes

BOOKS:
Recycled String Band Songbook

Cathy Fink and Marcy Marxer

E-MAIL: info@cathymarcy.com
WEB SITE: http://www.cathymarcy.com
PHONE: (301) 891-1228
FAX: (301) 891-3130

ADDRESS: Community Music, Inc.
P.O. Box 5778
Takoma Park, MD 20913

RECORDINGS:
Help Yourself; Air Guitar; Cathy and Marcy Collection for Kids; A Parent's Home Companion; Blanket Full of Dreams; Changing Channels; and *All Wound Up*

BOOKS:
Cathy Fink and Marcy Marxer's Kids' Guitar Songbook: For Ages 5–10 and Beyond

---

Doug Goodkin

E-MAIL: Goodkindg@aol.com
PHONE: (415) 564-1597

ORDERS (recordings not sold commercially):
E-MAIL: info@sfschool.org
PHONE: (415) 239-5065
ADDRESS: The San Francisco School
300 Gaven St.
San Francisco, CA 94134

BOOKS:
A Rhyme in Time; and *Name Games*

Red Grammer

Contact Maria at Red Note Records:
E-MAIL: maria@redgrammer.com
PHONE: (800) 824-2980

For concerts, workshops, or conference presentations, contact Marge and Cris Ghilarducci:
E-MAIL: margecris@aol.com
PHONE: (508) 822-3735

RECORDINGS:
Can You Sound Just Like Me?; Teaching Peace; Hello World; Down the Do Re Mi; and *Red Grammer's Favorite Sing Along Songs*

BOOKS:
Teaching Peace Songbook and Teacher's Guide

Greg & Steve

WEB SITE: http://www.gregandsteve.com
PHONE: (800) 548-4063 or (661) 269-5407
FAX: (661) 269-4322
ADDRESS: Greg & Steve Productions
33309 Santiago Rd., PMB 212
Acton, CA 93510

RECORDINGS:
We All Live Together, Vol. 1; *We All Live Together,* Vol. 2; *We All Live Together,* Vol. 3; *We All Live Together,* Vol. 4; *On the Move with Greg & Steve; Quiet Moments with Greg &*

Steve; Kidding Around with Greg & Steve; Kids in Motion; Holidays and Special Times; Playin' Favorites; We All Live Together, Vol. 5; *Rockin' Down the Road;* and *Big Fun*

VIDEOS:
Musical Adventures of Greg & Steve

BOOKS:
We All Live Together

Monty Harper

E-MAIL: cmw@cowboy.net
WEB SITE: http://www.montyharper.com
PHONE: (405) 624-3805

ASSEMBLY PROGRAM:
  E-MAIL: monty@cowboy.net

RECORDINGS:
Jungle Junk; Imagine That; Halloween Madness; and *Magical Madcap Tour*

Tom Hunter

E-MAIL: Tom.Hunter@ecunet.org
WEB SITE: www.nas.com/sgc
PHONE: (360) 738-0340
ADDRESS: The Song Growing Company
1225 E. Sunset Dr.
Bellingham, WA 98266

RECORDINGS:
We've Been Waiting for You; Come on Over; I Have a Box; In the Air; Bits and Pieces; and *Memories*

Jill Jarnow

E-MAIL: jjarnow@aol.com

BOOKS:
All Ears (currently out of print but may be found in some libraries)

Ella Jenkins

ADDRESS: Adventures in Rhythm
1844 N. Mohawk St.
Chicago, IL 60614

RECORDINGS:
Adventures in Rhythm; You Sing a Song and I'll Sing a Song; Counting Games & Rhythms for the Little Ones; Call and Response Rhythmic Group Singing; And One and Two; Growing Up with Ella Jenkins; Travellin' with Ella Jenkins; Jambo and Other Call & Response Songs; Seasons for Singing; Play Your Instruments (And Make a Pretty Sound); We Are All America's Children; Songs, Rhythms and Chants for the Dance; Rhythms of Childhood; This-A-Way, That-A-Way; My Street Begins at My House; Early Childhood Songs; Little Johnny Brown & Other Songs; Rhythm & Game Songs for the Little Ones; Come Dance by the Ocean; A Long Time to Freedom; African American Folk Songs & Rhythms; Songs and Rhythms from Near and Far; This Is Rhythm; Multicultural Songs for Children; Nursery Rhymes; Holiday Times; Songs Children Love to Sing; and *Ella Jenkins & A Union of Friends Pulling Together*

Anne Laskey PHONE: (510) 436-1234
ADDRESS: Kodály Music Program
Holy Names College
3500 Mountain Blvd.
Oakland, CA 94619

Lois (*see* Sharon, Lois & Bram)

Marcy Marxer (*see* Cathy Fink and Marcy Marxer)

Bob McGrath E-MAIL: kgreengrass@aol.com
WEB SITE: http://www.bobmcgrath.com
PHONE: (212) 421-8415
ADDRESS: Greengrass Enterprises
38 E. 57th St.
New York, NY 10022

BOOKINGS:
ADDRESS: The Brad Simon Organization, Inc.
122 E. 57th St.
New York, NY 10022

RECORDINGS:
The Baby Record; The Toddler Record; Sing Along with Bob, Vol. 1; *Sing Along with Bob,* Vol. 2; *Bob's Favorite Street Songs;* and *Sing Me a Story*

BOOKS:
Uh Oh! Gotta Go!: Potty Tales from Toddlers; and *Oops! Excuse Me, Please, and Other Mannerly Tales*

Mary Miché E-MAIL: marymiche@marymiche.com
WEB SITE: http://www.marymiche.com
Address: 2600 Hillegass Ave.
Berkeley, CA 94704

RECORDINGS:
Nature Nuts; Earthy Tunes; Holly Daze; Peace It Together; Kid's Stuff; Animal Crackers; and *Easy Sing Alongs*

BOOKS:
Weaving Music into Young Minds

Deborah Moore E-MAIL: DebLMoore@aol.com or fpmusic@magicnet.net

---

Jeff Moran (a.k.a. Dr. Chordate)
E-MAIL: scimusic@tranquility.net
WEB SITE: http://www.tranquility.net/~scimusic
ADDRESS: 2071 CR 246
Fulton, MO 65251

RECORDINGS:
Dr. Chordate: Parts Is Parts; The Notochords; Songs of Science; and *Dr. Chordate: The View from the Pad*

BOOKS:
The Notochords; Science Songs and Body Poetry

José Luis Orozco

E-MAIL: Joseluis@dnai.com
WEB SITE: http://www.Joseluisorozco.com
PHONE: (888) 354-7373
FAX: (510) 526-8555
ADDRESS: P.O. Box 7428
Berkeley, CA 94707

RECORDINGS:
Lírica Infantil, Vol. 1–13

BOOKS:
12 songbooks that accompany his albums; and the bilingual songbooks *De Colores* and *Diez Deditos,* illustrated by Elisa Kleven

---

Hap Palmer

E-MAIL: hap@netwood.net
WEB SITE: http://www.happalmer.com
ADDRESS: P.O. Box 323
Topanga, CA 90290

RECORDINGS:
Peek-a-Boo; Rhythms on Parade; Can a Cherry Pie Wave Goodbye?; Quiet Places; Child's World of Lullabies; We're on Our Way; So Big; Holiday Magic; Can Cockatoos Count by Twos?; Can a Jumbo Jet Sing the Alphabet?; Early Childhood Classics; Turn on the Music; Best of Baby Songs; Learning Basic Skills, Vol. 1; *Getting to Know Myself; Sally the Swinging Snake; Walter the Waltzing Worm; Classic Nursery Rhymes; Witches' Brew;* and *Singing Multiplication Tables*

VIDEOS:
Baby Songs; More Baby Songs; Baby Songs Goodnight; Baby's Busy Day; Baby Songs ABC, 123; Baby Songs Animals; and *Play Along Songs*

Annie Patterson (*see* Peter Blood and Annie Patterson)

Sarah Pirtle

E-MAIL: sarahpirtle@juno.com
PHONE: (413) 625-2355
ADDRESS: Discovery Center
63 Main St.
Shelburne Falls, MA 01370

RECORDINGS:
Two Hands Hold the Earth; The Wind Is Telling Secrets; Magical Earth; and *Linking up: Music and Movement to Promote Co-operation*

BOOKS:

An Outbreak of Peace; Linking up: Using Music, Movement and Language Arts to Promote Caring, Co-operation and Communication pre-K–grade 3; Discovery Time for Co-operation and Conflict Resolution K–8; and *Partnership Education in Action*

Raffi

WEB SITE: http://www.raffinews.com
PHONE: (604) 682-8698
FAX: (604) 682-4291
ADDRESS: Troubadour Records
1075 Cambie St.
Vancouver, BC, Canada V6B 5L7

RECORDINGS:

Let's Play (forthcoming); *Raffi's Box of Sunshine; The Singable Songs Collection* (20th Anniversary Special Ed.); *Raffi Radio; Bananaphone; Evergreen, Everblue: An Ecology Album; Raffi in Concert with the Rise and Shine Band; Everything Grows; One Light, One Sun; Raffi's Christmas Album; Rise and Shine; Baby Beluga; The Corner Grocery Store; More Singable Songs;* and *Singable Songs for the Very Young*

BOOKS:

Rise and Shine; Raffi's Top Ten Songs to Read; Bananaphone Songbook; Like Me and You; Spider on the Floor; Raffi Children's Favorites Songbook; Evergreen, Everblue Songbook; Baby Beluga; Everything Grows; The Raffi Everything Grows Songbook; Tingalayo; Five Little Ducks; The Wheels on the Bus; One Light, One Sun; The Raffi Christmas Treasury; Shake My Sillies Out; Down by the Bay; The Second Raffi Songbook; The Raffi Singable Songbook; Baby Beluga Book; and *The Learning with Raffi Series for Parents and Teachers: Singable Songs for the Very Young, More Singable Songs, Baby Beluga, Bananaphone*

VIDEOS:

Raffi on Broadway; Raffi in Concert with the Rise and Shine Band; and *A Young Children's Concert with Raffi*

Nancy Raven

E-MAIL: nancyraven@earthlink.net
WEBSITE: http://home.earthlink.net/~nancyraven
PHONE: (831) 649-6080
ADDRESS: 136 Spray Ave.
Monterey, CA 93940

RECORDINGS:

Nancy Raven Sings Her Favorites; You Gotta Juba; Singing, Prancing, and Dancing; Friends and Family; The House We Live In, Vols. 1 and 2; *Sky Bears; Jambalaya Songs for the Holiday Season; People and Animal Songs; Singing in a Circle; Activity Song Hop, Skip, and Sing; Thoroughly Modern Mother Goose;* and *Lullabies and Other Children's Songs*

Sally Rogers

E-MAIL: salrog@neca.com
WEB SITE: http://www.sallyrogers.com
PHONE: (860) 974-3089
ADDRESS: P.O. Box 98
Abington, CT 06230

AGENT:
E-MAIL: ShermanArt@aol.com
PHONE: (412) 323-9023
ADDRESS: Joan Sherman Artist Management
835 Western Ave.
Pittsburgh, PA 15233

RECORDINGS:
Peace By Peace; Sally Rogers Sings for Children; A Quiet O'Clock; A Child's Holiday; Piggy Back Planet; What Can One Little Person Do? and *Of Farms and Famous People*

Dennis and Linda Ronberg

PHONE: (800) 949-3313
ADDRESS: Linden Tree
170 State
Los Altos, CA 94022

The Linden Tree store carries 52,000 titles, and 5,000 of them are recordings.

Joe Scruggs

E-MAIL: joescruggs@aol.com
WEB SITE: http://www.hellojoe.com

RECORDINGS:
Late Last Night; Traffic Jams; Abracadabra; Deep in the Jungle; Even Trolls Have Moms; Bahamas Pajamas; Merry Christmas; and *Ants*

VIDEOS:
Joe's First Video and *Joe Scruggs in Concert*

Pete Seeger

ADDRESS: P.O. Box 431
Beacon, NY 12508

RECORDINGS:
Abiyoyo (and other songs and stories) 1967; American Folk Songs for Children; Birds, Beasts, Bugs and Little Fishes; Birds, Beasts, Bugs and Bigger Fishes; Songs to Grow On; Folk Songs for Young People; and *Camp Songs*

Sharon, Lois & Bram

E-MAIL: slb@total.net
ADDRESS: P.O. Box 609
Station C
Toronto, ON, Canada M6J 1J0

RECORDINGS:
Singing and Swinging; Sing A to Z; Let's Dance!; Candles, Snow and Mistletoe; The Elephant Show; One Elephant Went out to Play; Sing around the Campfire; and *Elephant Party*

P. J. Swift   E-MAIL: pickle@well.com

P. J. owns approximately 5,000 albums (CDs and cassettes). She probably has one of the largest English language collections of children's music in the United States. She is also developing a collection in Spanish.

Tickle Tune Typhoon (*see* Dennis Westphall)

Jane Timberlake   E-MAIL: Timberlake@earthlink.net
    PHONE: (510) 654-0322
    ADDRESS: 109 Echo Ave.
          Oakland, CA 94611

RECORDINGS:
Al the Alligator; Nine Green Fingers and Forty-Seven Toes; Our Songs; and *Carpet of Dreams*

Steve Van Zandt   E-MAIL: solarsteve@bananaslugstringband.com
    WEB SITE: http://www.bananaslugstringband.com
    PHONE: (888) 327-5847
    ADDRESS: P.O. Box 1162
          Santa Cruz, CA 95063

RECORDINGS:
La Tierra y el Mar; Goin' Wild; Penguin Parade; Adventures on the Air Cycle; Singing in Our Garden; Dirt Made My Lunch; and *Slugs at Sea*

VIDEOS:
Dancing with the Earth

BOOKS:
Songbooks are available for all albums.

Norman M. Weinberger   E-MAIL: nmweinbe@e4e.oac.uci.edu
    WEB SITE: http://www.musica.uci.edu
    ADDRESS: Center for the Neurobiology of Learning and Memory
          University of California
          Irvine, CA 92697-3800

Dennis Westphall   E-MAIL: ttyphoon@oz.net
    WEB SITE: http://www.tickletunetyphoon.com
    PHONE: (800) 490-0871
    FAX: (206) 632-9548
    ADDRESS: Tickle Tune Typhoon
          4649 Sunnyside Ave. N., #122
          Seattle, WA 98103

RECORDINGS:
Circle Around; Hug the Earth; All of Us Will Shine; Keep the Spirit; Hearts and Hands; Pattycakes and Peek-a-boo; Healthy Beginnings; and *Music for the Whole Child*

VIDEOS:
Let's Be Friends

Joy Yelin

E-MAIL: musicmos@aol.com
PHONE AND FAX: (941) 751-9426
ADDRESS: 6410 Sun Eagle Ln.
Bradenton, FL 34210

BOOKS:
Potpourri for Music and Movement and Improvisational Study; Recipes for Improvisation; Grow with Music and Movement; The Joy of Children's Favorites; Ring around the Development Tree; and *Movement That Fits*

Diana Zegers

PHONE: (360) 698-0706
ADDRESS: P.O. Box 3510
Silverdale, WA 98383

BOOKS:
Discover Music

Distributors

Roxan, Inc.

WEB SITE: http://www.roxan.com
PHONE: (800) 228-5775
ADDRESS: 5425 Lockhurst Dr.
Woodland Hills, CA 91367

Distributor of 10-minute tapes.

Supreme Audio

WEB SITE: http://www.supremeaudio.com
PHONE: (800) 445-7398

A large distributor of square dance music.

Time-Life Music®

WEB SITE: http://www.timelife.com
PHONE: (888) 294-7696
ADDRESS: P.O. Box 85720
Richmond, VA 23285-5720

Song Lyrics

(In Order of Appearance on CD)

Rapp Song*

by Red Grammer

Now all across this big wide world
There are lots of boys and lots of girls
With different eyes and different noses
Different hair and different clothes
It's a magical thing, it's a wonderful game
We all look different but we're all the same.

Chorus:
Hello, Hola, Jambo, Ching Tien Nee How Ma (2×)

Now the differences are great and the differences are small
But that's just part of the beauty of it all
We're all like notes that make up a song
We need everybody, so come on, sing along!

(Chorus)

Now some folks think that they are the best
They don't know how to get along, they say to heck with the rest
So they go the wrong way and they do the wrong thing
But the song sounds weak when it's time for them to sing.

(Chorus)

Now you gather up folks from all kinds of places
With different ways of talkin', And different color faces
There's something special each one brings along
And when they sing together, Now you've really got a song.

(Chorus)

Instrumental: Marimba
So open your eyes and take a look around
There's all kinds of kids that live in your town
Maybe black, maybe white, maybe rich, maybe poor
You gotta get to know 'em all, That's what friends are for.

(Chorus)

Cause the differences are great and the differences are small
But that's just part of the beauty of it all
We're all like notes that make up a song
We need everybody, so come on, sing along!

(Chorus)

*Recorded as "The Peace Rap" by Mary Miché.

Mooey Mooey Ma

by Mary Miché

(I said) Mooey mooey ma (2×)
(I said) Mooey mooey me (2×)
(I said) Mooey mooey mi (2×)
(I said) Mooey mooey mow (2×)
(I said) Mooey ma, mooey me, Mooey mi, mooey mow,
Mooey ma, me, mi, mow, moo!

Nooey na, ne, ni, no, new!
Kooey ka, ke, ki, ko, koo!
Gooey ga, ge, gi, go, goo!
Chewy cha, che, chi, cho, chew!
Thewy tha, the, thi, tho, thew!
Sooey sa, se, si, so, soo!
Tooey ta, te, ti, to, too!

Ms. Spider

by Linda Arnold

There's a spider on my knee, And she's crawling over me.
Oh what Oh what should I do?
Should I brush her on the floor, And sweep her out the door?
Should I shake hands and say "How do you do?"

Chorus:
Well, Hey Ms. Spider, want some apple cider?
How about a cookie or two, three, four?
Well, I'd like to be polite and treat this spider right,
She's a living thing and she's got feelings too.

Now she's crawling on my chin, And I'm trying to keep a grin.
Oh what Oh what should I do?
Should I give a little sneeze? (ah choo), And blow her in the breeze?
Should I hold my breath until I'm turning blue?

(Chorus)

Well, Hey Ms. Spider, want some apple cider?
How about a cookie or two, three, four?
But wait, now she's crawling out of sight, with a smile so polite
Guess she knows I'm a living thing with feelings too.

(Chorus)

Nine Green Fingers and Forty-Seven Toes

by Jane Timberlake

As I was walkin' down Tiddly Tum Street
I met a monster with 13 feet
He had 3 orange eyes and his knees on his nose
He had 9 green fingers and 47 toes

He was weird, he had a purple beard
He ate snakes wrapped up in chocolate cakes
He could fly 50 mountains high
He chewed gum with his thumb

Well, as I was running from Tiddly Tum Street
I heard the pitter patter of 13 feet
I turned around, and to my surprise
I saw 3 big tears roll out of 3 orange eyes

He was sad, he was feelin' bad
No one would stay, they all just ran away
So I smiled and we played a while
Then we flew (whoosh) to the zoo.

Well, we got to the zoo and we looked all around
And we saw a new creature that the zoo had just found
It had 3 orange eyes and its knees on its nose
It had 9 green fingers and 47 toes

She was weird, she had a purple beard
She ate snakes wrapped up in chocolate cakes
She could fly 50 mountains high
She chewed gum with her thumb

Well, they flew away together and they lived happily
They had two little monsters as cute as they could be
They each had 3 orange eyes and their knees on their noses
They had 9 green fingers and 47 toeses

They were weird, they had those purple beards
They ate snakes wrapped up in chocolate cakes
They could fly just 30 mountains high
They chewed gum with their thumbs.

Spiders and Snakes

by Gerry Axlerod

Chorus:
Spiders and snakes, spiders and snakes
I'm gonna learn to love them, No matter how long it takes.
Spiders and snakes, spiders and snakes
I'm gonna learn to love them, No matter how long it takes.

Some snakes eat insects, some eat rodents too
If they're in your garden, they're probably helping you
Most snakes won't bite anyone, of course there's some that do
But if you do not bother them, they will not bother you.

(Chorus)

Spiders catch flies in their webs this is what I've been taught
Some of the strands are sticky and some of them are not
Spiders have eight legs, they have eight eyes too
They'd rather munch on insects than taking a bite of you

(Chorus)

Instrumental: Mandolin and Jew's harp
Some people don't like spiders, some don't even like snakes
But if they knew how important they were
What a difference that would make.

(Chorus)

I Want to Eat 8 Apples and Bananas

version by Mary Miché

I want to eat, I want to eat
    eight apples and bananas
I want to eat, I want to eat
    eight apples and bananas
Short a: A wat tat at, A wat tat at
    at apples and bananas
Short e: E wet tet et, E wet tet et
    et epples end benenes
Short i: I wit tit it, I wit tit it
    it ipples ind bininis
Short o: O wot tot ot, O wot tot ot
    ot oppoles ond bononos
Short u: U wut tut ut, U wut tut ut
    ut upples und bununus
Long a: A wate tate ate, A wate tate ate
    ate apples and bananas
Long e: E weet teet eet, E weet teet eet
    eet eeples eend beeneenees

Long i: I wite tite ite, I wite tite ite
    ite ipples ind bininis
Long o: O wote tote ote, O wote tote ote
    ote opples ond bononos
Long u: U wute tute ute, U wute tute ute
    ute upples und bununus
Combine oi: OI woit toit oit, OI woit toit oit
    oit oipples oind boinoinois
Combine ow: OW wowt towt owt, OW wowt towt owt
    owt owpples ownd bownownows
Combine er: ER wert tert ert, ER wert tert ert,
    ert erpples ernd bernerners

Romp in the Swamp

by Bill Brennan

Chorus:
Go romp in the swamp, go squish not stomp, wear pants and shoes.
You better get set to get a little wet, and use some bug juice.

Walk right in where life abounds.
Shut your mouth and listen to the sounds.
Ribet, ribet, quack, quack
Cattails bouncin' off your back.
Boom diddle diddle diddle boom (3×)

(Chorus)

Watch where you walk, don't step on the nest.
Big green grass that the mamas like best.
Little muskrats, baby Northern pike.
Swamps are what those mamas like.
"Junior, get back in the swamp," "yes, Mama."

(Chorus)

I wouldn't go there with my bathing suit on.
Mosquitoes are so bad, it wouldn't take long.
They bite and bite, you wouldn't have a chance.
Make you do the mosquito dance.
One, two, three, four, I can't stand it anymore.

(Repeat song)

Go romp in the swamp, go squish not stomp, wear pants and shoes.

The Haunted House

by Gerry Tenny

As I walked into the Haunted House
Trying to be quiet as a mouse
Then I started to climb the stairs
The room was cold, the walls were bare
And who do you think was standing there?
Standing there at the top of the stairs
Standing there with a whole lot of hair

Chorus:
It was King Kong the gorilla
Playing ping pong with Godzilla
It was King Kong the gorilla
Playing ping pong with Godzilla

Can you imagine my surprise
I could hardly believe my eyes
'Cause they were having such a good time
That I wished I had brought my own monster disguise

Chorus 2:
So I could play, Ping pong with King Kong the gorilla and Godzilla
So I could play, Ping pong with King Kong the gorilla and Godzilla

Well all I could do was sit and stare
But I did not want them to see me there
So I hid behind a chair
Till I felt a hand on my hair
All of the sudden I started to scream
Then I woke up, it was only a dream

Chorus 3:
I dreamt that King Kong the gorilla
Was playing ping pong with Godzilla
I dreamt that King Kong the gorilla
Was playing ping pong with Godzilla

The Pumpkin Man

by John McCutcheon

There's something in my garden, So big and orange and round
It started just a little seed, When I stuck it in the ground
Now it doesn't look at all, Like what it did last spring
Hey won't somebody tell me, What the heck you call this thing

Chorus:
Oh the pumpkin man with the big round head
Smile so bright and eyes so red
I wish jack-o-lanterns hung from the sky
And the seas were made of pumpkin pie

My daddy and my mommy and my dog and my pal John
Walked out to the garden to see what was 'a goin' on
My daddy said "it's squash," my momma called it spice
John just laughed and my dog just barked and jumped up once or twice

(Chorus)

Then John said, "Haven't you ever seen a pumpkin plant before?
Why, you carve 'em up for Halloween and stick 'em right by your door
With two big eyes and a funny nose and a toothy smile below
And stick a candle in its head for to make the whole thing glow"

(Chorus)

So now I grow up pumpkins for my neighbors all around
Still I don't quite understand how they got so big and round
My daddy says, "It's nature," my momma says a miracle,
But John just laughs and my dog just barks, and I like that best of all

(Chorus 2×)

The Thanksgiving Song

by Hap Palmer

There are many things I am thankful for
They're around me near and far
There are many things I am thankful for
Let me tell you what they are

I am thankful for . . . (chocolate)
I am thankful for . . . (my dog)
I am thankful for . . . (my new school bag)
And I'm thankful to be me.

Christmas Mouse

by Linda Arnold

Downstairs by the Christmas tree, There's a Gingerbread House
Look who's found his way inside, It's a Chrismas mouse

Chorus:
It's a Christmas mouse, in a Christmas house, Chewin' on a candy cane
It's a Christmas mouse, in a Christmas house, Nibbling the window pane

Well if you listen like an elf
You will hear him singing to himself:
I'm a little mouse who likes to eat, Lots of things that are very sweet
I like gumdrops, candy canes too, Even licorice will do

(Chorus)

Well that mouse he ate and ate, For he was having such fun
And suddenly he found out, He'd eaten every crumb

(Chorus)

Well if you listen like an elf
You will hear him cryin' to himself:
I'm a little mouse and I feel bad, Oh my tummy feels so sad
I guess I should have tried to stop, Before I ate that last gumdrop

(Chorus)

Now there's not much house
Just a fat little mouse with a tummy full of pain

Newts, Salamanders & Frogs

by Steve Van Zandt

Chorus:
Newts, salamanders and frogs. (oh yah)
Newts, salamanders and frogs. (oh yah)
Livin' in ponds and lily pads and logs,
Newts, salamanders and frogs. (oh yah)

Amphibian life is livin' in ease,
Munchin' down bugs just as free as you please
A fly fricassee, I'll have another one please,
Right here on the tip of my tongue (mmm)

(Chorus)

A smile and a grin is what amphibians wear.
They're livin' a life with hardly a care.
But that big black snake who lives over there
Is eating frogs à la king. (Yuk!)

(Chorus)

Legs and lungs and sticky tongues.
They've got pores on their skin and they like to swim.
They hop and they bop,
They walk and they crawl eatin' insects à la carte. (Yum!)

(Chorus)

So the next time you feel like you haven't a friend,
You can go to the pond and you can jump right in.
It won't be long 'til you'll be wearing a grin,
Like newts, salamanders and frogs. (oh yah)

(Chorus)

Reprinted with permission from Banana Slug String Band, P.O. Box 2262, Santa Cruz, CA 95063, (888) 327-5847, http://www.bananaslugstringband.com.

It's a Very Good Day

by Tom Hunter

It's a very good day for (playin' in the sun)
    (playin' in the sun) for (playin' in the sun)
It's a very good day for (playin' in the sun)
    Why? Cause it's a (sunny) day
I can feel all the (sun) comin' down on me
Down on the flowers and down on the trees
I think the (sun) is gonna make me grow, you just wait and see.

Verses:
1. playin' in the sun
2. walkin' in the rain
3. playin' in the mud
4. playin' in the dirt
5. climbin' a tree
6. takin' out the garbage
7. eatin' lots of chocolate
8. givin' people love

Reprinted with permission from Tom Hunter, Minstrel, Consultant.

Roots, Stems, Leaves

by Steve Van Zandt

Intro.:
Roots, stems, leaves, flowers, fruits, and seeds
Roots, stems, leaves, flowers, fruits, and seeds
Roots, stems, leaves, flowers, fruits, and seeds
That's roots, stems, leaves, flowers, fruits, and seeds

Chorus:
That's six parts, six parts, six plant parts that plants and people need

The roots hold the plant into the ground
They gather up the water that falls around
And there's a root inside of me, 'cause a carrot is a root that I eat.

(Chorus)

The stem is an elevator up from the ground
The water goes up and the sugar back down
And there's a stem inside of me, 'cause celery is a stem that I eat

(Chorus)

The leaves are the kitchens where the food is done
They breathe the air and catch the rays of sun
And there's a leaf inside of me, 'cause lettuce is a leaf that I eat

(Chorus)

The flowers are dressed so colorfully
They hold the pollen and attract the bees
And there's a flower inside of me, 'cause cauliflower is a flower that I eat.

(Chorus)

The fruit gets ripe and falls on the ground
It holds the seed and it feeds the ground
And there's a fruit inside of me, 'cause apple is a fruit that I eat.

(Chorus)

The seed gets buried in the earth
The cycle starts again with a new plant's birth
And there's a seed inside of me, 'cause sunflower is a seed that I eat.

(Chorus)

Now you know what this whole world needs
It's roots, stems, leaves, flowers, fruits, and seeds.
There's six plant parts inside of me, 'cause a garden salad is what I eat.

(Chorus)

Roots, stems, leaves, flowers, fruits, and seeds (repeat)
(in duet with): Six parts, six parts, six parts, six parts (repeat)

(Chorus)

Reprinted with permission from Banana Slug String Band, P.O. Box 2262, Santa Cruz, CA 95063, (888) 327-5847, http://www.bananaslugstringband.com.

A Tribute to Martin Luther King, Jr.

by Mary Miché

Chorus:
Martin Luther King, You make my spirit sing
You mean so much to me, 'Cause you taught us how to be free

You loved everybody black or white
And you taught us that it's no good to fight
But just to stand up for what's right
And let your love shine like a light

(Chorus)

You bravely walked the streets of this land
You marched with others hand in hand
You told us that we all should stand
Together for equality in this land

(Chorus)

You spoke of justice loud and long
With patience and love you fought against wrong
As brothers and sisters we'll be strong
And so to you we give this song

(Chorus)

Bats Eat Bugs

by Steve Van Zandt

Bats eat bugs, they don't eat people.
Bats eat bugs, they don't fly in your hair.
Bats eat bugs, they eat insects for dinner.
That's why they're flyin' up there.

Chorus:
Nothing out there, wants to eat you.
Nothing out there, wants to make you its meal.
Nothing out there, eats people for dinner.
'Cause they know how sick they would feel.

Coyotes eat rabbits, they don't eat people.
Coyotes eat rabbits, 'cause you're too big to bite.
Coyotes eat rabbits, they eat rabbits for dinner.
That's why they're out at night.

(Chorus)

Snakes eat mice, they don't eat people.
Snakes eat mice, that's why they're on the ground.
Snakes eat mice, 'cause you're too big to swallow.
And they don't want you hangin' around.

(Chorus)

Bears eat berries, they don't eat people.
Bears eat berries, they don't eat you or me.
Bears eat berries but they'll steal your dinner.
So you better tie it up in a tree.

(Chorus)

Lotta Seeds Grow

by Tom Hunter

Lotta (trees) start from seeds so small
Ya gotta look close or you can't see 'em at all
It's hard to believe (trees) grow so tall
From seeds that start so small

Well the sun comes up, the sun comes up
And the rain comes down, and the rain comes down
And the seeds get planted in the fertile ground
If you listen real close, you can hear the sound
Of (trees) startin' to grow.

Verses (substitute in parentheses):
1. trees
2. flowers
3. corn
4. stories
5. banjo instrumental
6. songs
7. kids
8. love

Reprinted with permission from Tom Hunter, Minstrel, Consultant.

Fried Ham

version by Mary Miché

Fried ham, fried ham, cheese and bologna
After the macaroni, we'll have onions, pickles and peppers.
Then we'll have some more fried ham, fried ham, fried ham.
Second verse same as first, silly accent only worse
Third verse same as first, whining accent only worse
Fourth verse same as first, angry accent only worse
Fifth verse same as first, baby accent only worse
Sixth verse same as first, kitty accent only worse
Seventh verse same as first, doggie accent only worse
Eighth verse same as first, piggy accent only worse
Last verse same as first, all the accents only worse.

Dirt Made My Lunch

by Steve Van Zandt

Chorus:
Dirt made my lunch, dirt made my lunch
Thank you dirt, thanks a bunch
For my salad, my sandwich, my milk and my munch
Cause dirt you made my lunch

Dirt is a word we often use
When we talk about the earth beneath our shoes
It's a place where plants can sink their toes
And in a little while a garden grows

(Chorus)

A farmer's plow will tickle the ground
You know the earth has laughed when the wheat is found
The grain is taken and flour is ground
For makin' a sandwich to munch on down

(Chorus)

Instrumental: Tenor guitar

(Chorus)

A stubby green beard grows upon the land
Out of the soil the grass will stand
But under the hoof it must bow
For makin' milk by way of a cow

(Chorus)

Reprinted with permission from Banana Slug String Band, P.O. Box 2262, Santa Cruz, CA 95063, (888) 327-5847, http://www.bananaslugstringband.com.

Find a Peaceful Thought

by Linda Arnold

It's an old-fashioned word and it's been all around
'Cross every ocean, every mountain or town.
Thinking this word is lots of fun to do
Here is what some children said when they'd thought it through:
Peace is quiet countryside.
Peace is jumping on the moon.
Peace is a little kitten on your lap.
Peace is a happy birthday party.
Peace is fun but sometimes boring.
Peace is shaking hands and stuff like that.
Peace is planting flowers on a clear day.
Peace is blowing bubbles.
Peace is when you pray.
So find a peaceful thought and plant it in your heart
Maybe then a peaceful world will really start to grow.

Peace is a furry Easter bunny.
Peace is when your Daddy's funny.
Peace is sleeping with your teddy bear.
Peace is never having homework.
Peace is yummy chocolate sundae.
Peace is showing someone that you care.
Peace is feeling happy.
Peace is feeling free.
Peace is full of magic.
Peace is you and me.
So find a peaceful thought and plant it in your heart
Maybe then a peaceful world could really start to grow.

Glossary

A

absolute pitch—the ability to produce the exact same note or pitch each time it is requested, also called perfect pitch.

allegretto—musical term meaning playfully.

American Sign Language—an established system of communication that uses the hands to convey letters, words, and ideas to someone with a hearing disability.

anecdotal information—information gathered from true stories or observations of real-life occurrences.

animato—musical term meaning animated.

artistic medium—the materials for production of a piece of art; may include metal, paint, or film.

Attention Deficit Disorder (ADD)—an inability to control behavior due to difficulty in processing neural stimuli, characterized by the ability to hyperfocus on only one task while tuning other things out; may appear with or without hyperactivity (Attention Deficit Hyperactivity Disorder [ADHD]).

audio production—the process by which sounds are recorded in order to be played again.

auditory—of, relating to, or experienced through sound.

autism—a physiological disorder resulting in a lack of language development, social interaction difficulties, and a preference for routines and rigid structure.

autoharp—a small wooden harp with chord bars that dampen the strings that are not part of the chord.

B

babbling—long strings of sounds such as "da, da, da, da" that babies make as a part of language acquisition.

background music—music that is played secondarily to something else, such as scenes in a film, acts in a play, or even shopping.

ballad—a very old tradition of songs that tell stories.

bar—a group of beats (often four, depending on the style and piece of music) that repeats throughout a musical piece; also called a measure.

baroque music—of, relating to, or having the characteristics of expression prevalent in the 17th century; identified by its use of complex forms, bold ornamentation, and the juxtaposition of contrasting elements.

beat—the basic rhythmic pulse that steadily undergirds the music.

beat patterns—patterns of short and long beats that fall within one measure.

bilingual songs—songs that include lyrics from two languages.

blues—simple music of lamentation and melancholy characterized by repetition.

Bodily-Kinesthetic intelligence—the ability to use the mind to coordinate bodily movements.

C

call and response—a format in which the teacher claps or sings a rhythm and the children repeat back the same rhythm.

carry a tune—the ability to sing a song on pitch and in rhythm.

causality—a causal relationship between two occurrences, meaning that it can be proven that one occurrence actually causes the other.

choral readings—group recitations of a poem or the words to a song.

classical music—music from the late 18th to early 19th centuries; characterized by an emphasis on balance, clarity, and moderation; may include forms of chamber music, opera, and symphony.

cognitive development—the development of a child's intelligence and base of knowledge.

compact discs—also referred to as CDs; thin, flat discs for playing music that are more reliable and less fragile than records and audio tapes.

compassion—a quality whereby a person exhibits care and concern for oneself and other people and animals.

conducting pattern—the pattern that musical conductors use with their hands or conducting wands to signify the beat of a piece of music.

context dependent memory—the phenomenon that people remember information better when recalled in the same context in which it was learned; for example, information learned while listening to a certain piece of music will be more easily recalled while listening to that same musical piece.

contra dances—folk dances that incorporate calls into the music, which direct dancers to perform a specific move; couples face each other in two lines; for example, the Virginia Reel.

control group—a group used as a means of comparison in a scientific study.

correlation—a relationship between two occurrences that often occur together, but are not proven to cause one another.

country music—similar to folk music; generally having simple melodies and choruses that repeat.

creative dance—dance characterized by freely adapted patterns of movement.

creativity—the ability to take two or more known ideas, put them together, and create a new viewpoint or product.

cross-cultural dances—any common form of dance that is native to another country; may include Chinese Lion dances, Jewish circle dances, and Mexican folk dances.

cultural diversity—a way to teach cultural appreciation by exploring the unique differences of another society; the study may include beliefs, clothing, food, music, speech, and songs.

cutoff—the motion conductors makes with their hands to signify that the music should stop.

D

Dalcroze method—a form of music education developed by the Swiss educator Émile Jaques-Dalcroze in the 1890s; uses movement to teach the basic elements of music: rhythm, dynamics, tone, and form; its three branches include eurhythmics, solfège, and improvisation.

dance—a stylized form of movement.

decomposers—organisms in nature that break down plant and animal material into usable soil; some examples are slugs, worms, and fungi.

developmental delays—delays in the development of basic skills such as speaking or walking as compared to the norm.

developmental milestones—the approximate age when babies and children should acquire certain abilities such as lifting the head or turning the head toward sound.

developmental steps—the sequence of events that take place in the development of a skill; for singing, the steps are: hearing the sound, imitating the rise and fall of the melody, approximating the pitches, and singing the tune with the correct pitches and rhythms.

developmentally appropriate activity—an educational activity that is well-suited to the ages and developmental stages of the children participating.

developmentally appropriate practices (DAP)—presenting the right skill to the right child at the right time.

diatonic scale—a musical scale consisting of seven notes, with half steps between notes three and four and between seven and eight; also called a major scale, this is the scale used in most Western music.

differences—qualities or distinctions that make one thing unique from another.

discrimination—the act of finely distinguishing between two things; for example, distinguishing between the sounds of *P* and *B* in language acquisition.

Down syndrome—a chromosomal abnormality resulting in specific developmental delays in muscle coordination and in understanding mathematical concepts and spatial reasoning.

dynamic levels—the loudness or softness of music.

E

educational children's music—music played in a variety of styles with educational lyrics appropriate for children.

electric piano—a smaller, more affordable version of a piano; this instrument has pre-programmed songs and rhythms that can be accessed by pressing a button.

emotional disabilities—emotional differences caused by circumstances such as living through difficult emotional situations.

Emotional intelligence—sometimes referred to as Personal intelligence; includes *Interpersonal intelligence,* which is the ability to understand communication between people, and *Intrapersonal intelligence,* which is the ability to understand one's own feelings and motivations.

environment—a grouping of plants, animals, and nonliving things such as rocks that coexist to form a natural community.

eurhythmics—a branch of the Dalcroze method of music education that trains the body in rhythm and dynamics.

evening activity—an outdoor activity to do with children during the evening hours, after dark.

extramusical positive effect—the positive effect music can have on skills that are not thought to be related to music.

F

factual songs—songs that contain accurate information in their lyrics.

fanciful songs—songs that contain incorrect or made-up information in their lyrics, often intended to be funny.

Fetal Alcohol Syndrome (FAS)—a syndrome caused by a mother's abuse of alcohol or drugs during pregnancy, which results in severe and permanent brain damage; the symptoms are often similar to those of ADHD but with more pronounced hyperactivity.

folk music—includes a wide variety of musical styles, but most often consists of simple songs sung by a single voice with minimal instrumental accompaniment.

foreign language learning—the process of learning to speak a language other than one's native language.

full body motion—using the entire body to imitate predescribed motions such as digging and wading through a swamp; used for acting out a song.

G

grammar—the system of rules that determines the proper use of a language.

H

hand motions—the movements of one's hands to symbolize the words of a song.

harmony—a second tune that matches or complements the melody.

hearing disabled—a person who has severe difficulty hearing or who has deafness.

I

improvisation—making up the music while performing and playing it.

infant directed speech—the high-pitched, singsong phrases people say to infants, such as "coochy coochy coo" and "hi there, sweetie."

initial consonant—the consonant sound that begins a word, such as *M* in *Mary.*

instruments—devices through which one can produce musical sounds; for example, a drum, piano, and trumpet are all considered musical instruments.

interval—the relationship or pitch step between two notes.

J

jazz—American music characterized by syncopated rhythms, ensemble playing, and improvisation.

K

Kodály method—a method of music education developed by Zoltán Kodály; the goal is to engage children in music at a young age and keep them interested in it; folk music and singing games are central to the method.

L

language acquisition—the process of learning to speak and understand a language.

language skills—the skills acquired in learning to speak a language.

larghetto—musical term meaning somewhat slowly.

learning differences—a range of difficulties concerning learning, which can include dyslexia, memory problems, auditory and visual processing, and attention disorders; also called learning disabilities.

learning disabilities—a range of difficulties concerning learning, which can include dyslexia, memory problems, auditory and visual processing, and attention disorders; also called learning differences.

legato—musical term meaning smooth and connected.

leggiero—musical term meaning lightly and airily.

line dances—folk dances similar to a contra dance, but done in one line rather than two.

listening skills—skills concerning listening, including the ability to sit quietly, listen closely and attentively, and retain information that is heard.

Logical-Mathematical intelligence—the ability to reason deductively, detect patterns, and think logically.

lullabies—songs to quiet children or lull them to sleep.

M

maestoso—musical term meaning majestically.

marcato—musical term meaning mark each note.

measure—a group of beats (often four, depending on the style and piece of music) that repeats throughout a musical piece; also called a bar.

melodic contour—the tune or the rise and fall of the melody, unrelated to the key in which the melody is played.

meno mosso—musical term meaning a little movement.

mood—an emotional state characterized by positive or negative feelings.

movement—the act of motion.

multiple disabilities—the concurrence of more than one disability in a child.

Multiple Intelligences—a concept developed by Howard Gardner suggesting that there are eight different kinds of intelligence, including: Logical-Mathematical, Verbal-Linguistic, Visual-Spatial, Musical-Rhythmic, Bodily-Kinesthetic, Naturalistic, Intrapersonal, and Interpersonal.

music appreciation—a comprehensive understanding of the various genres of music and their contributions to music as a whole.

music delivery systems—devices through which one can play previously recorded music; for example, a compact disc player, computer, record player, and tape recorder are all considered music delivery systems.

music story combination—a song that is related to the theme of a story and that accompanies the story.

music therapist—a specially trained professional who uses music to assist people in retraining impaired areas of their brains.

musical ability—the ability or talent one has to perform music well.

musical accompaniment—similar to background music; having music play while reading or watching a film or a play; increases ability to recall information as it relates to words, images, and emotions.

musical experiment—an experiment that tests how various people, animals, and even plants respond to different kinds of music.

musical expressions—words that accompany written music and relate to the rhythm and tempo of the music.

musical game—an activity in which music or songs serve as the structure for a game; for example, the game "musical chairs" or having children guess the name of a tune.

musical notation—the lines and symbols that make up written music.

Musical-Rhythmic intelligence—the ability to recognize and compose musical pitches, tones, and rhythms; including the ability to perform music.

musical training—technical education in the field of music.

musicals—plays or films that are accompanied by music.

N

Naturalistic intelligence—the ability to observe, understand, and organize patterns in the natural environment; including the ability to recognize and classify plants and animals.

nature appreciation—respect for nature.

neural development—development of the nervous system, including the brain.

niche—the specific role in a habitat that an organism is best-suited to occupy.

nocturnal animals—animals that are active at night and sleep during the day.

nonprofessional recording—a recording made using a basic tape recorder and microphone.

normal—a subjective and ever-changing characterization that depends upon geographic location and economic status, among other factors.

normal development—typical and expected development of abilities and strengths in a child.

number system—an alternative technique to the solfège system for teaching pitch; each step in the scale is assigned a number: "one, two, three, four, five, six, seven, one."

O

off beat—a rhythm that falls on the weak pulse or beat; in a measure spoken as "one and two and three and four and," a rhythm that falls on the *ands* rather than the numbers.

Omnichord—*see* QChord.

on beat—a rhythm that falls on the strong pulse or beat; in a measure spoken as "one and two and three and four and," a rhythm that falls on the numbers rather than the *ands*.

Orff instruments—percussion instruments created by Carl Orff especially for children.

Orff music—music composed by Carl Orff especially for children to perform.

Orff-Schulwerke—Carl Orff's approach to music education, which focuses on creative and elemental experimentation and expression in music and dance simultaneously.

ostinato—a regular pattern that repeats over and over, forming the basis of a musical piece.

P

parade—a musical activity characterized by costumes, marching, and decorations.

parts of speech—categories of words according to the function they serve in a sentence; examples include noun, verb, adjective, pronoun, and contraction.

pentatonic scale—a musical scale consisting of five notes (C, D, E, G, and A on the piano); used in the folk music of middle Eastern Europe.

Personal intelligence—sometimes referred to as Emotional intelligence; includes *Interpersonal intelligence,* which is the ability to understand communication between people, and *Intrapersonal intelligence,* which is the ability to understand one's own feelings and motivations.

phonemic ability—a measure of a child's ability to distinguish between closely related sounds; music training helps develop this ability in children.

phonemic awareness—concentration on the sounding out of words and the ability to distinguish closely related sounds.

phonemic clues—small differences in sounds; for example, the difference between *P* and *B.*

physical disabilities—disabilities in which a person experiences difficulty getting some part of the body to work properly.

pitch—the property of a musical sound determined by the frequency of the sound waves producing it; the highness or lowness of a musical note.

pitch development—the process of learning to match pitches.

pitch discrimination—in music, the ability to distinguish between closely related sounds, especially notes being sung or played; related to a child's phonemic ability.

pitch matching—the ability to hear a musical note, or pitch, and then imitate it exactly.

pitch range—the range of musical notes, or pitches, any particular human voice can produce; also called vocal range.

plant parts—the parts of a plant appropriate for children to learn: root, stems, leaves, flowers, fruits, and seeds.

plant processes—the life processes that plants carry out, including photosynthesis and growth from a seed to a sprout to a full-grown plant.

pollution—contamination of the natural environment with human-made waste and toxins.

procedural memory—remembering a skill by repetition and practice so that the skill becomes automatic, like typing or riding a bicycle.

pronunciation—the oral formation of words; saying words correctly.

Q

QChord Digital Songcard Guitar—an inexpensive instrument that allows you to play notes, chords, and rhythms by pressing buttons; also contains pre-programmed rhythms; manufactured by Suzuki Corporation. Note: The QChord replaced the original Omnichord model.

R

read-along sing-along book—a book that begins as a song and then is later published in book form, the words of the song are the text and are supplemented by illustrations.

readiness—the degree to which a child is developmentally ready for the skill being presented.

reading ability—a measure of a person's level of comprehension while reading; the ability to understand what one has read.

records—thin, flat, grooved discs on which sounds are recorded for playing on a phonograph.

recycling—processing materials so that they can be used again.

relative pitch—the ability to sing a note in relation to another note, so that when singing a song, one is able to sing each note correctly in relation to the first note.

rhythm—the relative duration and accentuation of notes in a piece of music.

rhythmic patterns—patterns of short and long beats, made by combining beat patterns.

rock 'n' roll—popular music usually played on electrically amplified instruments; characterized by a persistent, heavy beat and repetition.

rodent—small, gnawing mammal such as a squirrel, mouse, or hamster.

S

science concepts—ideas for children to learn in the science fields.

self-esteem—the ability to value oneself; accepting one's faults and acknowledging one's abilities.

self-image—the way a person views him/herself.

semi-professional recording—a recording made using a four-track recording machine or the equipment in a small recording studio.

sense of rhythm—the ability to follow a beat without racing ahead or falling behind.

sensitivity—the quality or condition of being receptive to other people's beliefs, concerns, and emotions.

sforzando—musical term meaning suddenly strongly accented.

singing around the pitch—a singing style used by children in which the pitches of the tune are approximated; when the melody goes up, the child will sing a higher pitch, but not the correct pitch.

social disabilities—social differences caused by circumstances such as living through a difficult emotional situation.

solfège system—the standard technique for teaching pitch in traditional singing methods; each step in the scale is designated by a syllable: "do re mi fa sol la ti do."

spirituals—simple folk songs written to convey important spiritual truths.

square dance—a folk dance that incorporates calls into the music, which direct the dancers to perform a specific move; couples face each other in a square.

staccato—musical term meaning short and disconnected.

T

tape recorder—a device for recording sound onto a small cassette; can also play recorded material from audio tapes.

tempo—the speed of the music.

tessatura—comfortable vocal range.

timbre—the characteristic quality of sound that distinguishes one voice or musical instrument from another.

V

Verbal-Linguistic intelligence—the ability to read well, to understand sophisticated vocabulary, to grasp concepts presented, to speak intelligently, and to write well.

visually disabled—a person who has severe difficulty seeing or who has blindness.

Visual-Spatial intelligence—the ability to visualize objects or movements through space.

vocabulary—the sum of words an individual can speak and understand in a given language.

vocal range—the range of musical notes, or pitches, any particular human voice can produce; also called pitch range.

vowel sounds—the long, vocalized parts of words, signified in English by the letters *A, E, I, O,* and *U.*

W

windows of opportunity—the span of time in a child's development when certain skills can be learned.

Z

zipper song—a song that is virtually the same from verse to verse, with only a single word change per verse; named by Pete Seeger because you just zip out one word and zip in a new one.

Index

Q

QChord Digital Songcard Guitar, 10, 216
quarter note, 67
"Qué buena suerte" (Diamond), 158

R

Raffi. *See* Cavoukian, Raffi
rallentando, 44
Ramsey, Marjorie, 55
"Ranger Rick" (Wood), 131, 143
Rapaport, Diane, 210
"Rapp Song" (Grammer), 171–72, 173, 266
Rauscher, Frances, 56–57
Raven, Nancy, 158, 261
read-along sing-along books, 239, 241
readiness, 84
reading
  exploring vocabulary, 241
  finding songs to go along with, 239
  music and, 235, 236–41
  music story combinations, 239
  read-along sing-along books, 239, 241
  song words, 241
  stories with musical accompaniment, 238–39
reading ability, 237
records, music, 6–7
Recycled String Band, 140
recycling songs, 128, 139–42
Reid, Bob, 178
  Marz Barz, 178
  We are the Children, 178
relative pitch, 62–63
Reynolds, Malvina, 131
rhythm, 36, 40, 98, 216, 218
rhythm band, 47–48
rhythmic notation, 67
rhythmic patterns, 42, 43, 216
rhythm sticks, 48
"Right Field" (Welch), 177
Rise Up Singing (Blood and Patterson), 21, 25, 26
ritardando, 44, 219
Ritchie, Lionel, 176
A River Ran (Cherry), 139
rock 'n' roll, 28, 30
Rogers, Sally, 199, 261–62
"Romp in the Swamp" (Brennan), 129, 131, 143, 222, 270
Ronberg, Dennis, 7, 262
Ronberg, Linda, 7, 262

"Roots, Stems, Leaves" (Van Zandt), 137, 144, 274–75
rounds, singing, 97–98
"Row, Row, Row Your Boat," 63

S

The Salamander Room (Mazer), 202
Scelsa, Greg, 171, 222
science
  animals' and plants' responses to music, 145–46
  concepts, 128
  listening to and recording nature sounds, 147
  musical sound, 148
  music and, 127–50
  teaching concepts through song, 128–45
  world of sound and music, 147
Scruggs, Joe, 218, 262
Seeger, Charles, 181
Seeger, Pete, 9, 25, 86, 136, 181–83, 221, 262
  "Abiyoyo," 27
  "Where Have All the Flowers Gone?", 182–83
Seeger, Ruth Crawford, 26
"Seeing with My Ears" (Hunter), 178
self-esteem, 170
self-image, 176–77
semi-professional recording, 206, 208–11
  instrumental tracks, 208–9
  location for, 208
  in recording studio, 209–11
  sound mixing, 209
  vocal tracks, 208–9
sense of rhythm, 94
sensitivity, to people with special needs, 178
Sesame Street® (television program), 82, 161
seven-year-old children, 95–98
  developmentally appropriate music, 100
  learning to play instruments, 95, 96–97
  performance and, 95, 97
  songs and, 97–98
sforzando, 66, 220
Sharon, Lois & Bram, 207–8, 262
Shaw, Gordon, 56
Silverstein, Shel, 247
Singable Songs for the Very Young (Raffi), 240
singing
  in children's vocal range, 165
  developmental steps, 74
  eight-year-olds and, 98, 100
  learning, 55, 57, 152
  three-year-olds and, 86–87

299